IMAGES
of America

St. George Reef Lighthouse

On the Cover: In this view, shot from the pitching deck of the Coast Guard cutter *Avoyal*, St. George Reef Lighthouse, guardian of the "Dragon Rocks" off the shore of Crescent City, is assaulted by hurricane-force winds and waves. Incredibly, but true to the Coast Guard motto *Semper Paratus*, meaning "Always Ready," the cutter is actually on a crew transfer mission. It was a love-hate relationship that kept the light burning for 84 years. (Doug Wilson, *Humboldt Times*.)

IMAGES
of America

St. George Reef Lighthouse

Guy Towers

ARCADIA
PUBLISHING

ISBN 978-1-4671-3317-3

Published by Arcadia Publishing
Charleston, South Carolina

Printed in the United States of America

Library of Congress Control Number: 2015935023

For all general information, please contact Arcadia Publishing:
Telephone 843-853-2070
Fax 843-853-0044
E-mail sales@arcadiapublishing.com
For customer service and orders:
Toll-Free 1-888-313-2665

Visit us on the Internet at www.arcadiapublishing.com

To my wife, Alice; my sons and their wives, Grant and Kathy and Glen and Lori; and my grandsons, Grant II and Greg.

Contents

Acknowledgments

First, I would like to acknowledge the Father of Lights. Just as the power of a Fresnel lens is measured in candlepower or individual points of light, so, too, has the successes of the St. George Reef Lighthouse preservation been measured by the efforts of hundreds of people, businesses, government, and private organizations who collectively illuminated the Dragon Rocks and made this book possible.

To light but a few of these candles, I would first like to thank Maggie and Joe Snowden; bless you, Maggie, for your tireless efforts molding the rough draft into computer format, your courteous editing, and friendship. Thank you, friend—Joe—for contributing to research. Thanks go to the pioneers of the lighthouse preservation movement: Ralph Shanks, Jim Gibbs, Wayne Wheeler, the US Lighthouse Preservation Society, "Mr. Lighthouse" Ken Black, Tim Harrison, and the *Lighthouse Digest*. Thank you Susan Karlshoej, TK Foundation; Tom Dozcos, Government Services Administration; National Park Service; US Fish and Wildlife Service; 11th Coast Guard District; Coast Guard Group Humboldt Bay; Chetco Lifeboat Station; Veterans of Foreign Wars, US Merchant Marines; Humboldt and Del Norte Counties boards of supervisors; City of Crescent City; the *Daily Triplicate*; *Curry Costal Pilot*; Harbor Art Gallery; Crescent City and Del Norte County Chamber of Commerce; *Eureka Times-Standard*; radio stations KCRE and KPOD; Ardis Vaughn; Holly Weir; Rick Heiser; Holly Austin, DNACA; Jeff Russel; Joanne Cady; Mary Bryan; Debbie Stover, owner, Del Norte Office Supply, with associates Gina and Samantha; Dan Brattain, Westlog Aviation/Cal-Ore Life Flight; Wrights Custom Framing; ACE Hardware; Crescent Electric; Woods Plumbing; and Home Depot; Eureka merchants Phil and Linelle Hasmer; the Crescent City Foursquare Church; and our "Partners in Light," the Del Norte County Historical Society.

Research help was given from the Del Norte County Library; the National Archives, in Washington, DC; the National Archives at San Francisco, in San Bruno, California; Barre, Vermont, Public Library; California State Library, Sacramento; Humboldt State Library and Media Department; and Humboldt County Historical Society.

This book would not be possible without family and friends: my sister Lillian and her friend Phyllis; my brother Ben; my brother Lee and his wife, Cathy; and in memory, my parents, James and Violet Towers. Credit is also due the Oregon Chapter US Lighthouse Society, Brookings Chamber of Commerce, City of Brookings, Del Norte Chapter AARP, Crescent City Woman's Club, Rotary Club, and Del Norte County Schools.

Finally, I am grateful to those who made special contributions but were only with us a short time: Terry and Martha Lewis, Maureen and Terry Limes, and Andy Hussari.

Introduction

In the summer of 2012, a group of travelers goes to the visitors' center in Crescent City, California, to inquire about historical sites. The people learn of Battery Point, the *Brother Jonathan*, the *Emedio* memorial, and the efforts of a local group to save the St. George Reef Lighthouse.

The chamber explains the connection between the *Jonathan* and the lighthouse, which is located near the wreck site, and gives the visitors a general chronology of the building and manning of St. George: 10 years to construct, the most expensive lighthouse in 19th-century America, storms, the dangers of getting on and off, the US Lighthouse Service keepers, and the Coast Guard, which assumed control just before World War II, the deaths of one Lighthouse Service keeper, and four from the country's oldest seagoing service, the Coast Guard, whose history dates to 1790.

The travelers skim through the book selection on lighthouses and find a few that mention St. George. There are quotes from famous authors that say this beacon on the Dragon Rocks is America's greatest lighthouse because of the difficulty of construction, the hardships of manning the beacon, the role it played in protecting mariners, and the fact that it was the last manned lighthouse on the Pacific coast.

They inquire about the group, the St. George Reef Lighthouse Preservation Society (referred to throughout this book as "SGRLPS"), and learn that the nonprofit organization was formed in 1986 and made great progress in spite of weather, finances, and the need to protect threatened species of mammals that seasonally inhabit the site.

They hear rave reviews from visitors who have flown the six miles out from the local airport by helicopter to tour the 16-story granite monolith built with 12-ton stones quarried 70 miles south and transported to the site by steamer. Docents at several levels explain the workings of an aid to navigation and the pleasures and trials of the men who lived there.

The visitors say it was well worth the fee, and they want to return, but the volunteers, who call themselves the Second Watch, are up against a new challenge. In March 2012, they were notified by the California Department of Transportation that, according to federal aviation rules, the landing space for helicopters (currently 50 feet) is not large enough, and an additional 30 feet will be needed. In the meantime, restoration can continue when they complete a permit application. The group has drawn up a plan for the extension and is currently seeking funding.

Reader, if the story so far has piqued your interest, read on to learn the whole incredible tale of master craftsmen who turned a small mountain of granite into a monument of 19th-century engineering and how men survived towering waves, loneliness, boredom, and being thrown into the sea. Learn also of the challenges and rewards of being the Second Watch at America's greatest lighthouse and join efforts nationwide to save our heritage.

Chronology of the Building of St. George Reef Lighthouse 1881–1892

October 1, 1881 – Surveyor lands on Northwest Seal Rock, but unable to take measurements.
April 1882 – A civil engineer makes survey of Northwest Seal Rock, produces three-foot-interval contour plot plan.
August 1882 – Congress makes first appropriation of $50,000. Plans formulated to prepare rock to receive foundation of pier.
March 1883 – Second appropriation of $50,000. Schooner *La Ninfa* chartered in San Francisco to act as barrack for work crew. Use of cable "trolly" system to transport workmen to rock. Towed to site, but due to mooring problems and storm that casts *La Ninfa* adrift, not in place until early May. Humboldt Bay, 75 miles south, is selected as headquarters, has resources and safe anchorage. Remainder of work season: quarrymen land, secure barrack. Rough outline of pier foundation ledges for oval-shaped pier accomplished by blasting.
July 1884 – Only $30,000 was approved but project moves forward. An office was established in San Francisco where stone patterns of zinc were to be cut. Capt. A.H. Payson, Army Corps of Engineers and chief engineer the 12th Lighthouse District, in charge of the St. George project, also made arrangements for a stone finishing facility on the Samoa Peninsula. Located near the Humboldt Bay Lighthouse and Life-Saving Station, which was thereafter dubbed "Paysonville." Rounding out the season, Ballantyne was astonished to find a high-grade deposit of granite on the Mad River (in present day McKinleyville) and made arrangements with the owner of a nearby railroad to haul it to a site where it was then barged to Paysonville. Over 5,000 cubic feet of dimension stone was quarried by October. In preparation for the following years work, the schooner *American Boy* was chartered and a derrick erected at the rock.
March 1885 – $40,000 appropriation, only enough to send work crew to rock to prepare against possible winters damage to moorings and to place markers where the stones would be set when funding allowed.
March 1886 – Allotment of $120,000 but no stones made it to the rock. Severe winter rains caused landslides at quarry which buried the derrick and granite slabs set near the rail spur. They would not have been able to receive them at Paysonville anyway, as teredos (shipworms) had bored into the pier.
March 1887 – Schooner *Sparrow* chartered in San Francisco to replace *La Ninfa. Santa Maria* towed *Sparrow* and carried men and equipment to moorings and rock now prepared to receive stones for first courses of caisson of pier. In June, steamer *Alliance* brings two loads of finely finished granite slabs. By September, nine courses raised the workers at least a few yards above the menacing waves.
April 1888 – Congress granted $150,000. With the newly chartered *Santa Maria* running even at night, by the end of the working season, 13 tiers of the caisson were completed.
March 1889 – The board had requested $200,000 for the 1888–1889 fiscal year and the steamer *Del Norte* was chartered in March. The first task the workers faced was repairing the damage done by winter storms to the heavily timbered barrack constructed the year before to provide living quarters on the rock. The season brought severe weather, but by June the outer walls of the caisson rose to 16 courses with the interior walls of the engine room, coal storage, and tower keeping pace. As the season progressed, the caisson rose to six stories but spray still dampened mortar and stalled work. Quarrymen wrested nearly all the stone needed for the pier from the quarry.
1890–1892 – No funds were allocated for 1890, but $80,000 came in September for fiscal 1891 and the Phoenix Iron Works of Trenton, New Jersey, was given the contract for all the metalwork needed for the lighthouse, such as the lantern room, handrails, and so forth. Working speedily, the *Sunol*-ferried workforce once again rebuilt the storm-mauled barrack, and completed the caisson by June. The brick-lined tower then received its cement floors, plastered walls, finishing touches on woodwork, and installation of machinery. All was done by October except for the light, awaiting delivery from France. The weather administered one final blow to the project, preventing the tired workers from leaving until November 8. The light was exhibited on October 20, 1892.

One

The Sinking of the *Brother Jonathan*

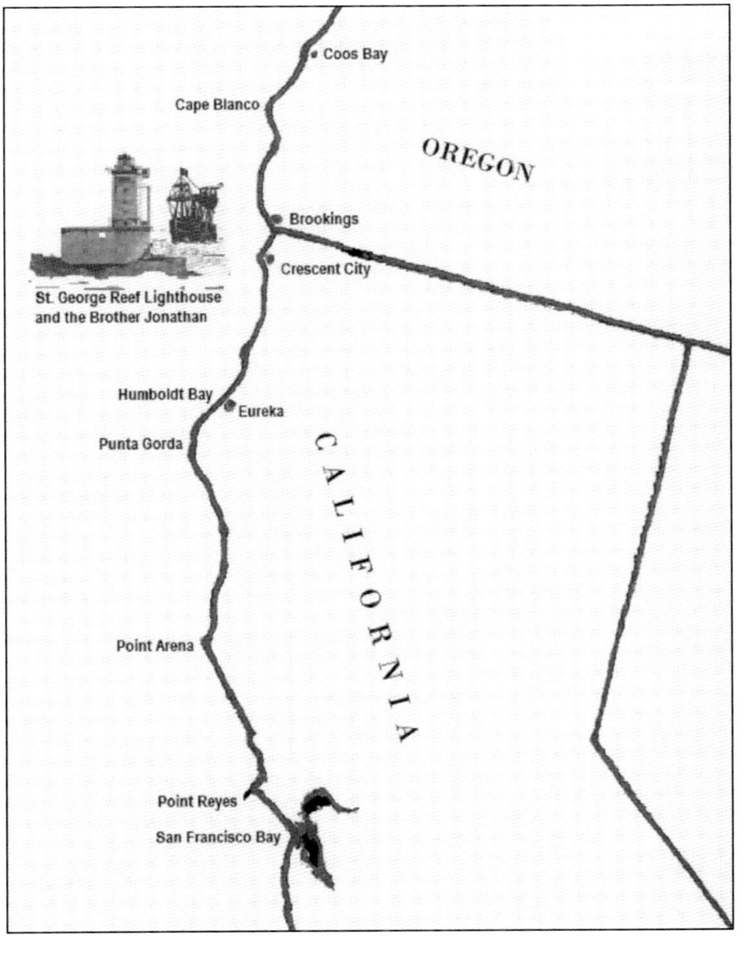

The northern California coast, shown here in this locator map, had little contact from early European voyagers but was buzzing with activity after the discovery of gold in 1848. Increased shipping led to the placement of lighthouses along the entire coast from San Diego in the south to Crescent City near the Oregon border. The first beacon on Alcatraz Island in San Francisco Bay was completed in 1853, to be followed by over 40 other stations and two lightships. (Author's collection.)

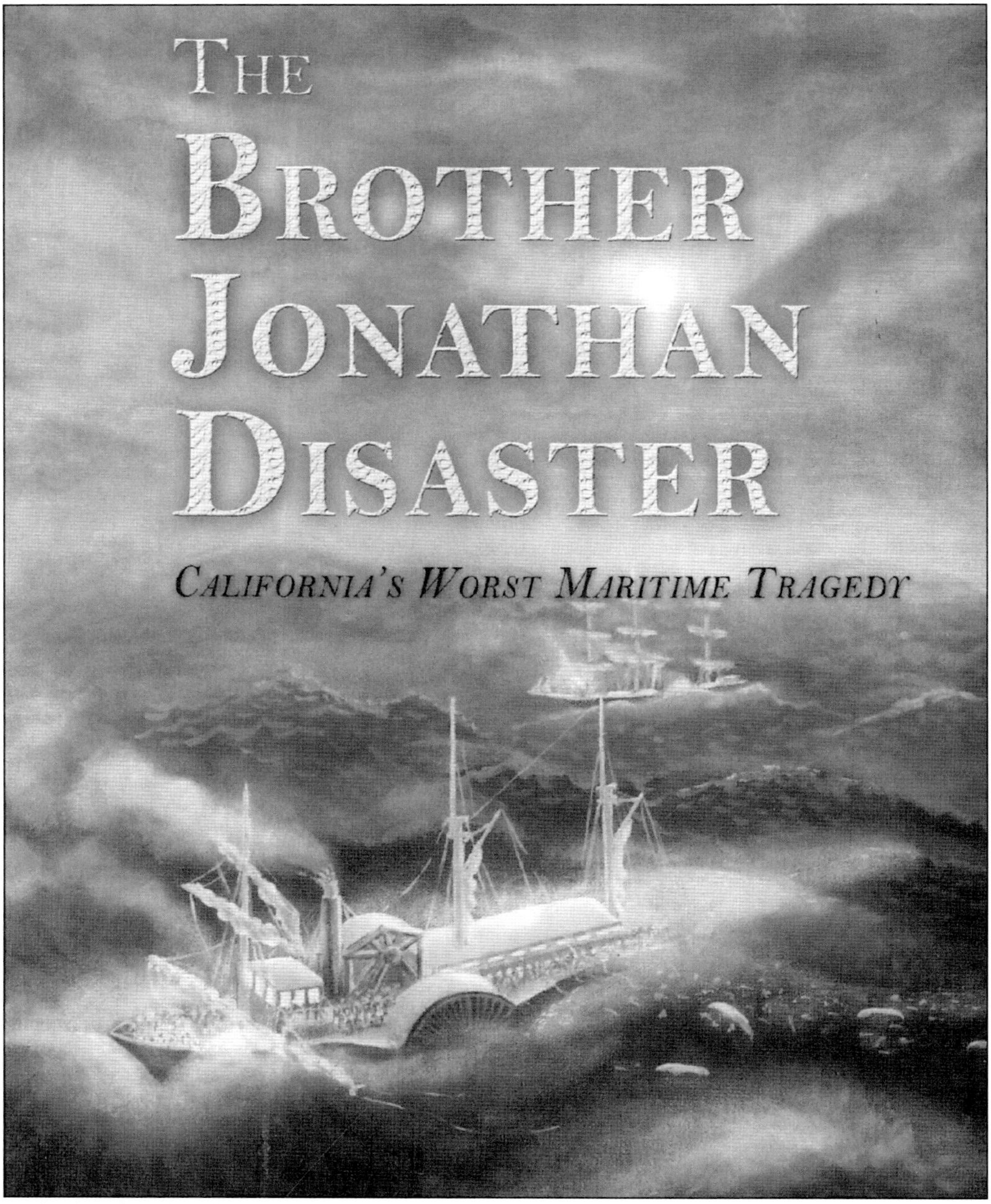

In the first decades after the Gold Rush, there was still an unlighted section north of Crescent City, which included the feared Dragon Rocks of St. George Reef, so named by Capt. James Vancouver on his way to the Columbia River in 1792. Twin-paddle coastal steamers made many safe transits of the reef, but one of these was destined to find a place in maritime history when it foundered on a semi-submerged pinnacle. Shown here is the coastal steamer *Brother Jonathan*, which met its doom in 1865, taking most of its passengers and crew to the bottom. It is an unfortunate truism that catastrophic loss of life is often necessary to prod public officials into taking action. The tragedy led to the building of St. George Reef Lighthouse to mark these dangerous waters. (Painting by and courtesy of Gene Olson.)

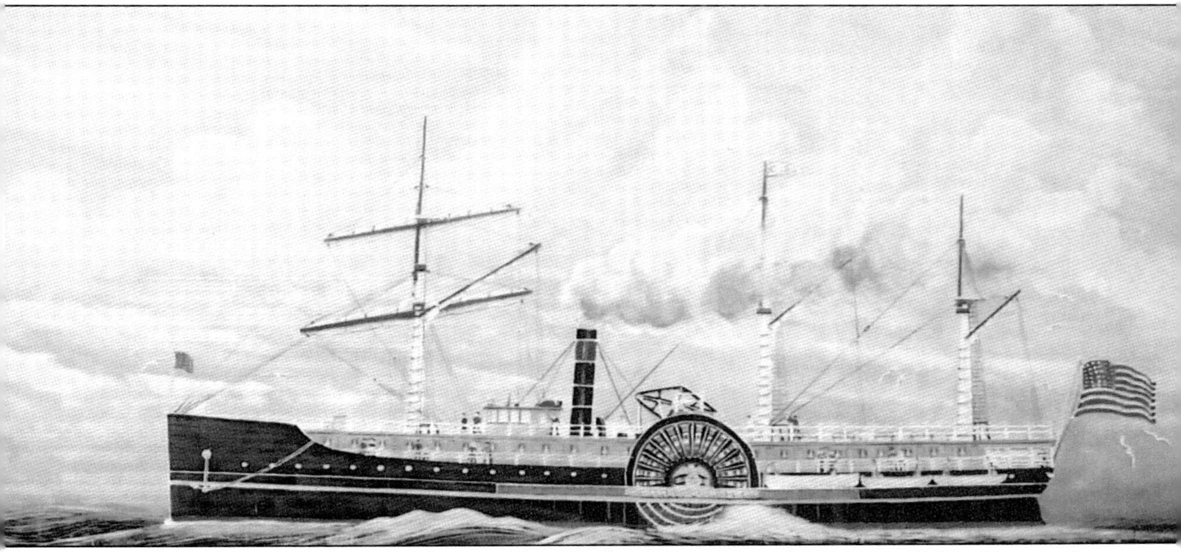

Originally built in 1850 and a veteran of hundreds of voyages on the East and West Coasts, the *Jonathan* sailed from San Francisco on July 28, 1865, with a fortune in gold, an Army payroll, and more than 200 passengers, including 54 officers and crew. In what was the worst nonmilitary maritime tragedy in California history, it sank on St. George Reef off Crescent City on July 30. (Painting by and courtesy of Gene Olson.)

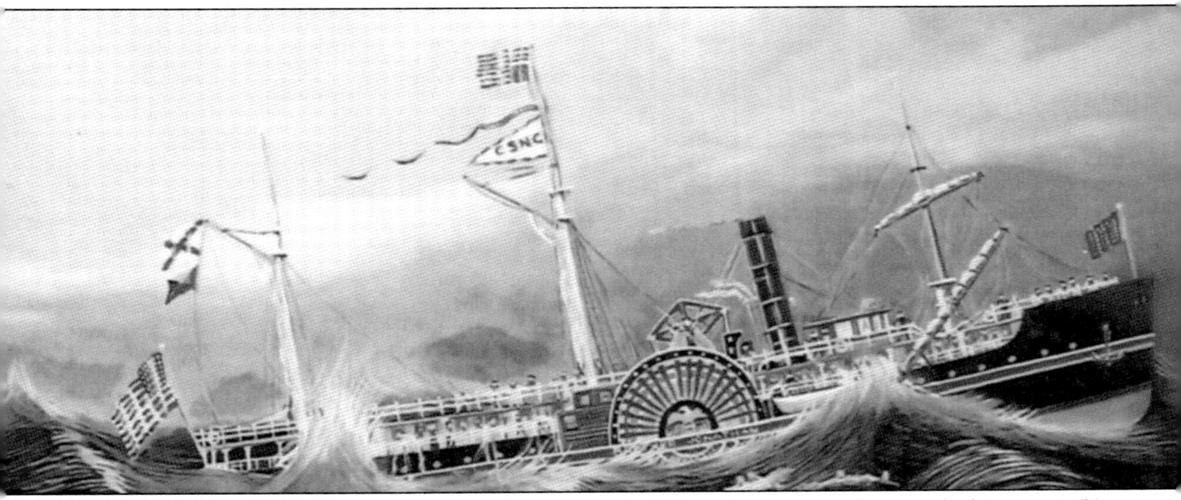

It took only 45 minutes from the time first officer W.H. Allen saw a submerged object at 1:50 p.m. until the hull was shattered and the main mast collapsed. Water gushed into the lower compartments, trapping passengers. Wave upon wave lifted and slammed the shattered hulk until it slid into 50 fathoms of brine. In this historical recreation, the once-elegant ship struggles to remain afloat. (Painting by and courtesy of Gene Olson.)

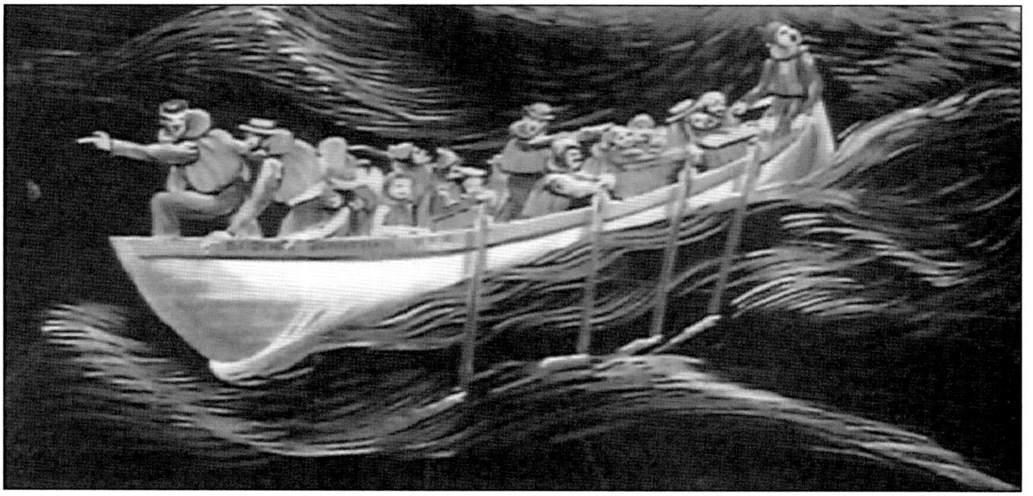

Depicted here pulling away from the screams of the doomed is the one lifeboat that managed to escape with 16 to 21 people aboard. Bodies of the victims later washed up along a wide stretch of coast from Cape Blanco, Oregon, south to Eureka, California. Seven crewmen were among the survivors and remarkably, given the racial prejudices of the time, a Chinese woman and her child. (Painting by and courtesy of Gene Olson.)

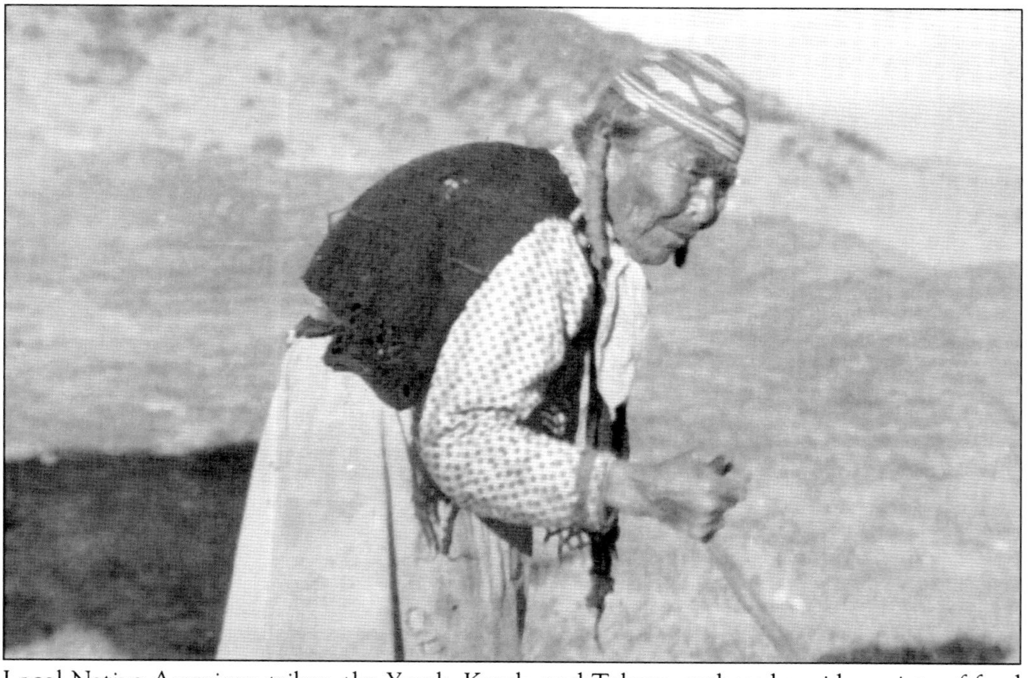

Local Native American tribes, the Yurok, Karok, and Tolowa, gathered a wide variety of food from the sea. Today on Point St. George, a historical display marks a former Tolowa settlement, and it was from this site that the tribe, represented by this photograph of a Tolowa woman, reported hearing the cries of *Jonathan* victims. However, an investigation by searchers turned up no evidence. (Private collection.)

Capt. Samuel J. DeWolf, true to the traditions of the sea, went down with his ship. According to testimonies, he acted commendably, looking after his crew and assisting passengers to lifeboats. Stories surrounding the sinking say he protested to owners that the vessel was overloaded when it left the docks in San Francisco. DeWolf's body was found, and he is buried in San Francisco. (Del Norte County Historical Society.)

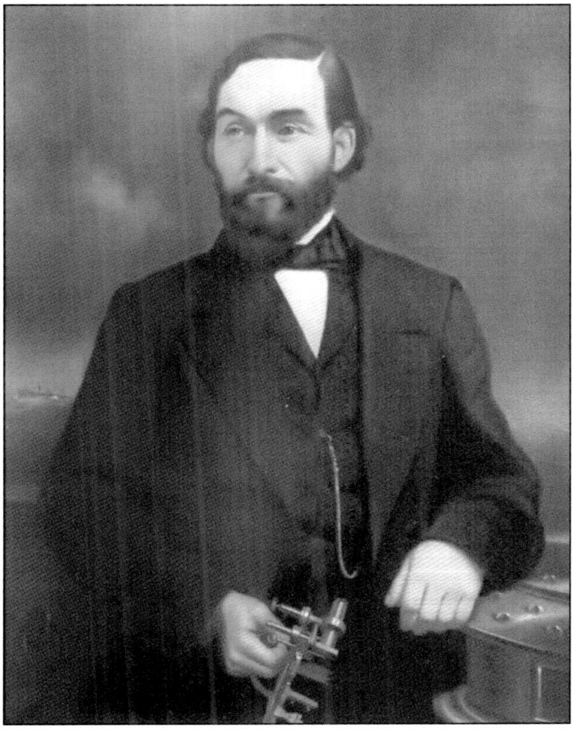

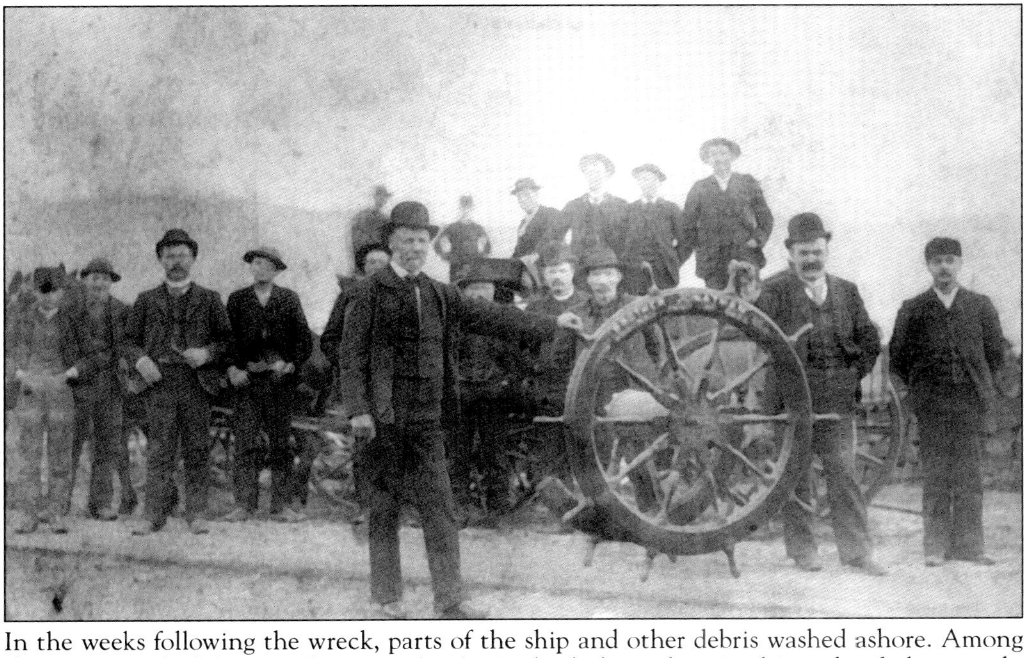

In the weeks following the wreck, parts of the ship and other debris washed ashore. Among the most prized of these artifacts was the ship's wheel, shown here in this undated photograph. Seaman Jacob Yates, a survivor, was the last of the crew to touch the wheel. After a stay in Crescent City, the wheel dropped anchor at the Oyster Bar in Portland, Oregon. (Del Norte County Historical Society.)

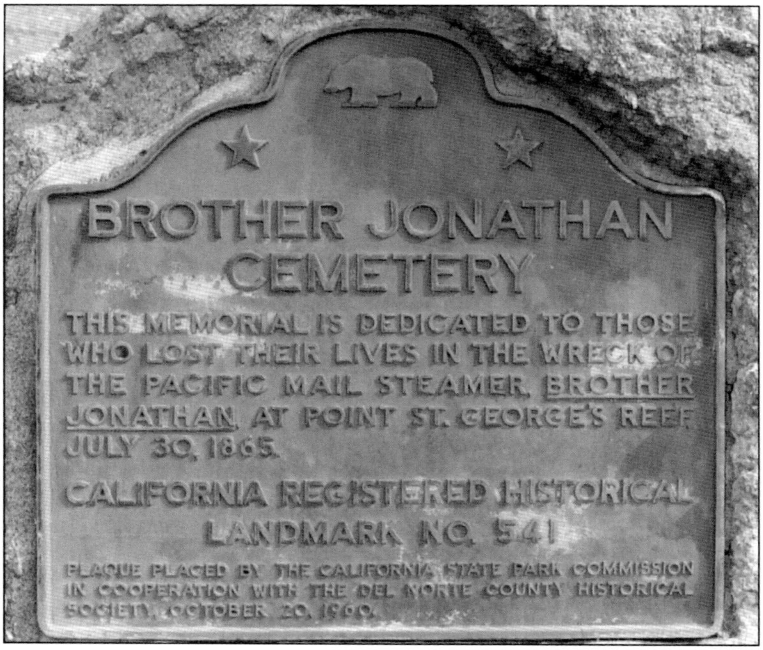

The remains of 22 passengers were eventually identified. Among them were Daniel and Paulina Rowell, who are buried at the Brother Jonathan Memorial in Crescent City. The Rowells and other victims of the tragedy were originally interred in the Crescent City Masonic Cemetery; but following years of neglect there, they were reinterred at the memorial. (Author's collection.)

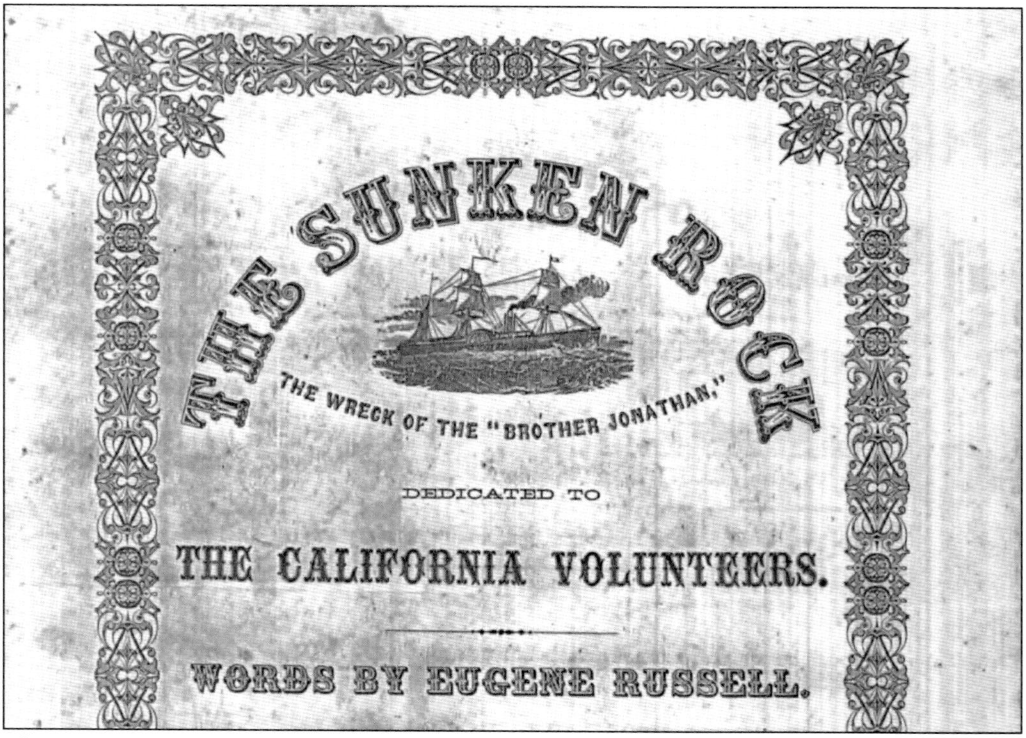

This song, "The Sunken Rock," was written by Eugene Russell with music by P.R. Preyor, and it is the only song known to the author that commemorates the *Jonathan* sinking. Lost to history, it was resurrected by sheet music collector Louis Revor and distributed through local museums. (Louis Revor.)

Two

STONE ON STONE

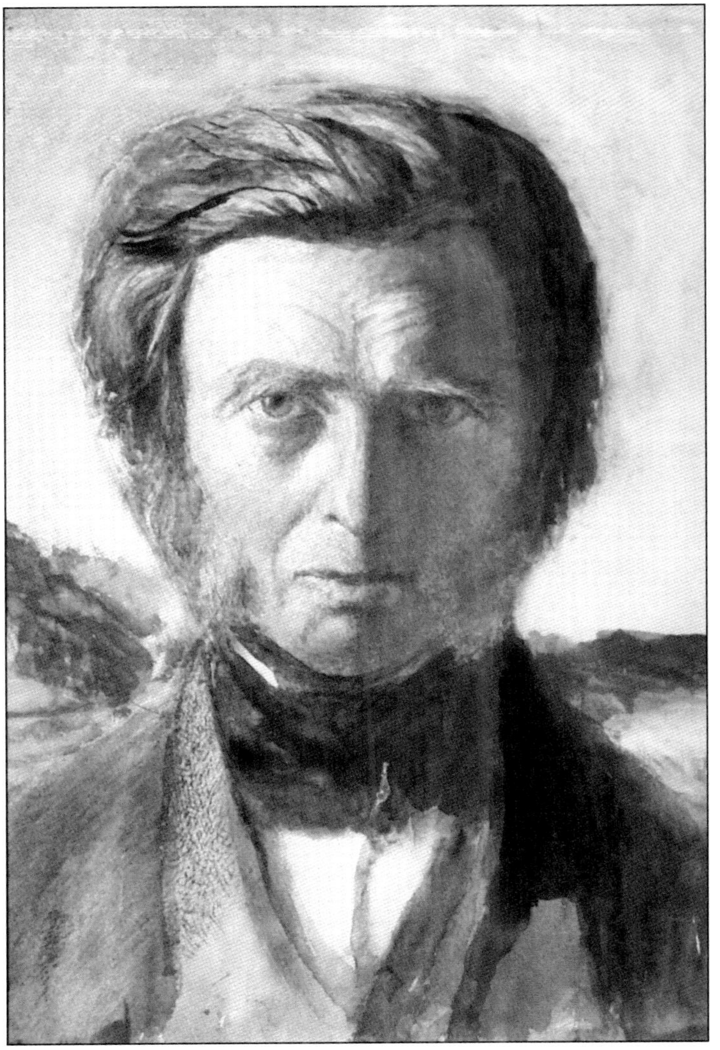

The theme of chapter 2, pride in workmanship, can be found in the writings of 19th-century art critic John Ruskin, who wrote: "When we build . . . Let it be such work as our descendants will thank us for; and let us think, as we lay stone on stone, that a time is to come when those stones will be held sacred because our hands have touched them."

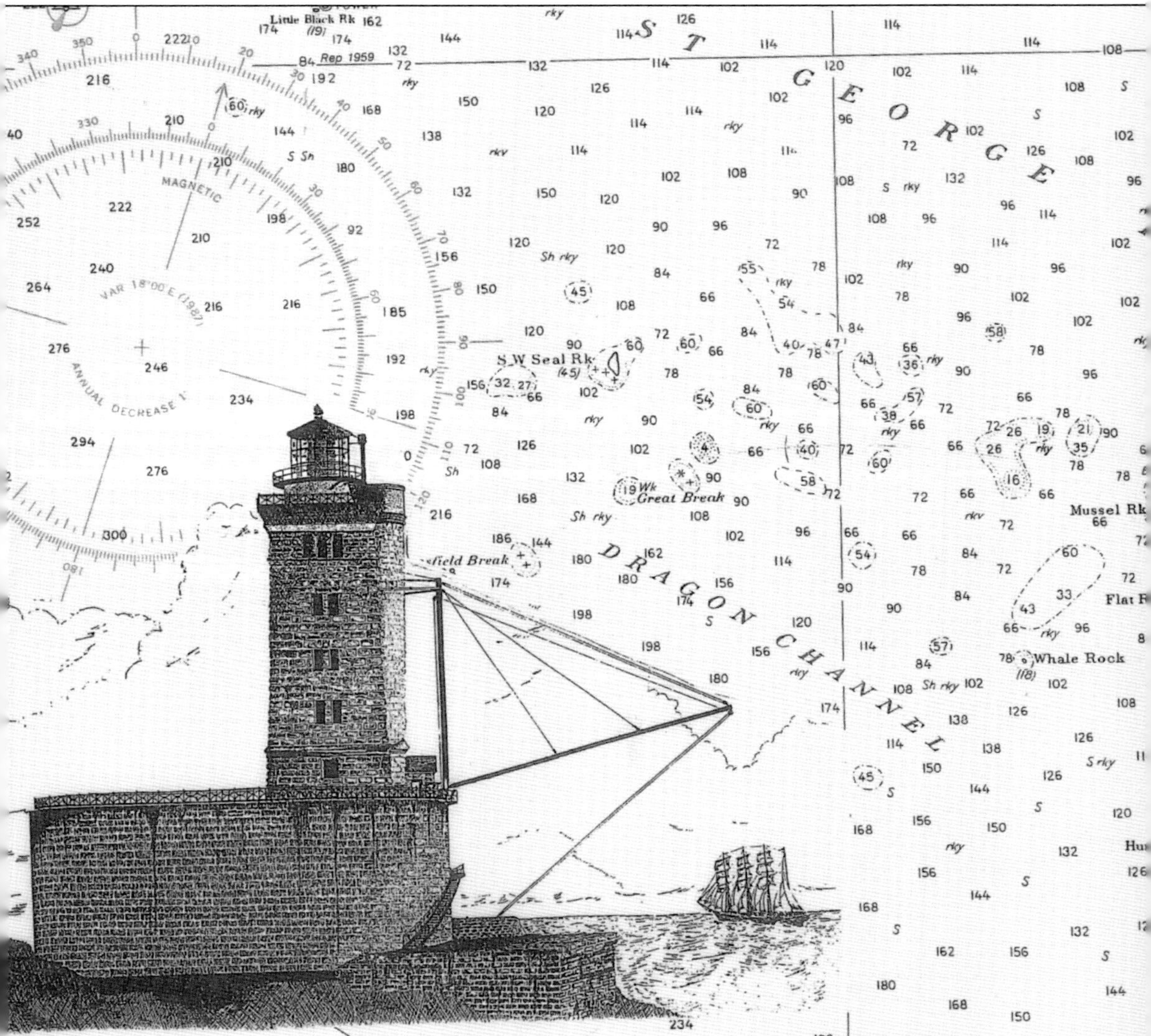

With the cries of the *Jonathan* victims still resonating from press coverage, the lighthouse board took the first step toward establishing a lighthouse in May 1866, when it requested the general land office to reserve land at Point St. George. Potential sites were later expanded to include what was described as "all the rocky islets off Pt. St. George," when it was argued that an offshore light was needed to warn mariners of the submerged reef. However, a pilot project was needed to prove that

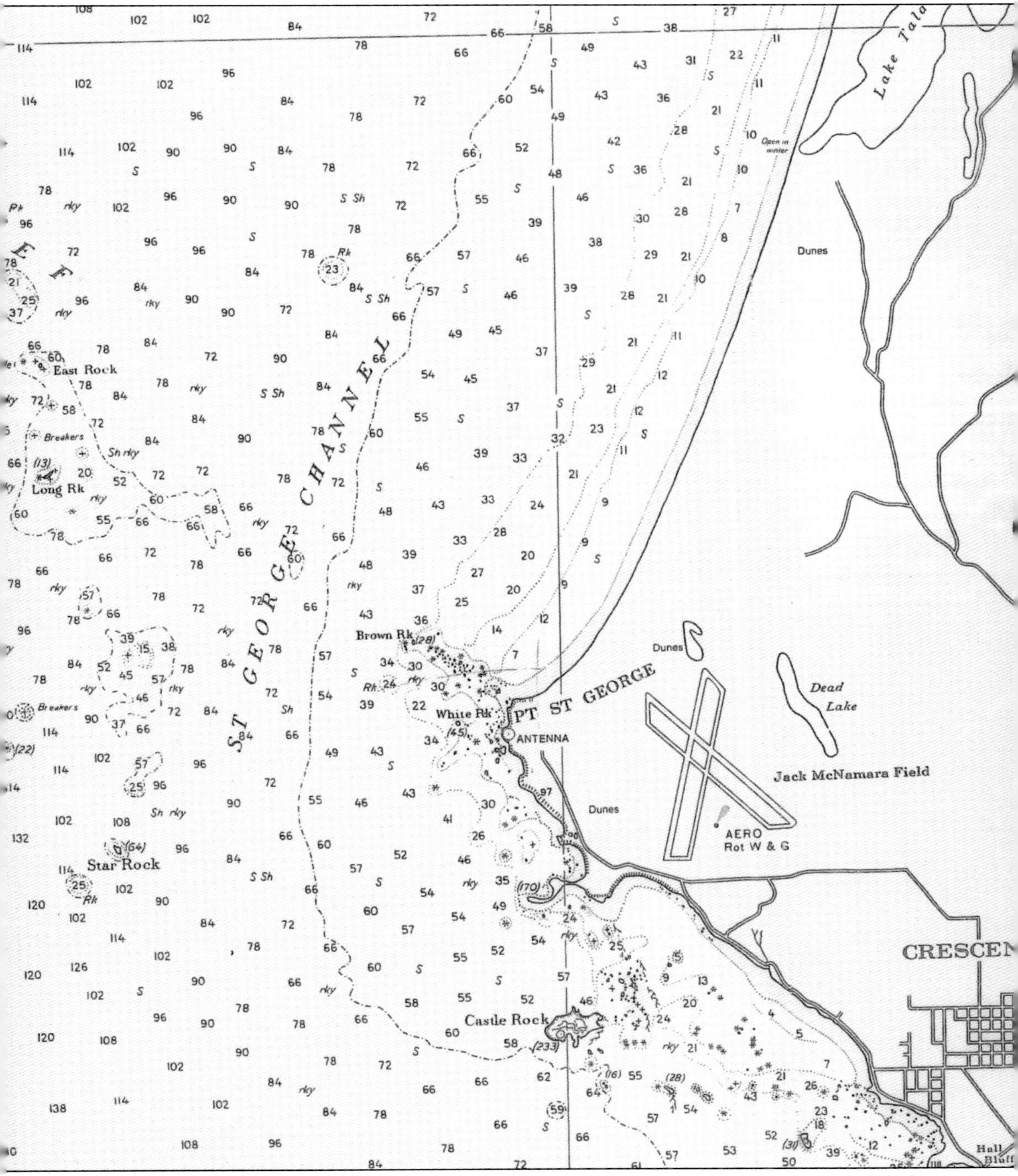

a lighthouse could be built on an exposed rock in the stormy Pacific Ocean; such an undertaking was transpiring hundreds of miles north in Oregon. Later, it was decided the lighthouse would be on Northwest Seal Rock instead of Castle Rock. Here is a NOAA coastal chart showing St. George Reef with the superimposed image of the lighthouse. (NOAA.)

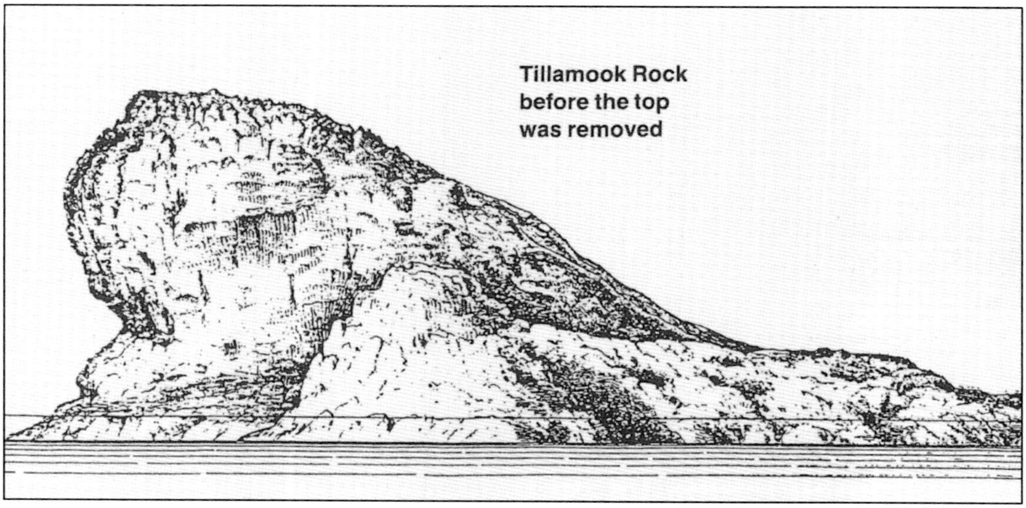

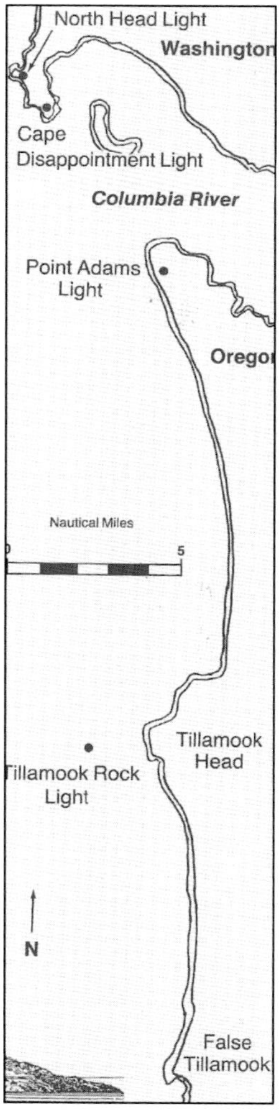

Destined to be the proving ground for the challenge at St. George Reef was Tillamook Rock, shown here as it appeared prior to being excavated for its lighthouse. As with St. George, the site was in an exposed location and pounded by huge seas and fearsome weather. Any builder who could prevail there could master similar conditions in California waters. (US Lighthouse Society.)

First proposals for a new light at "Terrible Tilly" were submitted in June 1878, and Charles A. Ballantyne was appointed civilian superintendent of construction. The building of the lighthouse on Tillamook Rock is an epic of endurance, ingenuity, and tragedy, foreshadowing events of St. George Reef a decade later. The light was turned on January 21, 1881, and the schematic shows the location of Tillamook Rock. (US Lighthouse Society.)

The plan of operation, first successfully employed at Tillamook and then at St. George, was to house the crew in a barrack ship moored nearby and transport the men to and from the worksite in a boatswain chair suspended from a line that was attached to the mast of the ship and a rock. Notice the arrangement of derricks for moving stone and the barrack ship moored nearby with a line running from the mast to the rock for transporting men and materials. (US Lighthouse Society.)

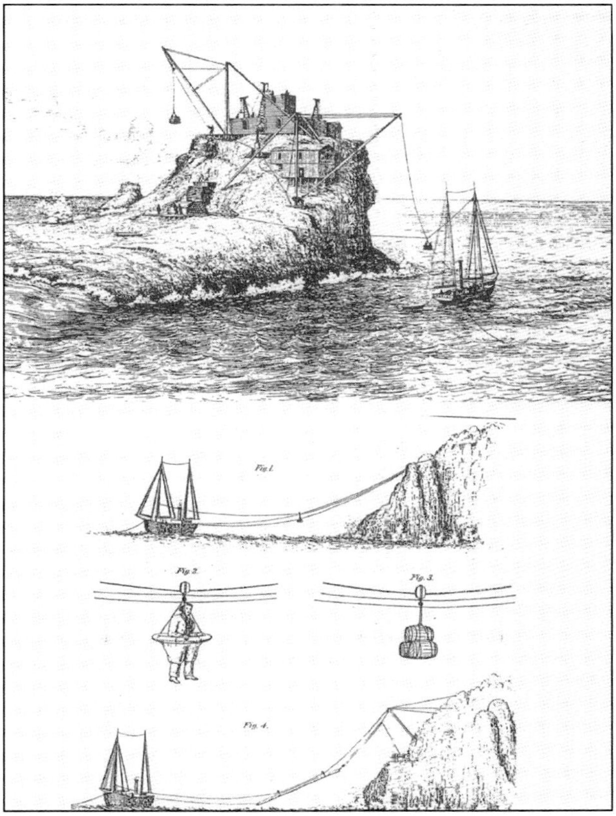

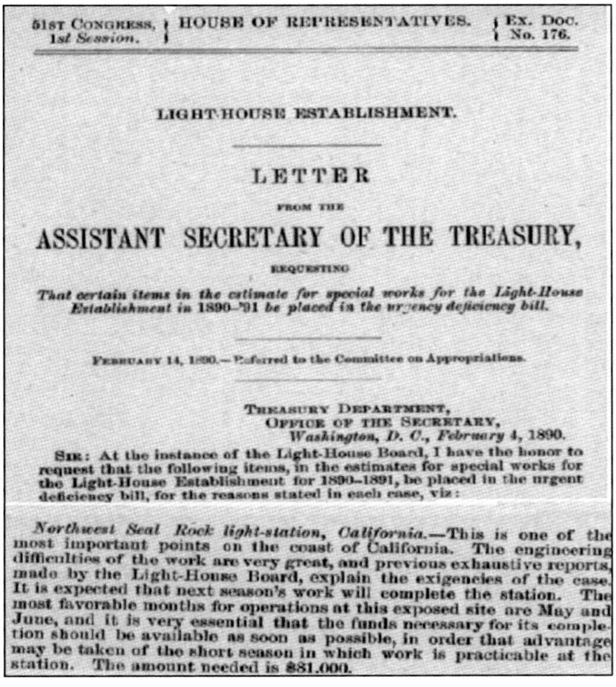

51st Congress, 1st Session. | HOUSE OF REPRESENTATIVES. | Ex. Doc. No. 176.

LIGHT-HOUSE ESTABLISHMENT.

LETTER

FROM THE

ASSISTANT SECRETARY OF THE TREASURY,

REQUESTING

That certain items in the estimate for special works for the Light-House Establishment in 1890-'91 be placed in the urgency deficiency bill.

February 14, 1890.—Referred to the Committee on Appropriations.

Treasury Department,
Office of the Secretary,
Washington, D. C., February 4, 1890.

Sir: At the instance of the Light-House Board, I have the honor to request that the following items, in the estimates for special works for the Light-House Establishment for 1890-1891, be placed in the urgent deficiency bill, for the reasons stated in each case, viz:

Northwest Seal Rock light-station, California.—This is one of the most important points on the coast of California. The engineering difficulties of the work are very great, and previous exhaustive reports, made by the Light-House Board, explain the exigencies of the case. It is expected that next season's work will complete the station. The most favorable months for operations at this exposed site are May and June, and it is very essential that the funds necessary for its completion should be available as soon as possible, in order that advantage may be taken of the short season in which work is practicable at the station. The amount needed is $81,000.

Following Ballantyne's success, Northwest Seal Rock, one of the Rocky Islets, was selected as the building site, and the lighthouse board made its case for funding in the annual report for 1874. An appropriation of $50,000 was finally granted in 1882. Although the document shown here is a request for funds at a later date, it is shown as an example of appropriation requests. (National Archives.)

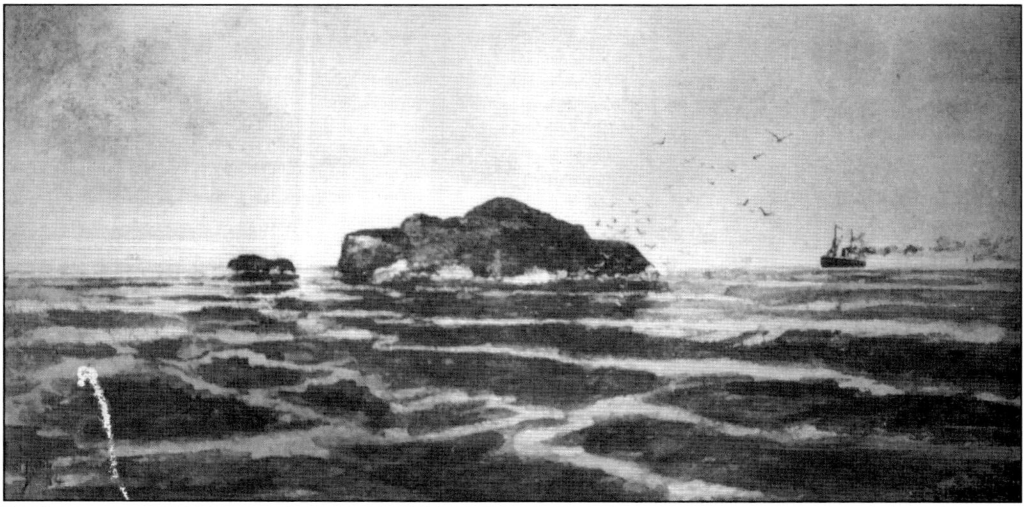

In the spring of 1882, civil engineer Alfred Craven performed the first survey of the islet that would become the home for the lighthouse. He produced a detailed drawing of the rock. His findings reported to Lieutenant Payson showed that the oval-shaped rock had an area of 46,000 square feet (1.6 acres). The rock had a high, central ridge 54 feet above sea level, and Craven recommended excavation to begin 30 feet lower. (Odonnell Entertainment.)

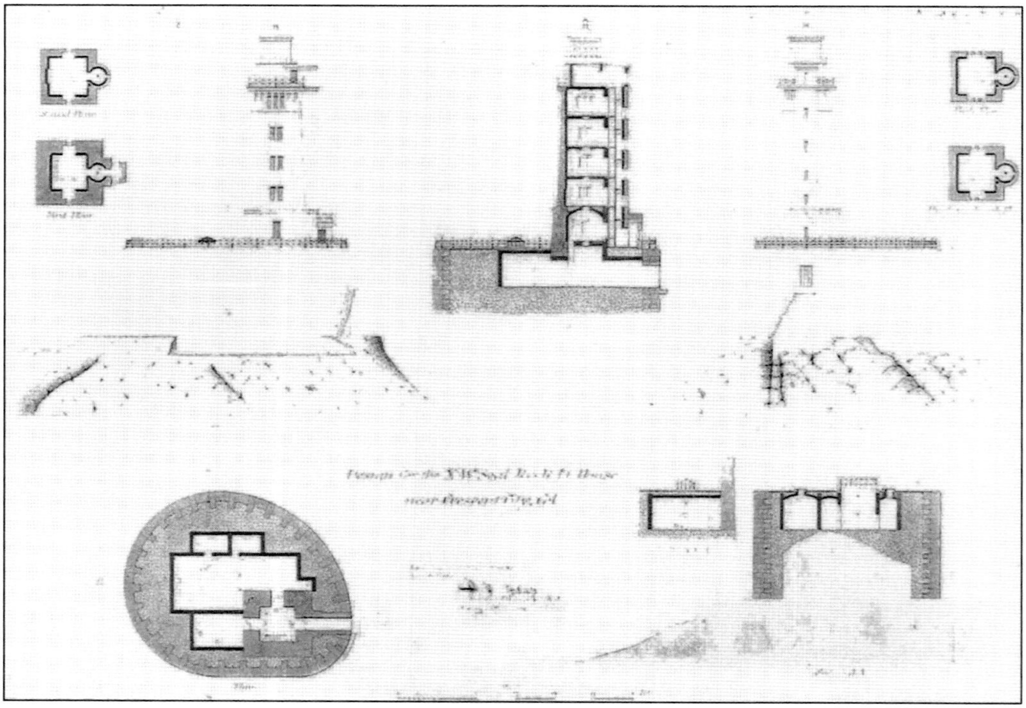

To Ballantyne's trained eye, this elevation would contain the overall plan for the light station at Northwest Seal Rock. A light of the first order needed to be established with a focal point 142 feet above mean sea level. The station would also feature a six-story tower containing keepers' rooms, a kitchen, and storage area, all atop a more than 60-foot caisson (pier) fitted to ledges cut into rock. The source of the building stone is yet to be determined. (National Archives.)

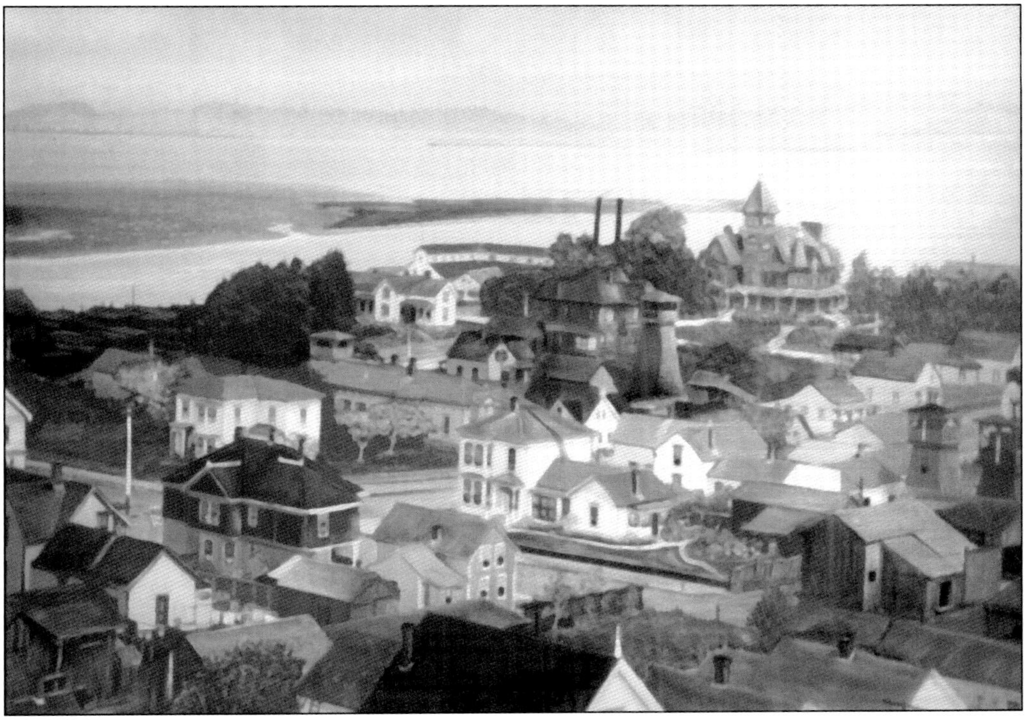

The lighthouse board selected Humboldt Bay, 70 miles south of the building site, as its logistical headquarters. The bay and its environs ultimately provided the vast amounts of granite, brick, lumber, and cement necessary for the undertaking off Crescent City. Here is an early scene, showing a portion of the harbor's chief city, Eureka, with its Victorian architecture and the bay in the background. (Sam Swanlund.)

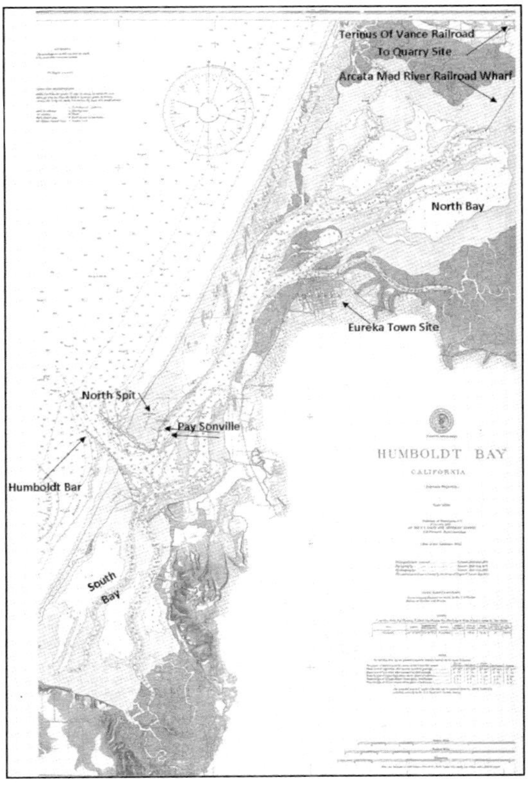

This 1901 map shows water depths of the main channels in Humboldt Bay and the surrounding ocean, important information for shipmasters transporting men and materials to and from the lighthouse construction site. The Humboldt Bay is known and feared worldwide for the mountainous swells produced in its narrow channel by tidal runoff colliding with Pacific surf, but the St. George vessels all did well. (US Coast and Geodetic Survey.)

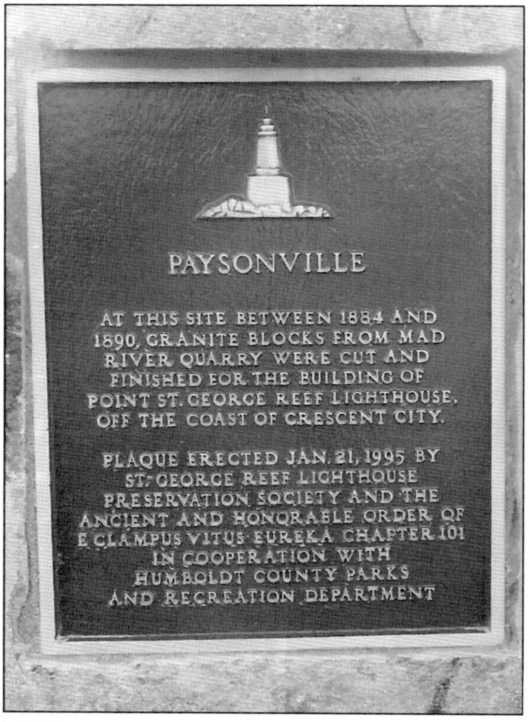

Ballantyne discovered a deposit of huge granite boulders near an existing railroad on the Mad River in present-day McKinleyville. The rail line terminated on Humboldt Bay, so the stone had to be ferried to a processing facility across the bay, which came to be known as "Paysonville" in recognition of the Army engineer in charge of the project. The St. George Reef Lighthouse Preservation Society placed a boulder from the quarry at the Paysonville site. (Author's collection.)

Pictured here is the granite quarry at Hannah's Crossing. A *Weekly Times-Telephone* article dated June 7, 1884, details operations at the site: "Ballantyne is currently overseeing the work at the quarry, but when the material arrives at the rock, Mr. Chalmers will be in charge of the quarry and Mr. Brown will supervise the building site." Note the system of booms that transported the stones to an awaiting railcar. (Humboldt County Historical Society.)

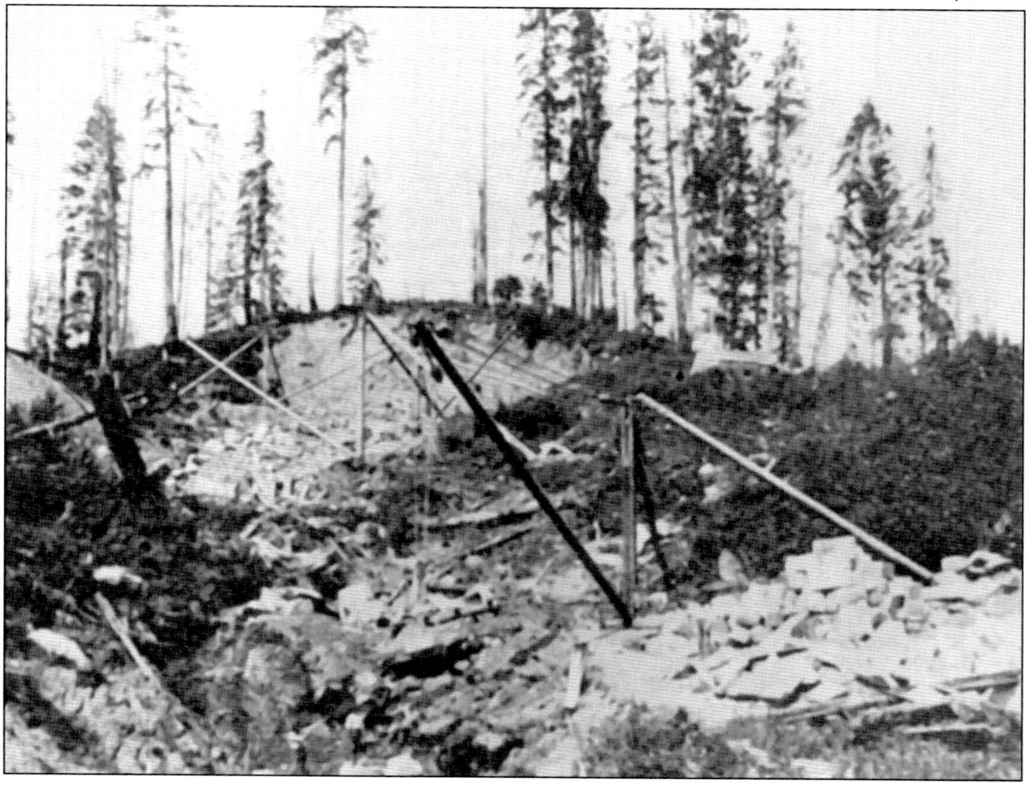

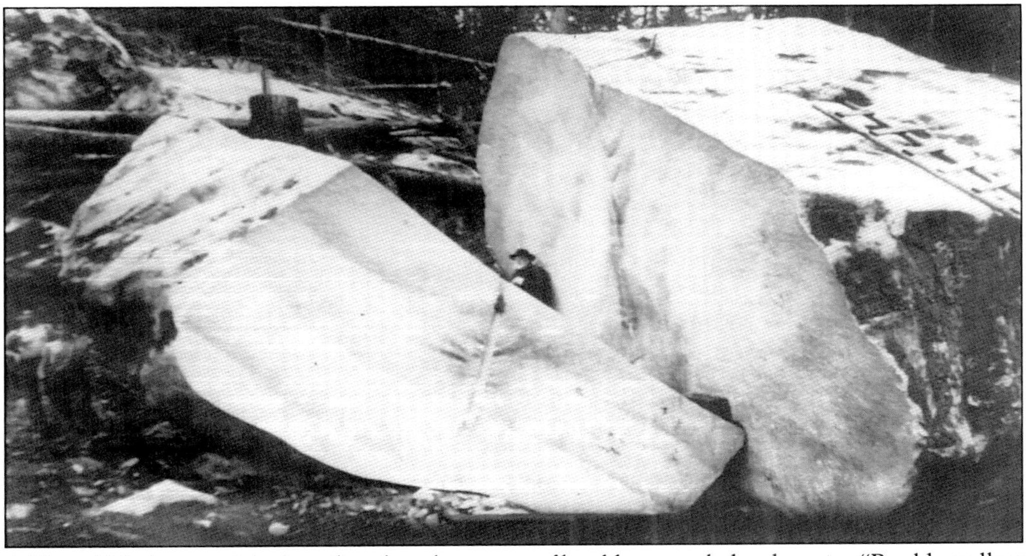

A *Times-Telephone* article describes the advantages of boulders over ledge deposits: "Boulders allow the workmen to attack the rock from several sides at once." This view, taken in the same time period as the work at St. George, is a scene showing the cleaving of a giant boulder in a nearby quarry owned by Isaac Minor, a pioneer businessman. (Humboldt County Historical Society.)

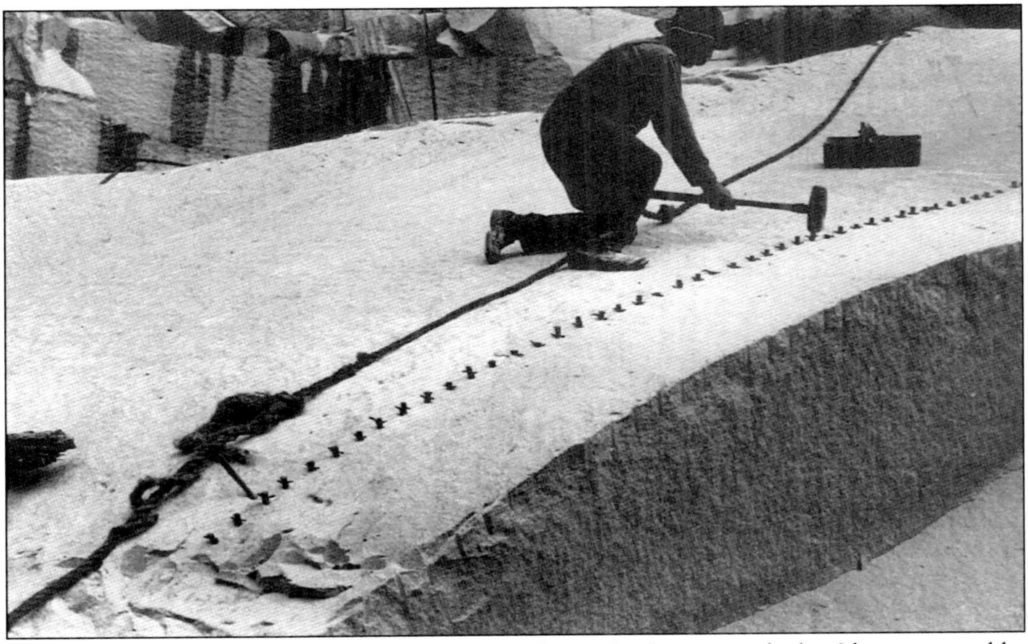

St. George is constructed of giant granite slabs, and to make the cuts in the boulders manageable, they are further reduced by being cut into dimension or pattern stones. It is a slow process of making six-inch-deep indentations in the stone with star drills inserted into metal sleeves and uncounted blows of the hammer, slicing off a nearly perfect slab. (Aldrich Public Library.)

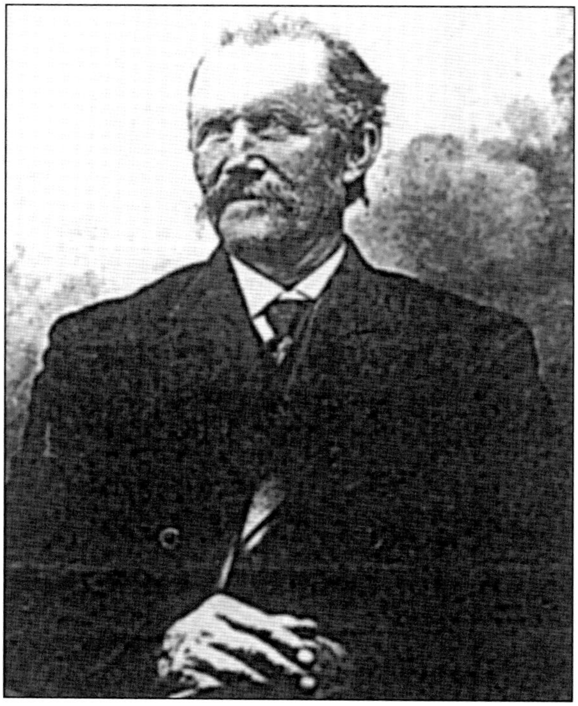

The photograph at left, provided by society members Bill and Betty Barton, is of Oscar Sjorn, who worked at the quarry. However, the more than 75 masons at St. George, the Mad River Quarry, and Paysonville remain for the most part unnamed. Yet research at the 11th Coast Guard District offices in Alameda, California, revealed a remarkable document, too large to fit in these pages. It is a scale drawing showing every stone in the exterior wall of the tower inscribed with the name of a mason. Their names are listed in the final report. In the drawing, each slab of stone is delineated and personally signed by the mason who finished it at Paysonville. Here is a composite drawing listing some of the names. (Left, Bill and Betty Barton; below, Dordy Round and the SGRLPS Archives.)

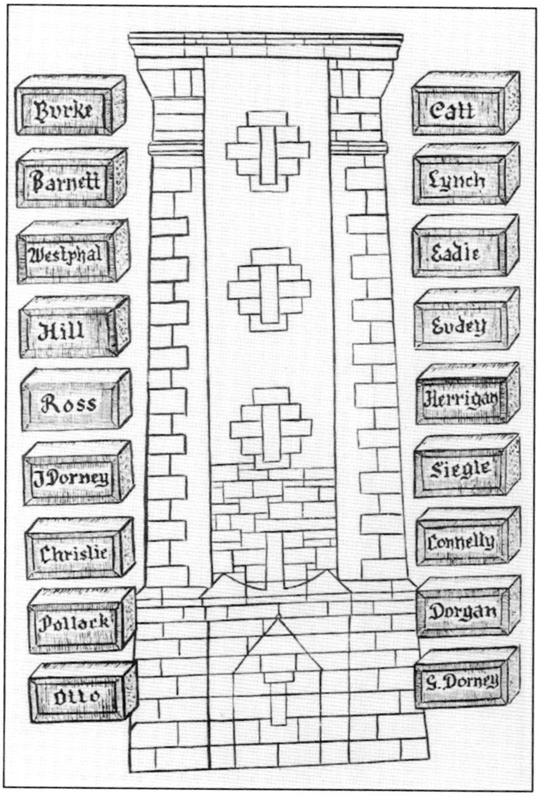

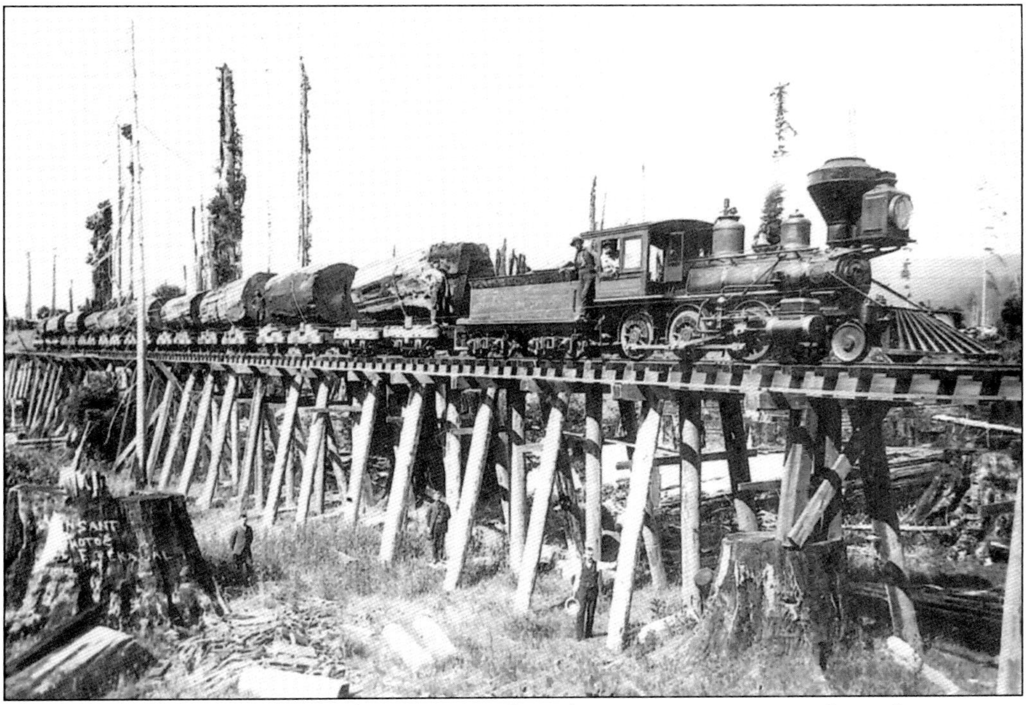

The rail line that carried the rough stone pieces from the quarry to an awaiting barge for transport to the finishing shed was owned and operated by pioneer businessman John Vance. The line was designed to transport redwood from Vance's operations to the east. Here, cars of redwood logs pulled by one of Vance's locomotives cross a trestle over a branch of the Mad River. (Humboldt County Historical Society.)

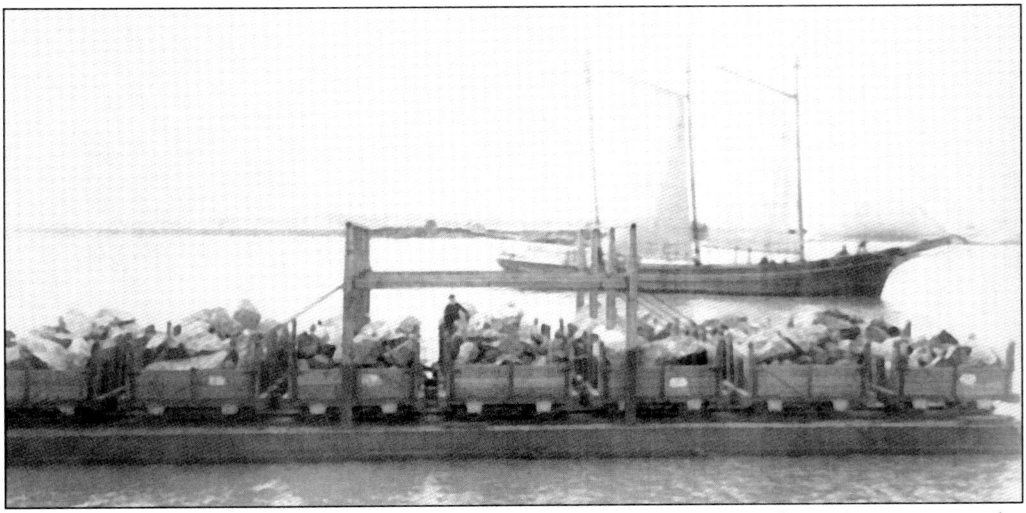

Capt. Harry Smith, with the steamer *Ada*, barged all of the cut stone from the quarry to the masons at the finishing facility. Vance, who had the contract for transporting the rock, built the scow for that purpose. An average haul was about 125 tons, similar to this barge and load of rocks being towed across Humboldt Bay for construction of jetties in the same time period. (Humboldt County Historical Society.)

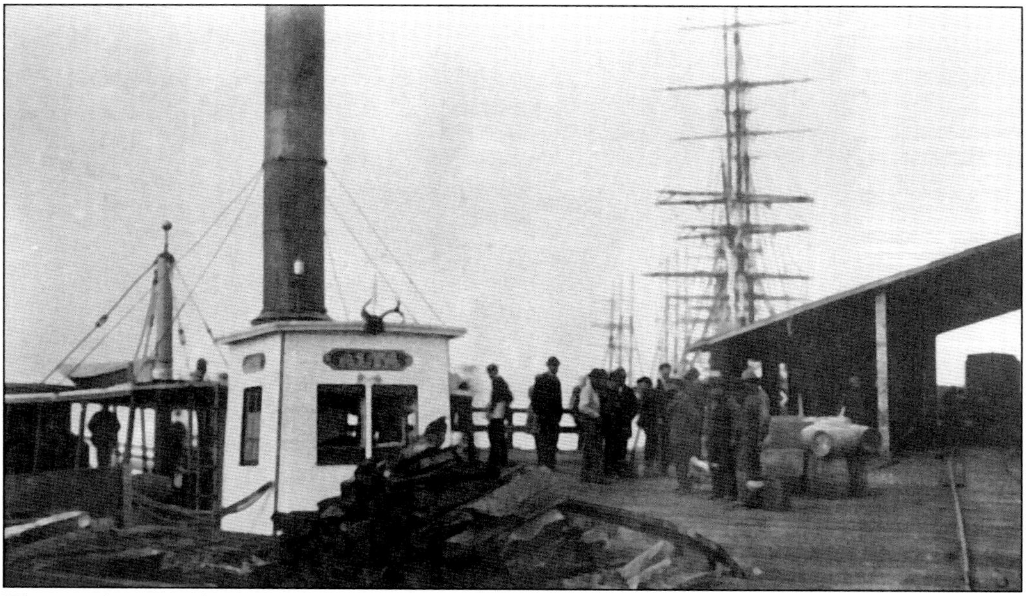

This 1883 image shows the steamboat *Alta* taking on passengers at the Arcata Wharf. In the background are the masts of some of the many sailing ships that frequented the bay. The Vance rail terminus was at the head of Mad River Slough, west of the Arcata Wharf. (Photograph by Edgar Cherry, private collection.)

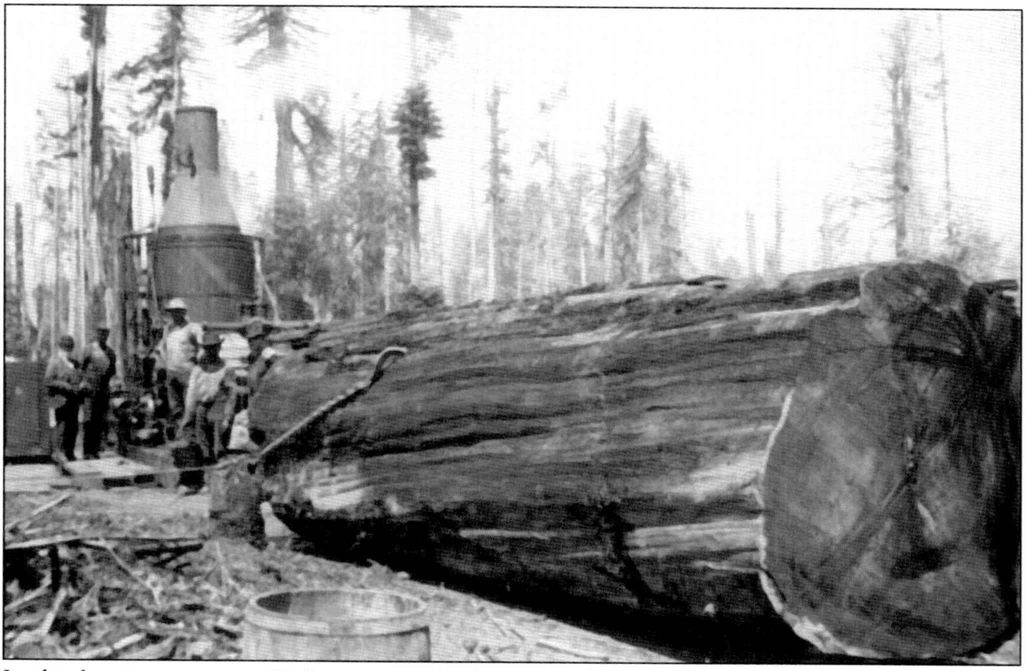

In this logging scene is a Dolbeer steam donkey, named for its inventor, James Dolbeer. Capable of moving strings of tethered giant redwoods, it logically found its way into the movement of stone. A variety of the Dolbeer was probably employed at Paysonville in conjunction with the type of derrick seen at the quarry. (Private collection.)

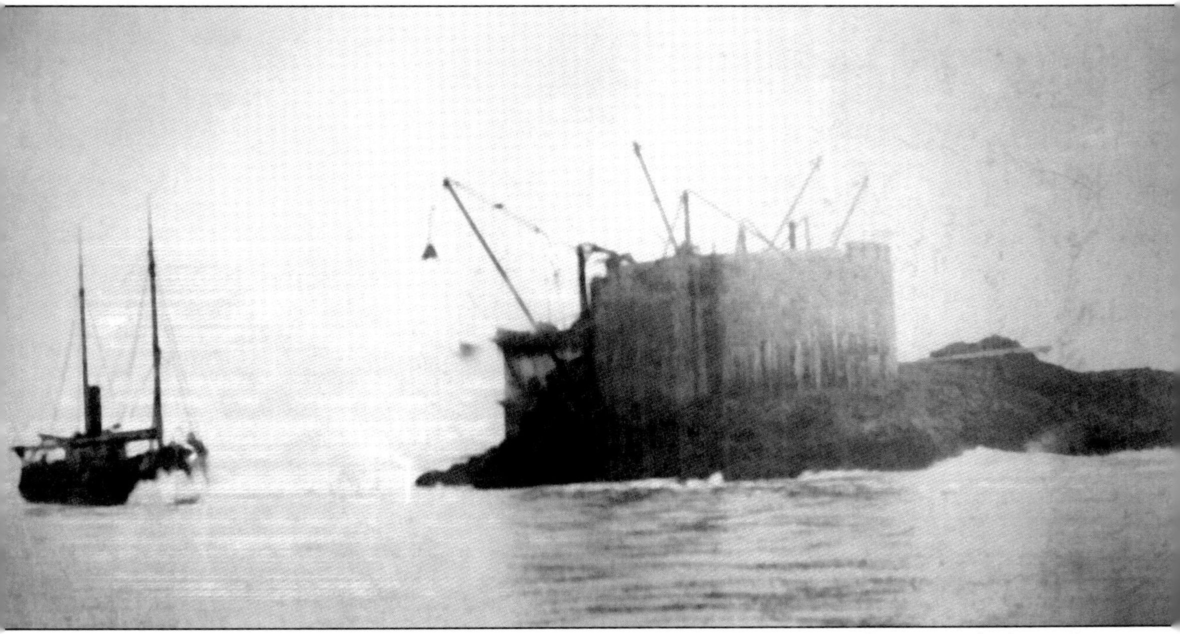

In March 1889, the first task the workers faced was repairing the winter storm damage to the barracks constructed the year before on the rock. The season brought severe weather and soakings for the men in the barracks, but by June the outer walls of the caisson rose high enough to reduce the threat of wave action, with the interior walls of the engine room, coal storage, and tower keeping pace. As the season progressed, the caissons rose to six stories, but spray still dampened mortar and stalled work. In this scene from June 1889, the steamer *Del Norte* completes the transfer of material from its rigging to the derrick positioned at the base of the caisson. The stone was then passed to a derrick with a flex extension, which allows it to bend and directly put the masonry in place or transfer it to a stone setter's boom. (National Archives.)

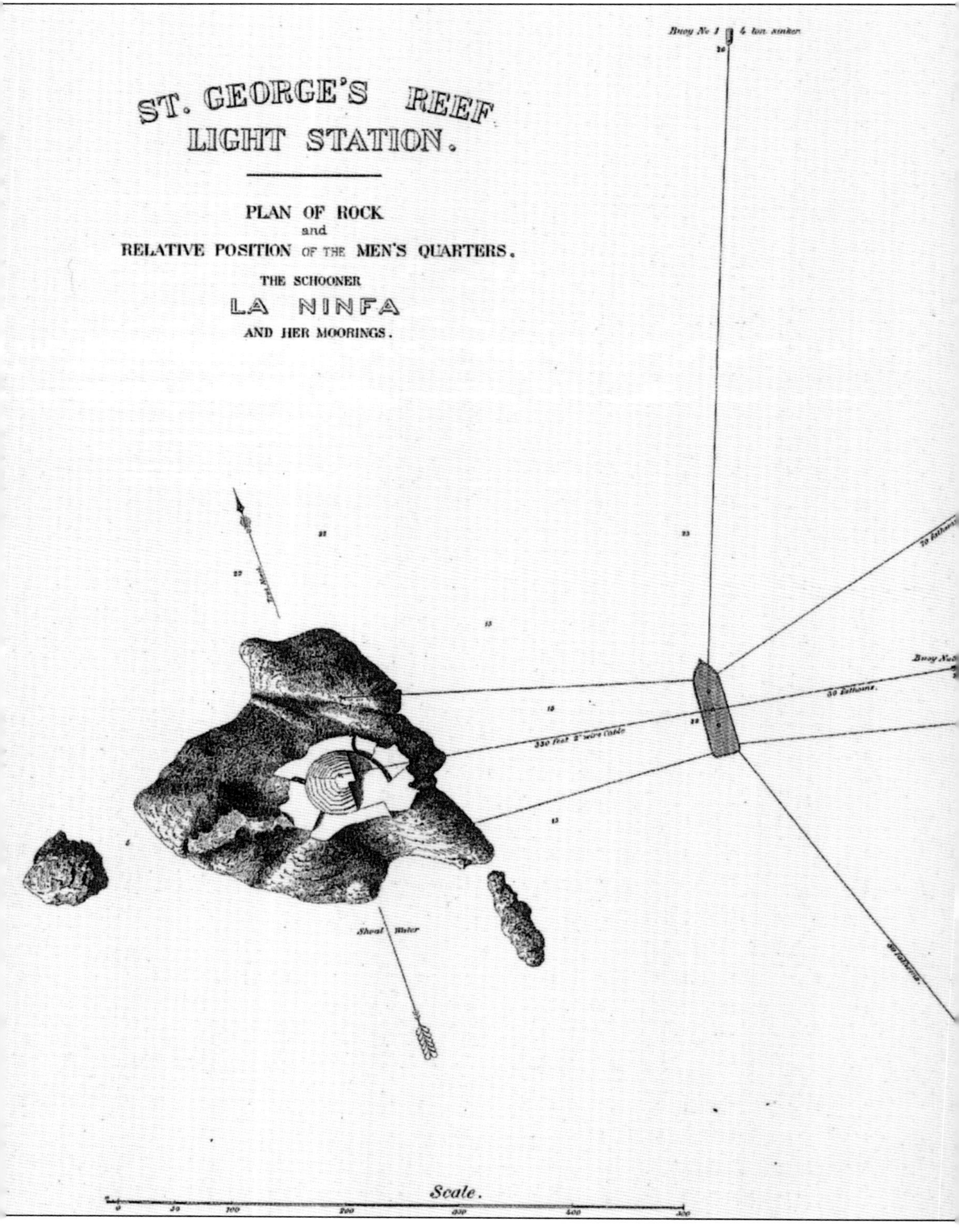
ST. GEORGE'S REEF
LIGHT STATION.
PLAN OF ROCK
and
RELATIVE POSITION OF THE MEN'S QUARTERS.
THE SCHOONER
LA NINFA
AND HER MOORINGS.
Buoy No 1
4 ton sinker
330 feet 2" wire Cable
30 fathoms
Shoal Water
Scale.

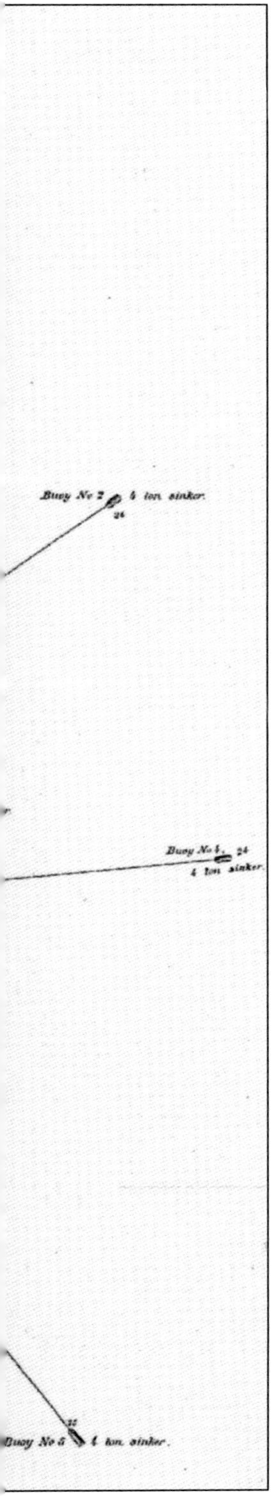

This engineering drawing, dated 1886, helps to show the role played by the barracks ship in the construction of St. George. In 1883, Ballantyne received the second round of funding for the project and chartered the steamer *LaNinfa* to act as housing for the work crew. As at Tillamook, the *LaNinfa* is depicted here at its moorings off of Northwest Seal Rock, with a line to act as a trolley running from the ship's mast to the islet for conveying the masons to and from the site. The ledges portrayed in the drawing have been cut into the rock for placement of the stone slabs quarried and finished at Paysonville. In 1887, *LaNinfa* was replaced by the steamer *Sparrow*, which carried the granite slabs safely to the stone setters. (Odonnell Entertainment.)

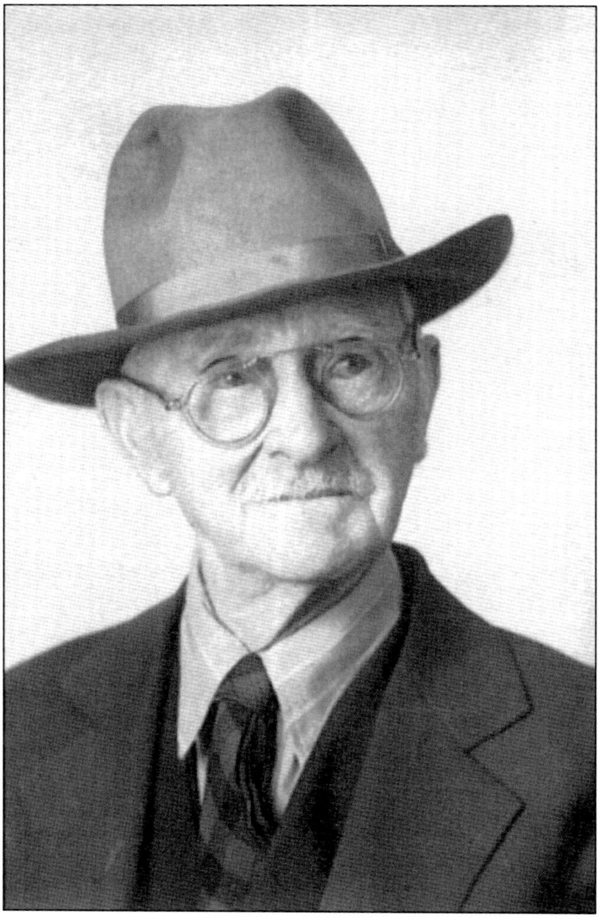

The quantity of brick used in the construction of St. George is known from the builder's report, but the supplier remained unidentified for some time. However, records were found at the National Archives that identify the businessman as Jessie Lentell of Eureka. Lentell, a prominent civil engineer, is best known for producing the first comprehensive map of Humboldt County. He is pictured here in his later years. (Humboldt County Historical Society.)

Thousands of board feet of timber would come from the dense stands of virgin forest surrounding Humboldt Bay for the seven-story scaffolding, floors, walls, windows, cabinets, doors, and trim that were needed at St. George Reef. The Lincoln Mill in Eureka received the contract from the 12th District office to provide the finished work. Located on Second Street between K and L Streets, it originally opened in January 1881. (Humboldt County Historical Society.)

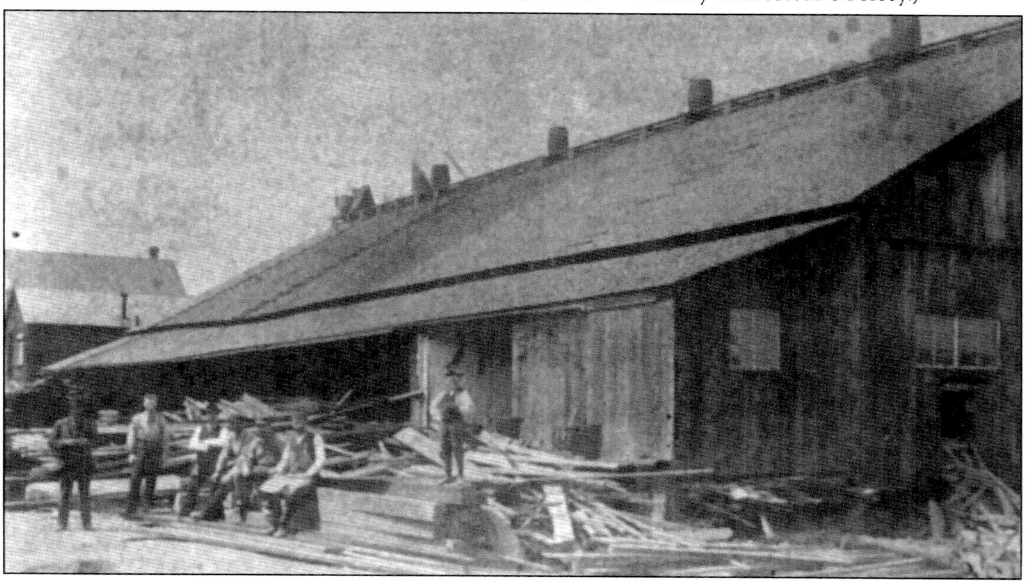

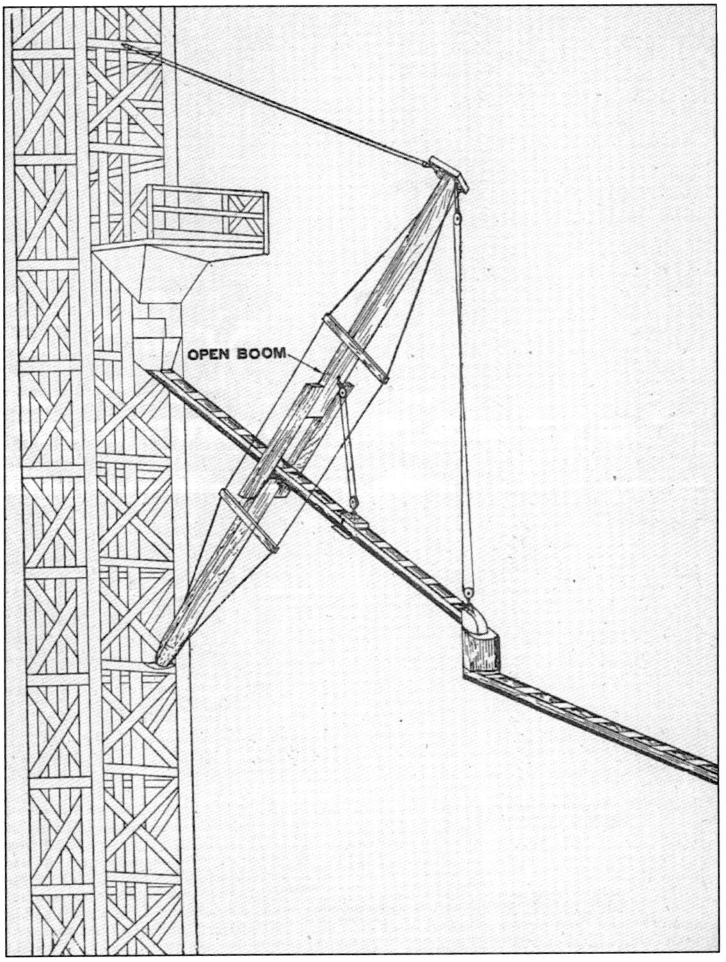

These two illustrations provide a hint as to how concrete was moved from ship to forms: an elementary conveying cableway and what is known as an open boom attached to scaffolding, similar to the scaffolding used for the lighthouse. A possible scenario is that concrete mixture was carried on the cableway and fed into the open boom for pouring into forms set up in the various rooms. (Both, *Audels Masons and Builders Guide*.)

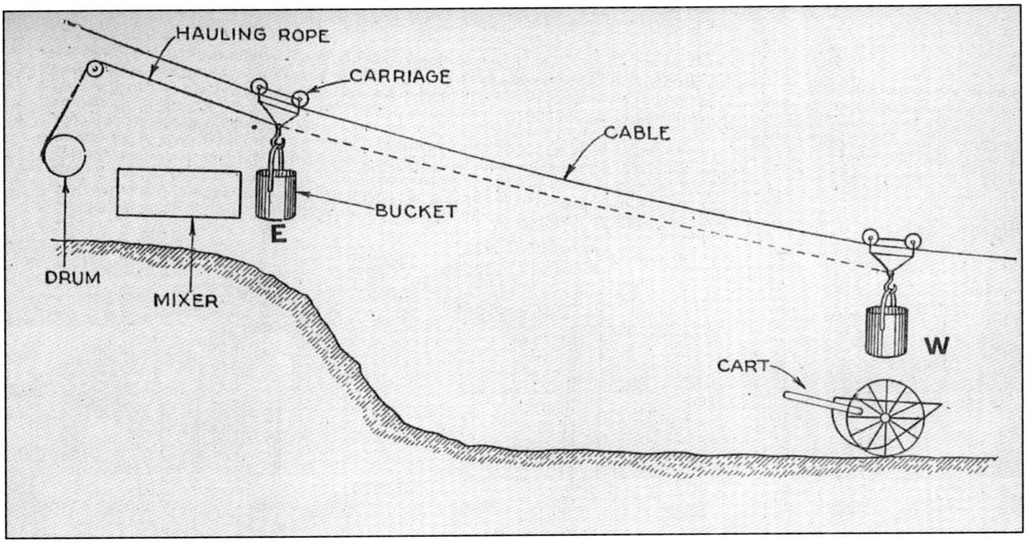

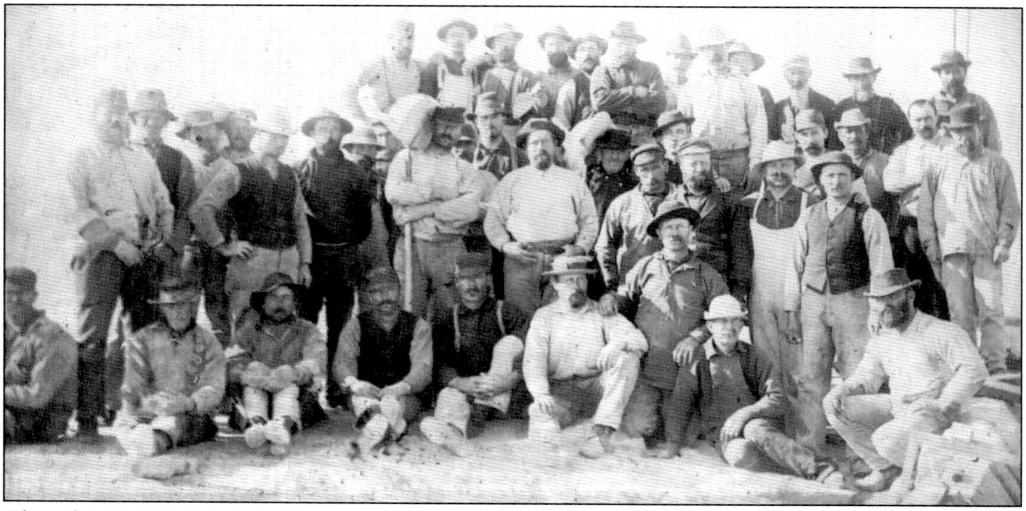

This photograph, one of only two known images of the work crew that built the lighthouse, was taken on-site at the outside wall of the caisson on which the tower stands. The longevity of St. George, enduring the pounding of legendary storms and waves for over a century, is a testimony to their creed of pride in craftsmanship. It is a legacy that motivates the efforts of the St. George Reef Lighthouse Preservation Society. (Humboldt County Historical Society.)

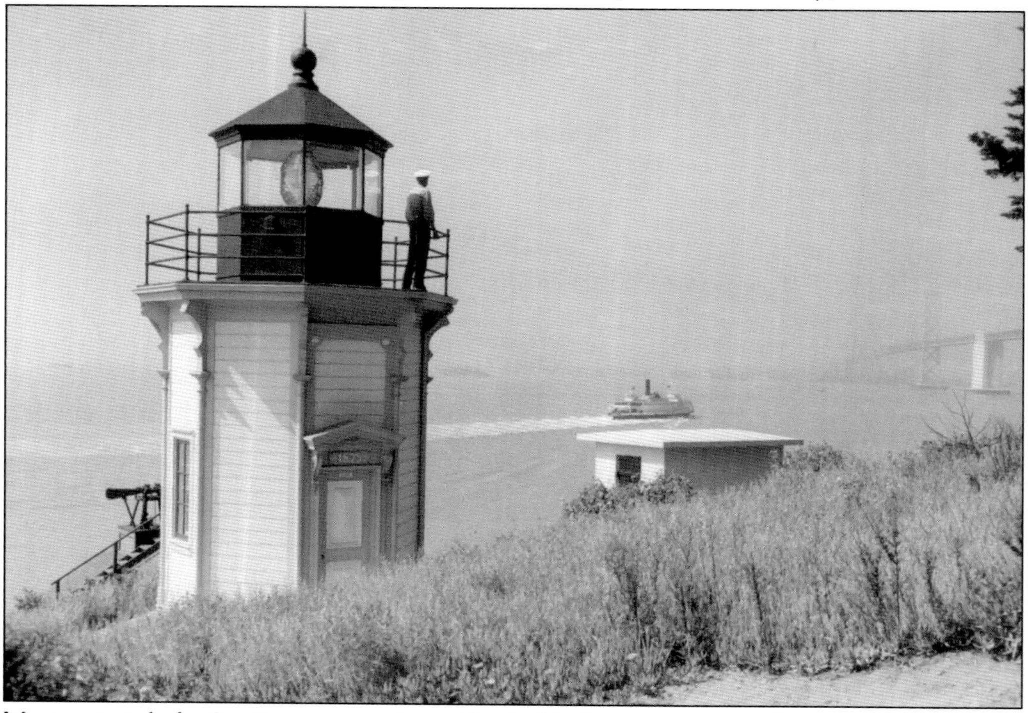

Most materials for St. George came from Humboldt County, yet specialized components were supplied by San Francisco merchants, including Davis & Cowell (lime), Morris Greenberg (brass), Charles J. Hendry & Son and G.M. Josselyn & Co. (ship chandlers), George H. Tay Co. (stoves, metals), Payne Bolt Works, Fulton Iron Works, and Moynihan & Aitkin Boiler Works. Pictured here is San Francisco Bay's lighthouse at Yerba Buena Island. (US Lighthouse Society.)

Pictured here is nearly completed Northwest Seal Rock Lighthouse in August 1891. Many tasks remain: installing woodwork, setting up steam boilers and whistles for fog signals, plastering rooms, painting metalwork, and preparing platforms for hoisting engine and boom. Ballantyne's final report states that all of the work was done, yet keepers were busy for many months after the last of the workforce departed in November. (Humboldt County Historical Society.)

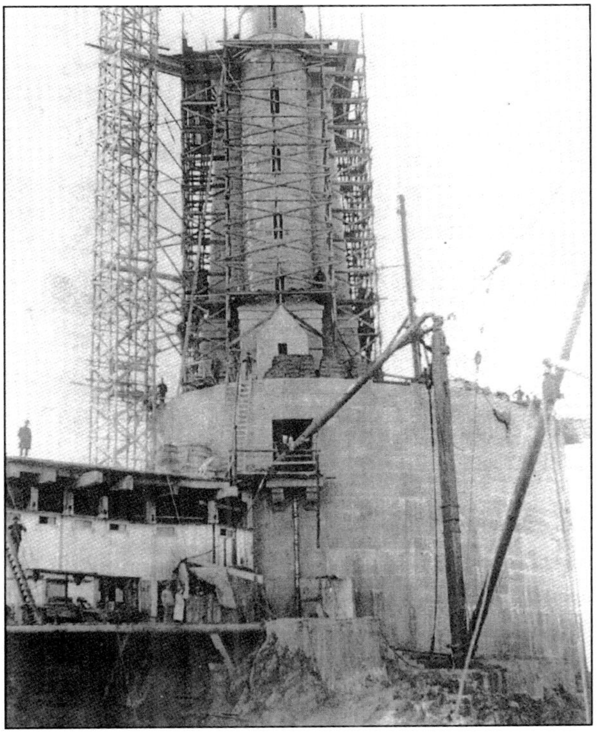

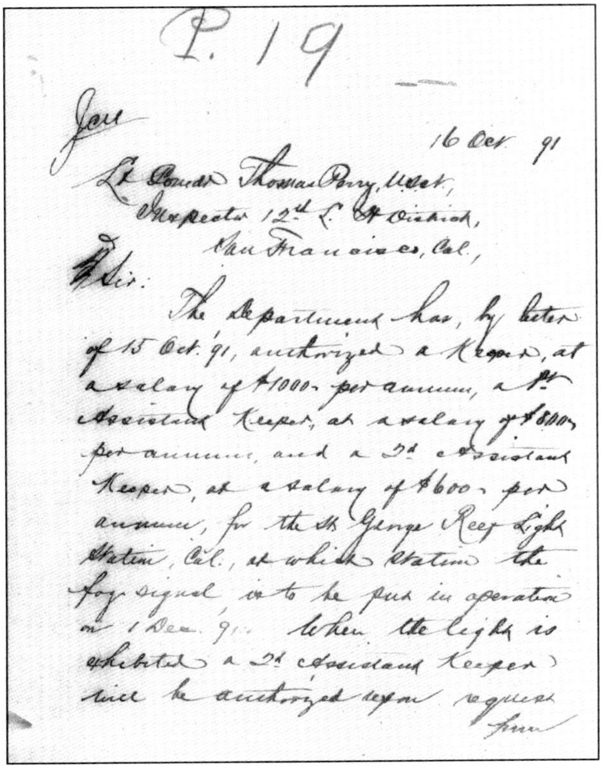

P. 19

16 Oct. 91

Lt. Comdr. Thomas Perry, U.S.N.,
Inspector 12th L. H. District,
San Francisco, Cal.,

Sir:

The Department has, by letter of 15 Oct. '91, authorized a Keeper, at a salary of $1000 per annum, a 1st Assistant Keeper, at a salary of $800 per annum, and a 2d Assistant Keeper, at a salary of $600 per annum, for the St. George Reef Light Station, Cal., at which station the fog signal is to be put in operation on 1 Dec. 91. When the light is exhibited a 3d Assistant Keeper will be authorized upon request from

There was a flurry of activity in the final months of construction to attend to last-minute details. Hurried letters were exchanged between engineers. This handwritten plea by Lt. Comdr. Thomas Perry in October for a keeper (at $1,000 per annum) and assistant keeper ($600) attests to the urgent need for men to operate the fog signal that would become operational on December 1, 1891. (National Archives.)

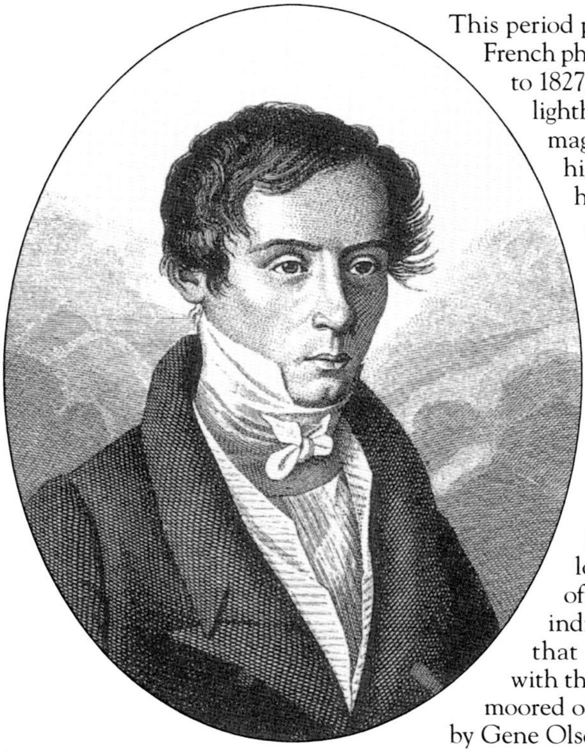

This period portrait is of Augustin Fresnel, a brilliant French physicist who revolutionized optics from 1788 to 1827, replacing ineffective gas and oil lamps in lighthouses with a system of cut-glass prisms that magnified light from a central source into a high-powered beam that could be seen to the horizon. They varied in size, and the largest, a first-order Fresnel, would be placed at St. George Reef. (US Lighthouse Society.)

The lantern room did not show until summer 1891, and the Fresnel, ordered from Henri Lepaut in France, took even longer to arrive. Although the lens was officially ordered on February 5, 1891, the log indicates that it was not until August 8, 1892, that the lighthouse tender *Madrono* arrived with the precious cargo. The *Madrono* is depicted moored off St. George in this historical recreation by Gene Olson. (Author's collection.)

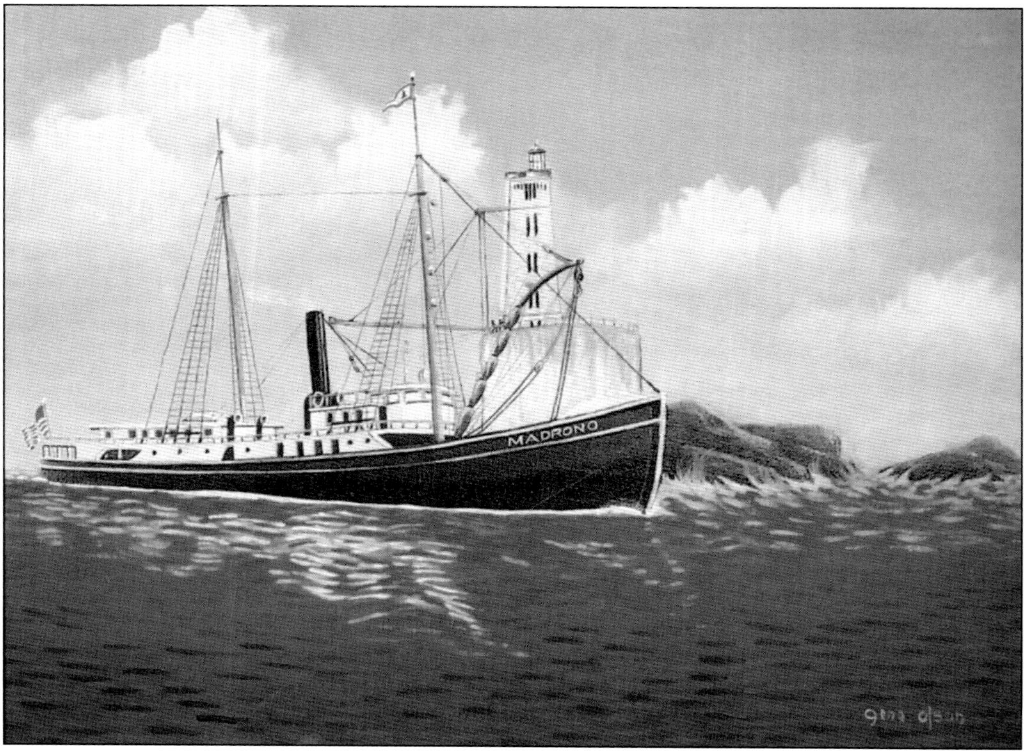

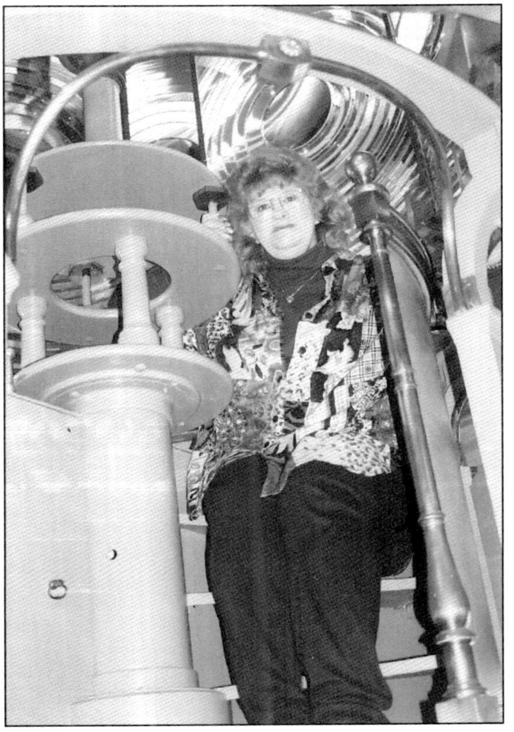

Board correspondence indicates that the first order Fresnel 360-degree red and white lens with 15-second intervals was recommended on November 20, 1885. With delays due to funding, a cost estimate and recommendation to order the lens did not come until the end of January 1891. The jewel-like quality and scale of the 12-foot-tall Fresnel is illustrated in these views taken in the Del Norte County Historical Society Museum in Crescent City. Society volunteers were visiting the exhibit and photographed inside the lens. Marilyn McLaughlin poses in the entryway next to the pedestal that connects the lens to the turning mechanism below. The author looks out of the missing bull's-eye that had been damaged when the apparatus was relocated to the museum. (Both, SGRLPS Archives.)

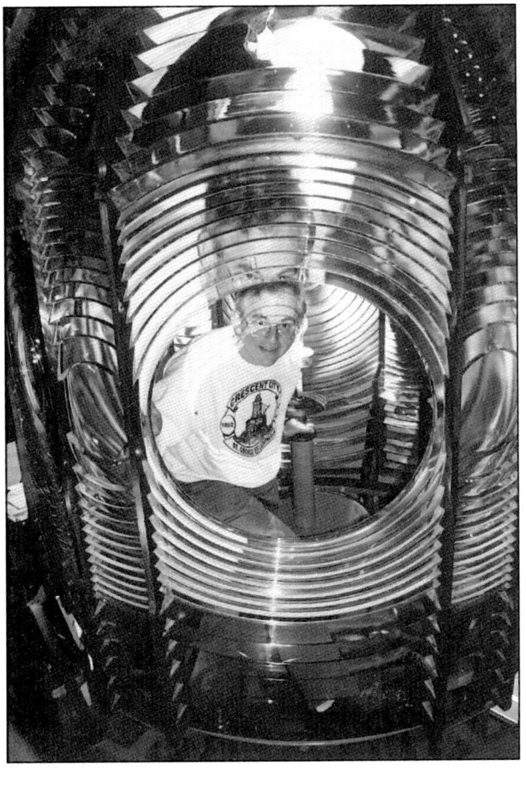

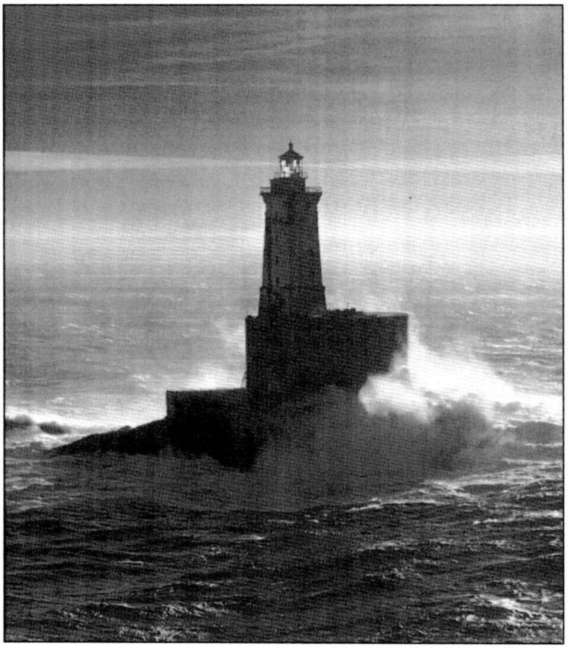

Following delivery of the lens by the *Madrono*, nearly a month of cleaning and assembling the Fresnel optics was required. Finally, at dusk on October 20, 1892, radiant red and white rays pierced the darkness with a flash seen by mariners 20 miles at sea and onshore for at least six miles. The log entry reads, "This is the first date when the light was first exhibited at the station." (Photograph by Dutch Dremmon.)

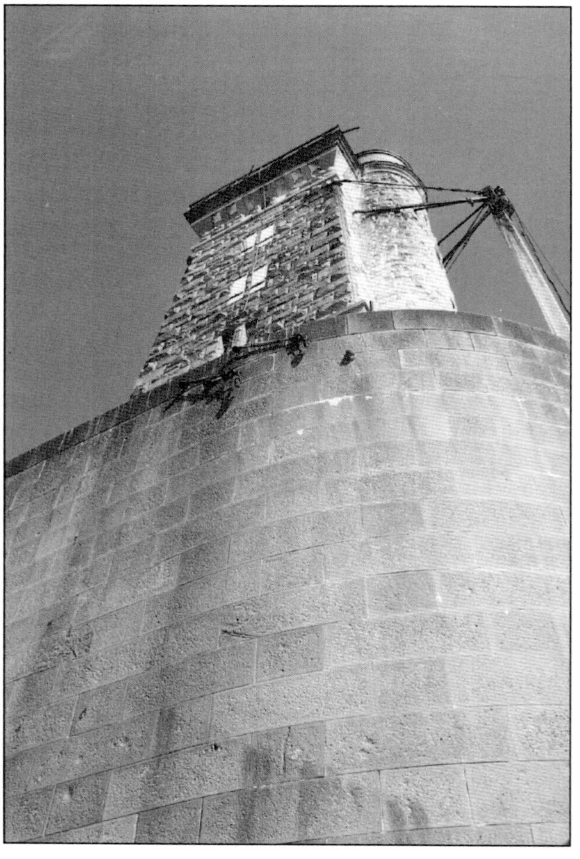

At the conclusion of the project, Ballantyne summarized materials and expenses in his report to the lighthouse board. Here are some examples: 175,200 cubic feet of granite, $15,007; cutting dimension stone, $92,220; preparing the site, $17,500; bricklaying, $840. According to the report, 94,000 bricks were used to line the stonework in the tower. Total costs exceeded $700,000. Sadly, one worker was killed. This is the completed structure shot from sea level. (Author's collection.)

Three

Keepers of the US Lighthouse Service

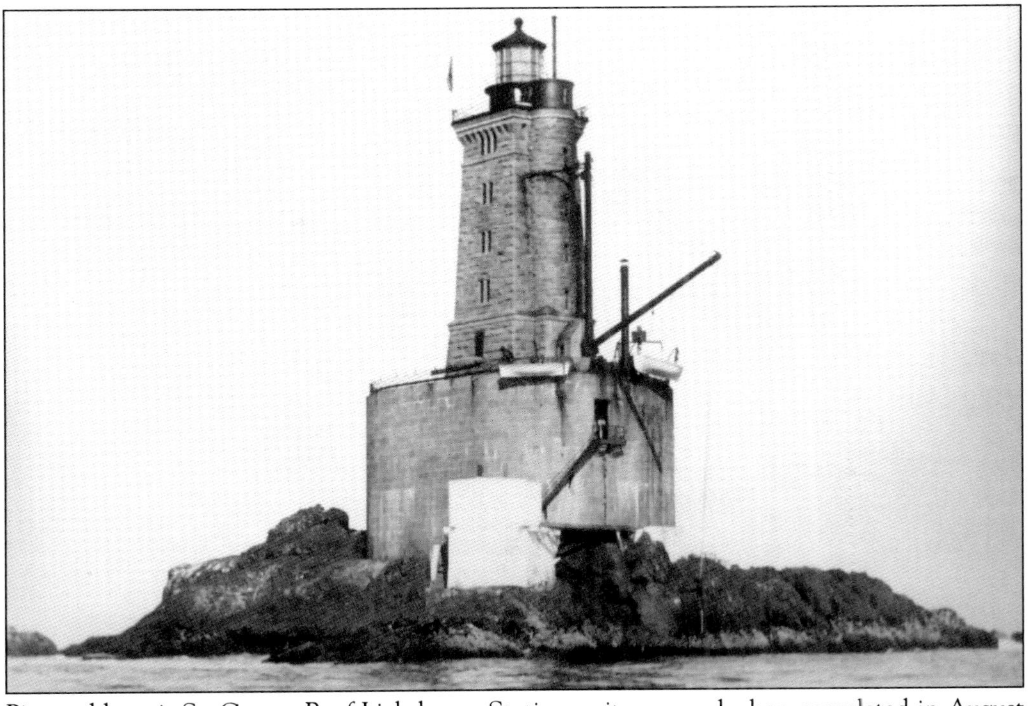

Pictured here is St. George Reef Lighthouse Station as it appeared when completed in August 1891. It must have been a heady experience for the new custodians of this castle at sea, the largest and costliest structure of its type in the United States, requiring the resources of an entire nation to complete. It was the tallest building and only wave-washed lighthouse on the Pacific coast. (Del Norte County Historical Society.)

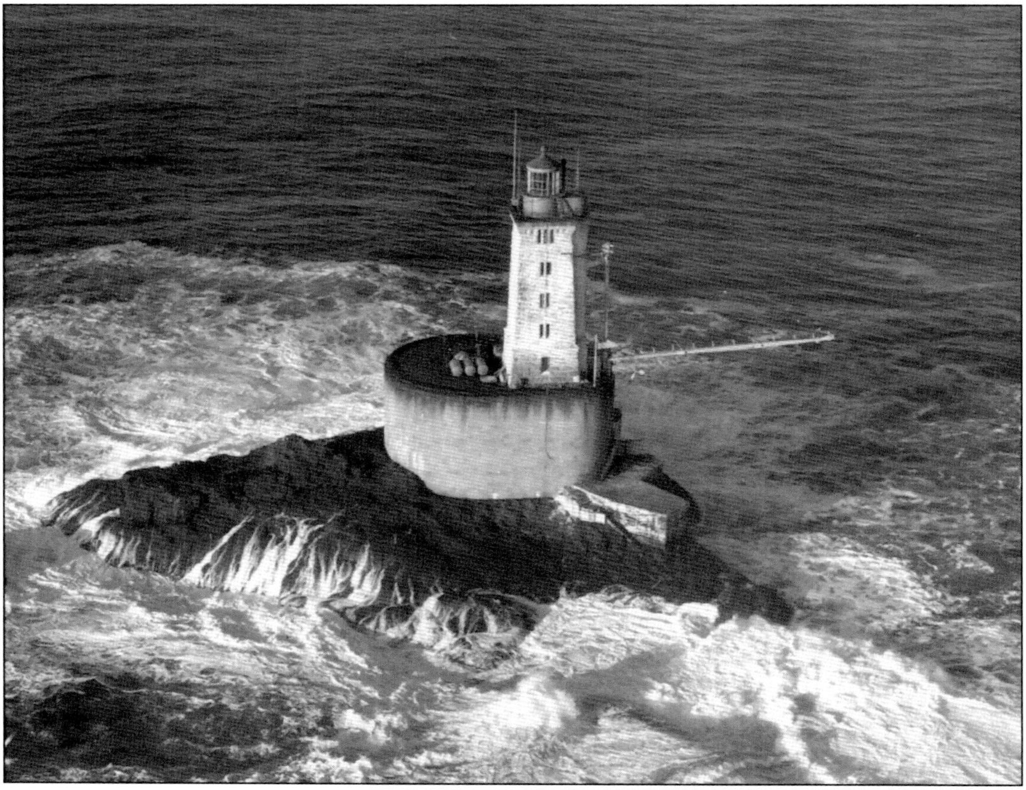

This aerial view was taken in the 1960s, and it offers a more revealing perspective for discussing the beacon as an aid to navigation. Also, excerpts from the *Pacific Coast Pilot 1945 Edition, U.S. Department of Commerce and Coast and Geodetic Survey* provide a cautionary guide to the reef and environs for the mariner approaching the Dragon Rocks. (Coast Guard Historian's Office.)

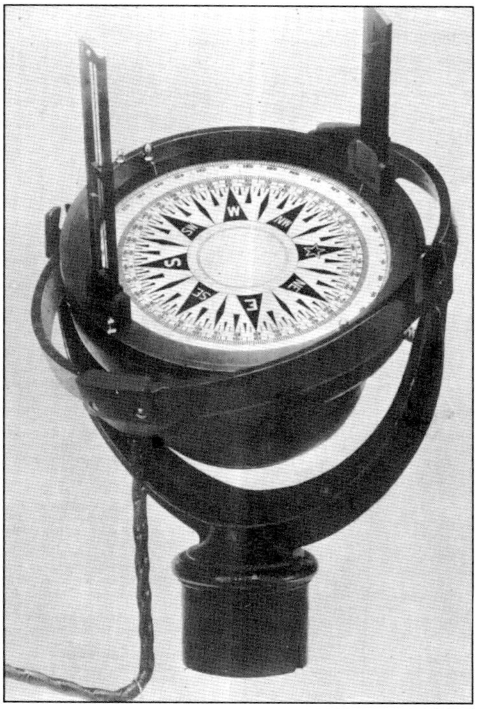

"Crescent City is located on the northern side of a small, rocky contracted bay about three miles southeastward of Point St. George . . . approaches to the harbor are bad . . . St. George Reef is a group of rocks and sunken ledges extending 6.5 miles northwestward . . . from Point St. George." The visible rocks vary from 18 to 45 feet in height. Early mariners relied on compasses such as this one shown here. (*American Practical Navigator*, Bowditch, Revised edition, 1938.)

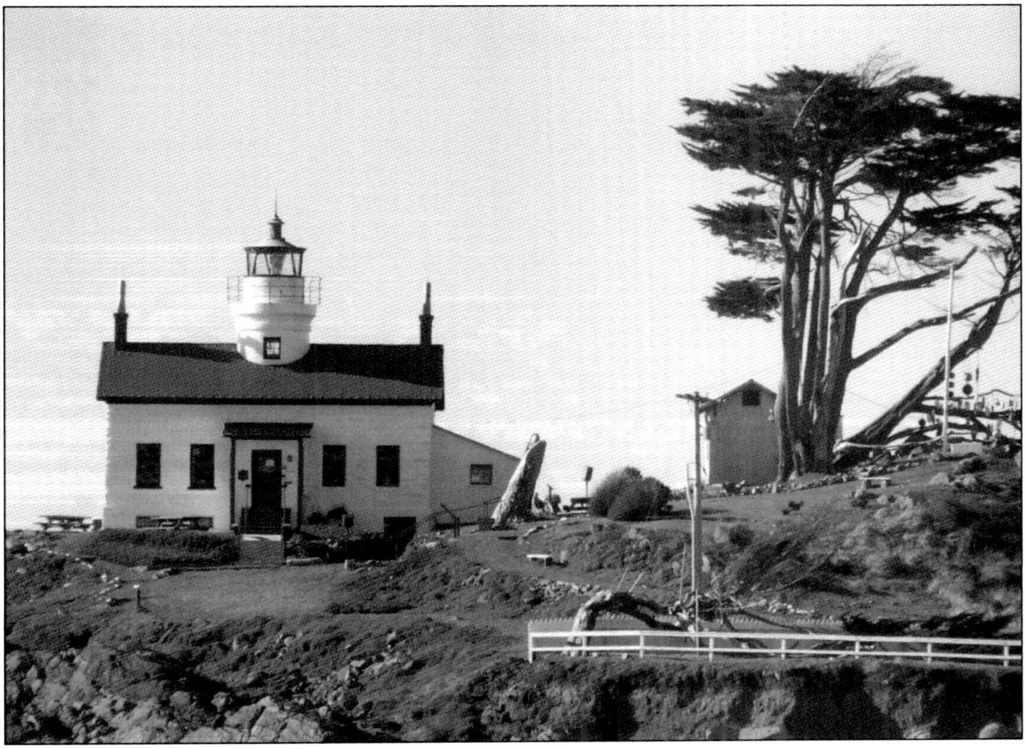

Battery Point Lighthouse, first lit on December 10, 1865, had a fourth-order lens and was used to guide mariners into the then unprotected harbor with a rocky entrance. First named Crescent City Light Station, it is one of the oldest original lighthouses on the West Coast and is currently operated by the Del Norte County Historical Society. It still proved to serve a needed purpose, even after St. George was built. (Maggie Snowden.)

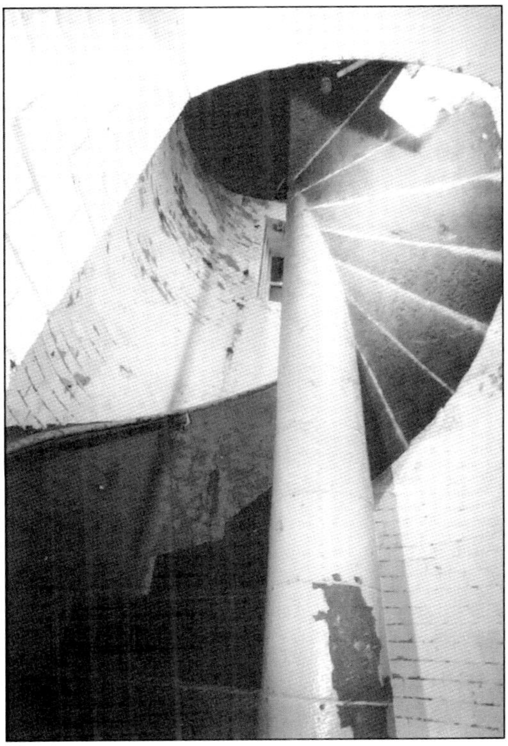

On December 1, 1891, John Olson was appointed head keeper, William Erickson first assistant, and George Goldsmith second assistant. Olson was head keeper until 1913. There is no available information about the preparation and training of the first keepers at St. George. It is also unknown if they had a planning session to assign areas of responsibility. This spiraling staircase, providing access to rooms in the tower, still echoes with their footsteps and voices. (Steve Corley.)

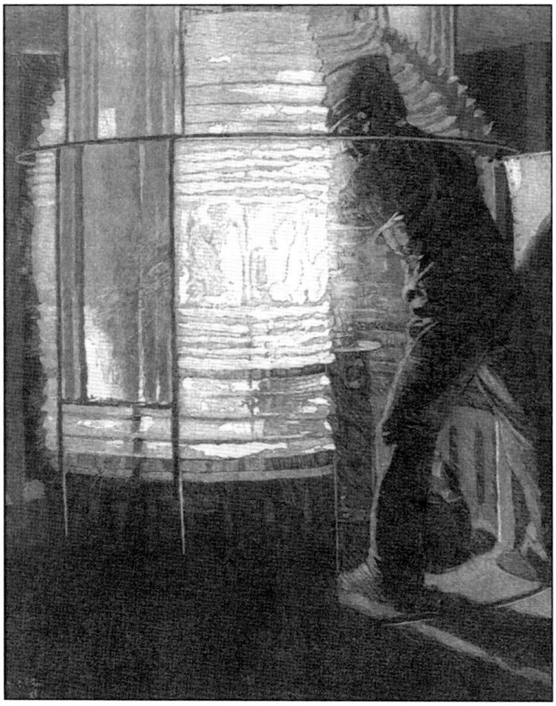

The average person would probably visualize something like this portrayal of the lighthouse keeper: trimming the wick in the oil lamp, adding fuel, keeping the Fresnel glass prisms and the lantern room windows spotless, winding the clockwork mechanism that turned the lens, and polishing the brass work. Yet, when examining the daily station logs, the time spent in the lantern room was minimal compared to a staggering list of other chores. (St. George Archives.)

Among the myriad tasks necessary to maintain the 6,000-square-foot facility with its lens, steam equipment, boom apparatus, and boats, this crew may have scraped and painted the lantern room, varnished woodwork, fixed the kitchen stove, and scraped the hull of the station launch. The only identified men are Frank Weller (left), Chester Johnson (fourth from left), and Georges Roux (right). (Author's collection.)

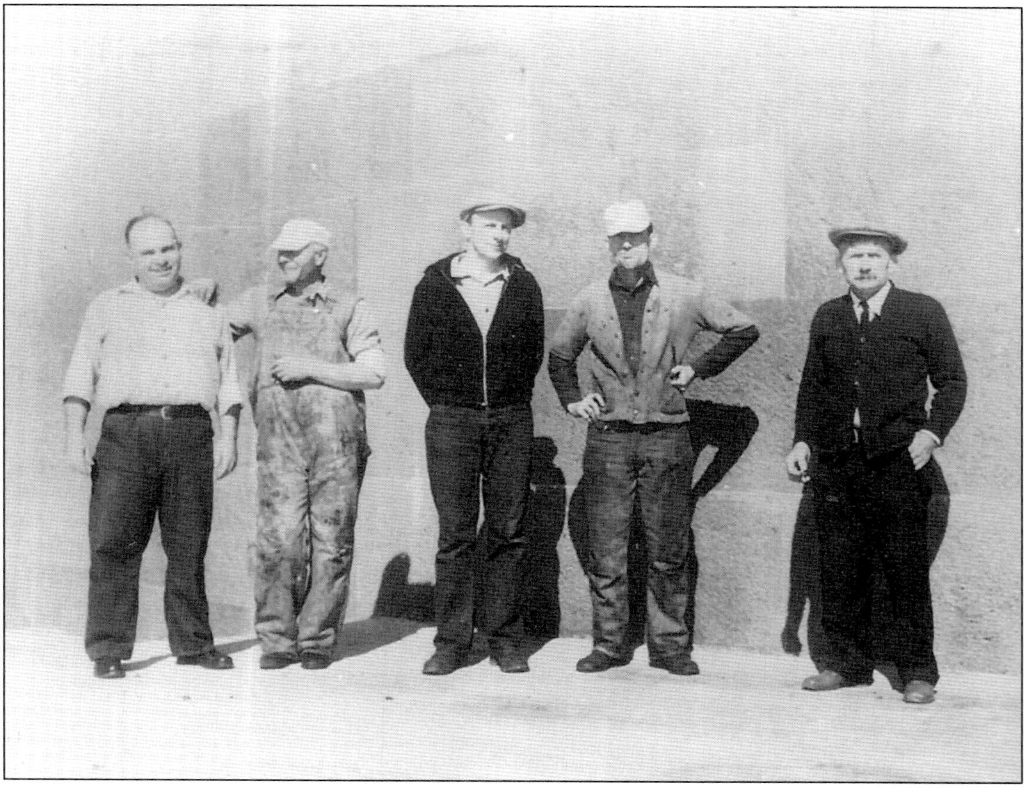

Pictured here is the ornate entrance of the Hurley-Wright Building in Washington, DC, which is marked Department of Commerce: Lighthouse Service, Aeronautics Branch, Bureau of Fisheries, Bureau of Mines. Until 1939, when control of aids to navigation was assumed by the Coast Guard, every detail of life and operations at Northwest Seal Lighthouse was closely monitored here. (St. George Archives and Clauflin and Sons Nautical Antiques.)

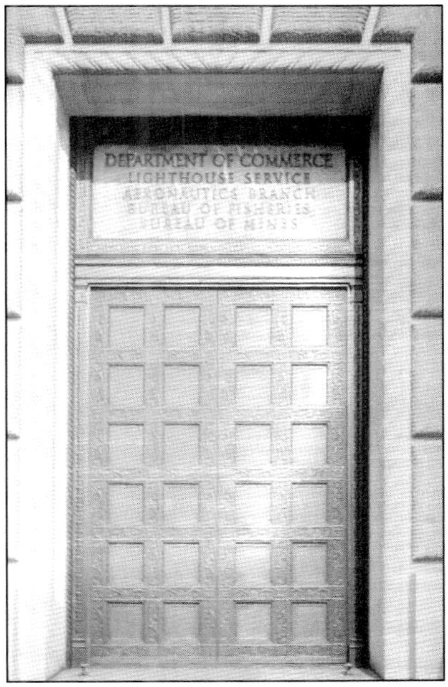

The Tomkinsville Depot in New Jersey probably received the Fresnel lens from France and then shipped it to St. George Reef by way of Yerba Buena Depot in San Francisco Bay. Pictured here is a ship at the Yerba Buena Supply Depot taking on a load from a coal storage shed. Buoys, by far the most numerous navigation aids, line the area near the dock in the lower part of the image. (US Lighthouse Society.)

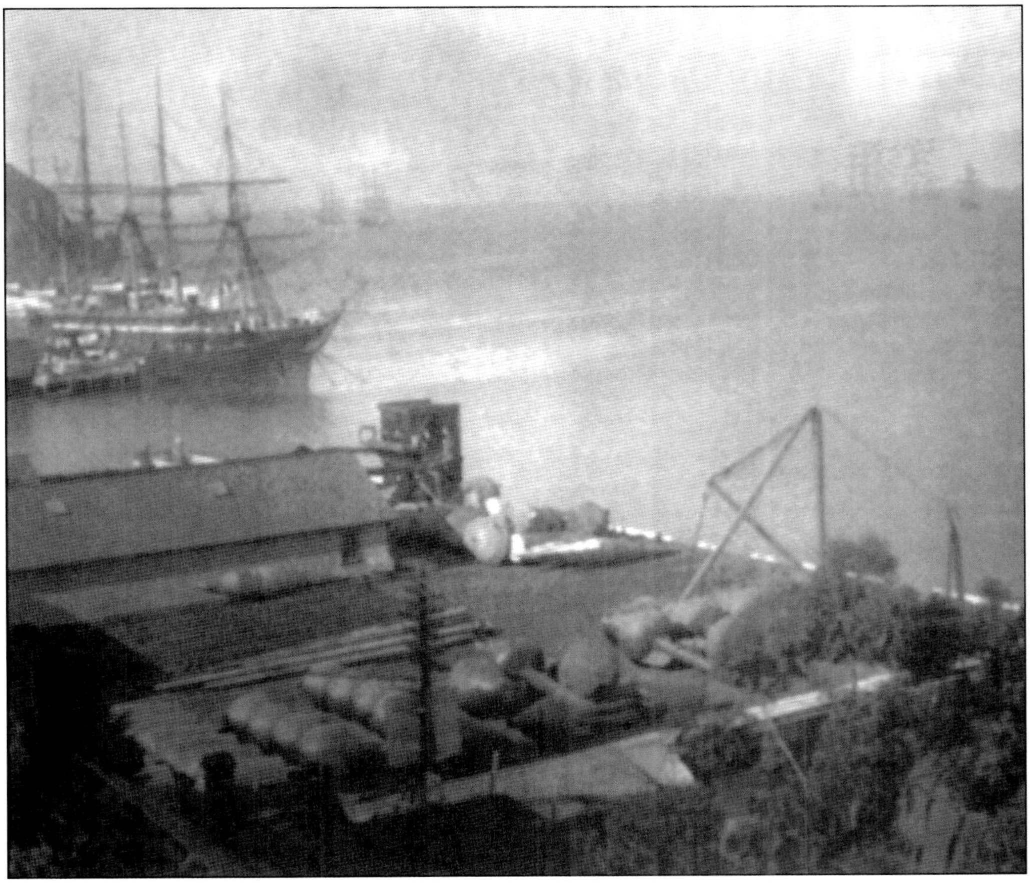

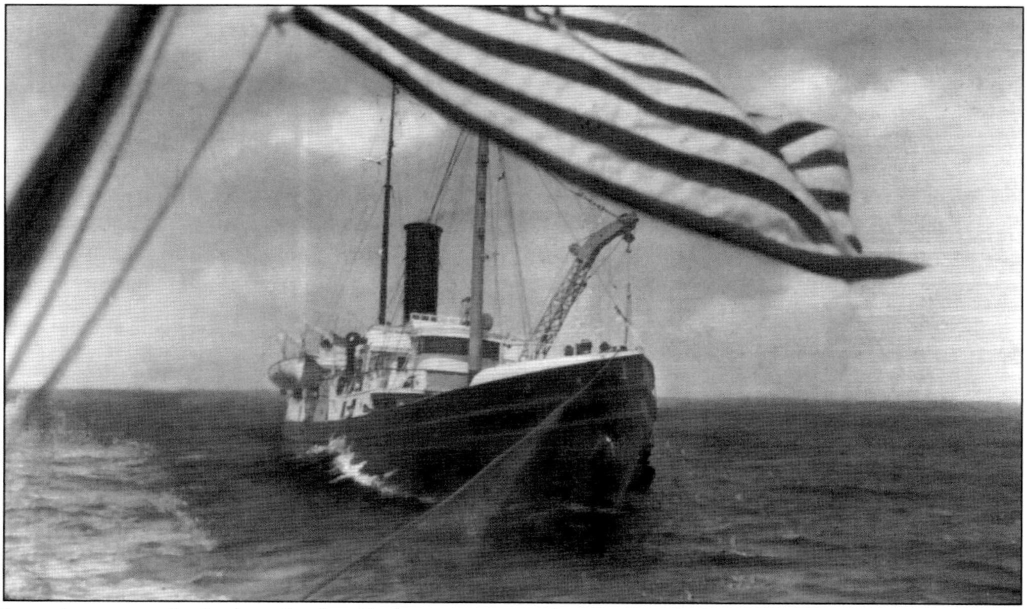

In order to supply the hundreds of light stations in the country, lighthouse tenders were assigned to each district. These scrappy little crafts established an unparalleled record of endurance and reliability during their 50-year tenure. Two tenders dominate the early history of St. George, the *Madrono* and the *Sequoia*. Shown here, the 150-foot, steel-hulled *Sequoia*, with a crew of 29, was launched June 4, 1908. (St. George Archives.)

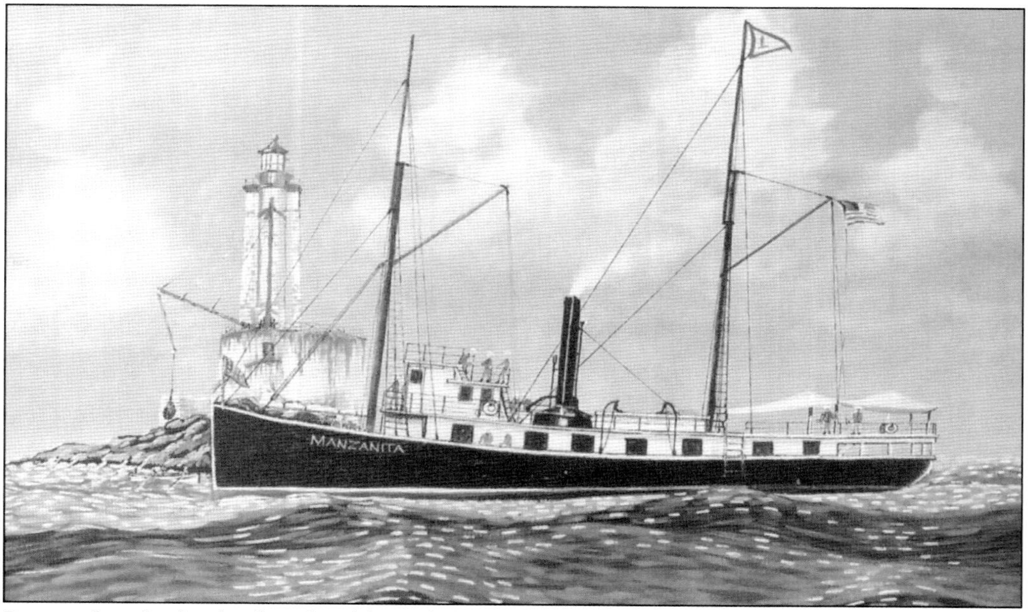

Braving hundreds of miles of rockbound, foggy coastline, the tenders maintained all of the aids to navigation, including the buoys, post lights, and daymarks. They also delivered a wide range of material to St. George such as coal, fuel oils, equipment, spare parts, and foodstuffs. Tender crews sometimes had to wait out bad conditions in the harbor at Crescent City before off-loading at the reef. (Painting by and courtesy of Gene Olson.)

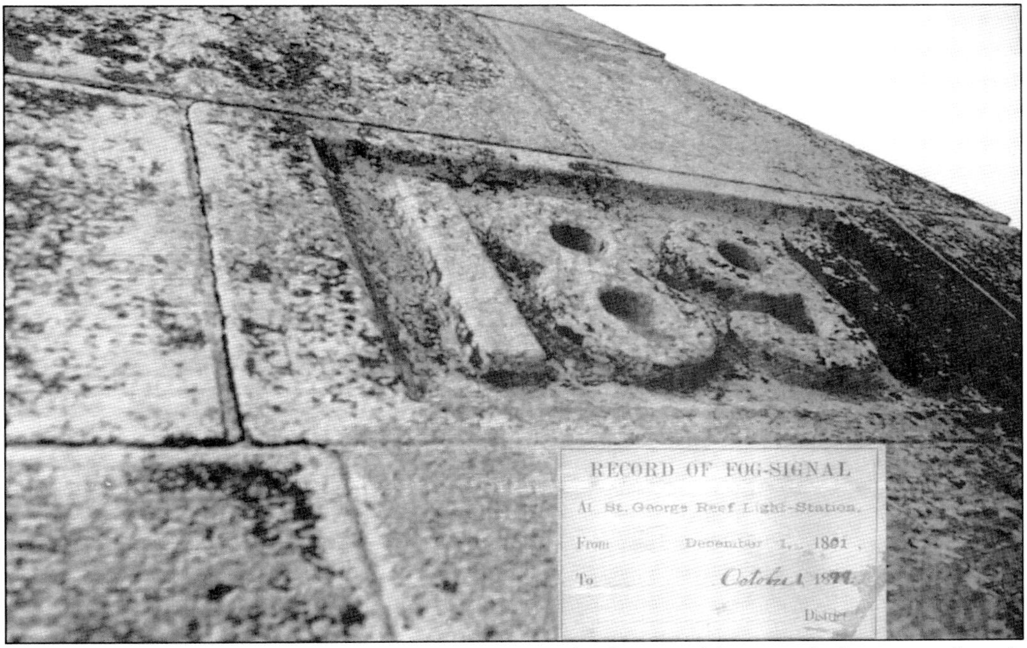

"This is the first day of the fog signal." This entry in the fog-signal log reveals that, even though the lens had not yet arrived, the station became an active aid to navigation on December 1, 1891. According to the station log, a "blast of 5 seconds duration at intervals of 35-40 seconds" was released through 12-inch whistles. Pictured here is completion date of 1891 engraved on the staircase masonry above the tower entrance door. (Author's collection.)

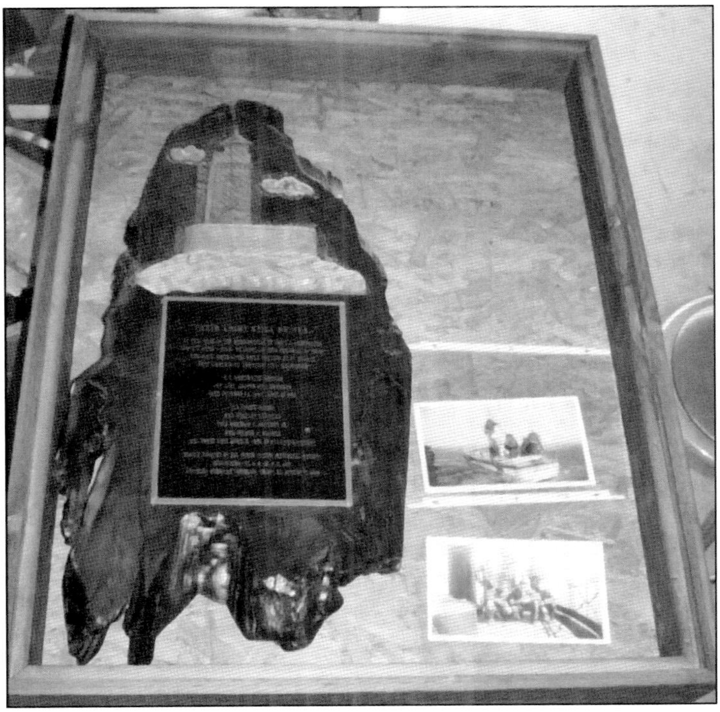

The first loss of a keeper at St. George occurred on October 17, 1893, when third assistant keeper William Erickson vanished when he left the lighthouse in the station's 18-foot sailboat on a routine visit to Crescent City. Four other men died on duty at St. George. Pictured here is a memorial plaque bearing the names of keepers who died in service. (Author's collection.)

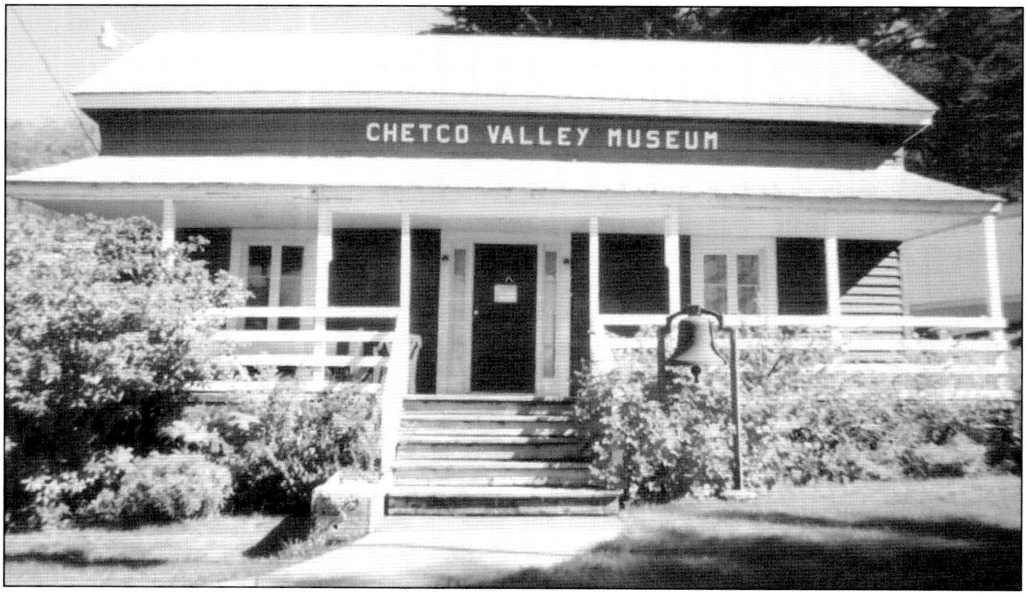

Brookings, Oregon, and its port on the Chetco River have always had a close association with St. George. The town, named after its founder, Robert Brookings, began sending shiploads of timber past the lighthouse in 1907 and, in later years, sent boats from the Chetco Life-Saving Station to provide standby assistance during crew transfers. The town and the Chetco Museum, shown here, are active supporters of St. George. (Author's collection.)

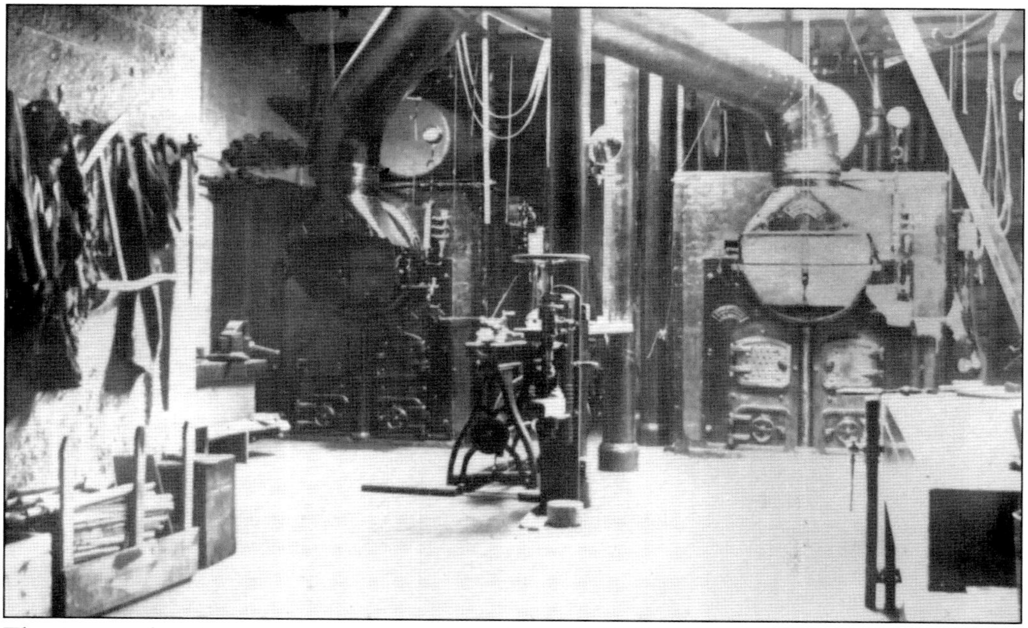

This image of engine room, as it appeared in the early 1900s, shows the double boilers against the western wall of the caisson. When visibility was reduced to critical limits, water was pumped into the coal-fired boilers. Pressure was brought to eight to 11 pounds per square inch to power the steam sirens at St. George. They were later replaced by a gasoline-driven compressed air system. (Marhoffer Album.)

Joseph Marhoffer is bedecked in his new uniform, complete with hat and the symbol of the service, a wreath-encircled lighthouse. Marhoffer had a long career at the station and kept a photo album recording his time at St. George Reef and other lighthouses in California. This album and other private collections offer a rare glimpse of life in a late 19th-century offshore lighthouse. (Marhoffer Album.)

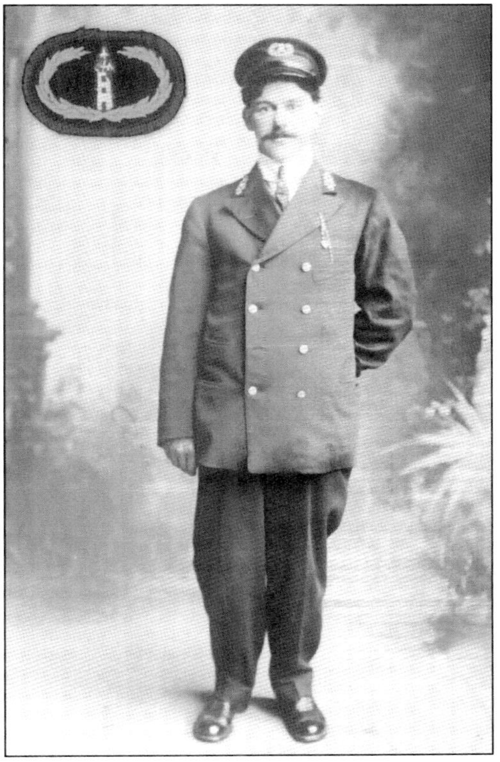

This undated family portrait shows the Crescent City pioneer family of keeper Joseph Marhoffer (standing, third from left). His father, Jacob (seated), was a well-known businessman and eventually became associated with the Hobbs-Wall Company, the largest redwood mill in town. (Del Norte County Historical Society.)

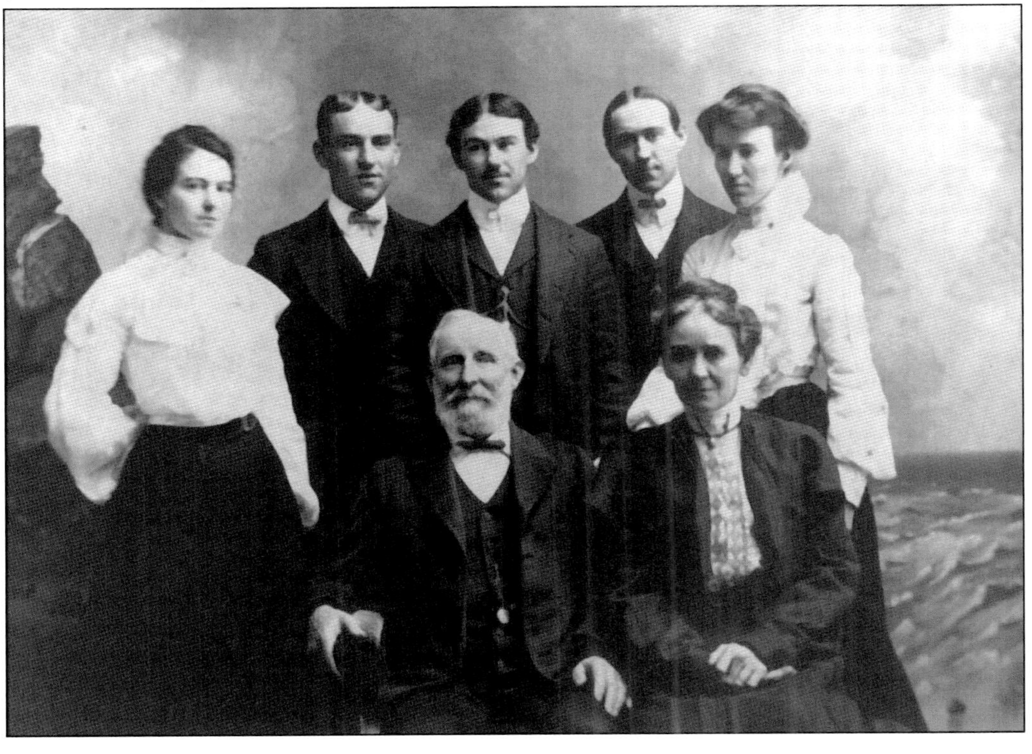

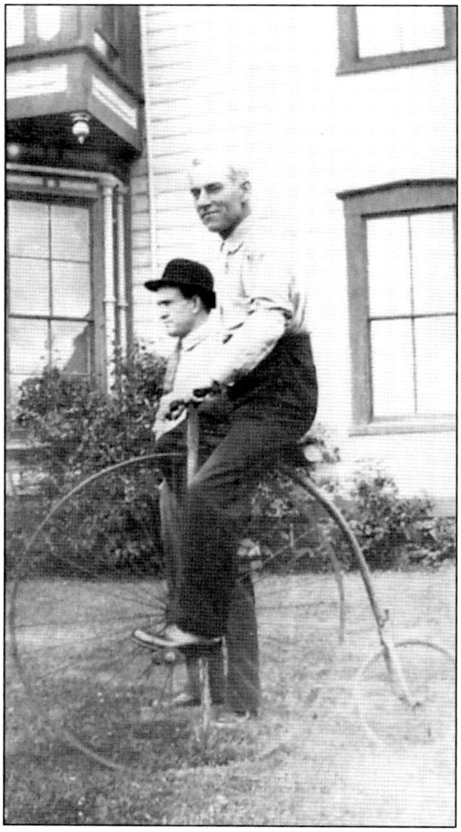

The two-story Victorian Marhoffer residence in Crescent City reflected the pioneer family's financial success. This scene shows the front of the home with family or friends riding a penny-farthing. Joseph, the future keeper at St. George, was born here in 1881 and began his career at St. George on August 20, 1913. Available records indicate he was at St. George until sometime in the 1930s, and he also served at other lighthouses. (Marhoffer Album.)

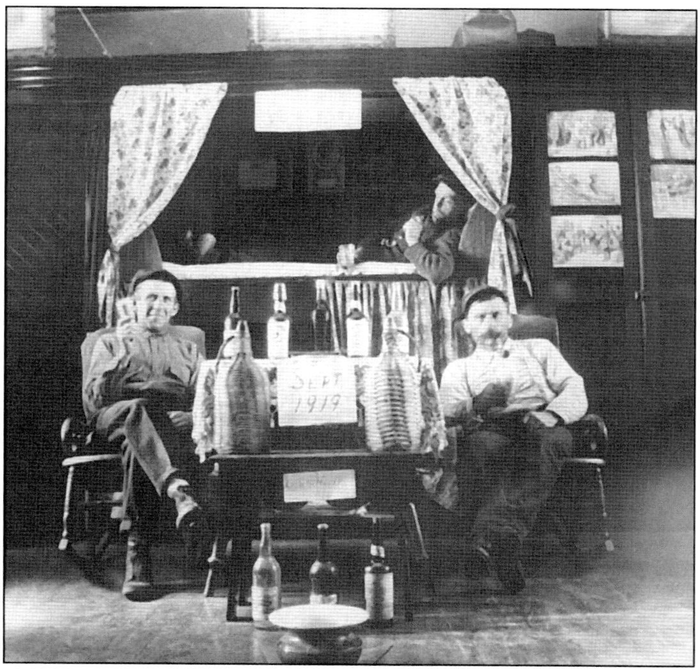

Here, three keepers are pictured in a room with built-in bunk beds, lacquered woodwork, and tongue-and-groove flooring. The dated sign and the wine bottles show that Prohibition has just started, and the men are registering a complaint. In reality, liquor was strictly prohibited at all lighthouses. Note that casual dress was the order of the day. The keeper seated to the right is Georges Roux. (Marhoffer Album.)

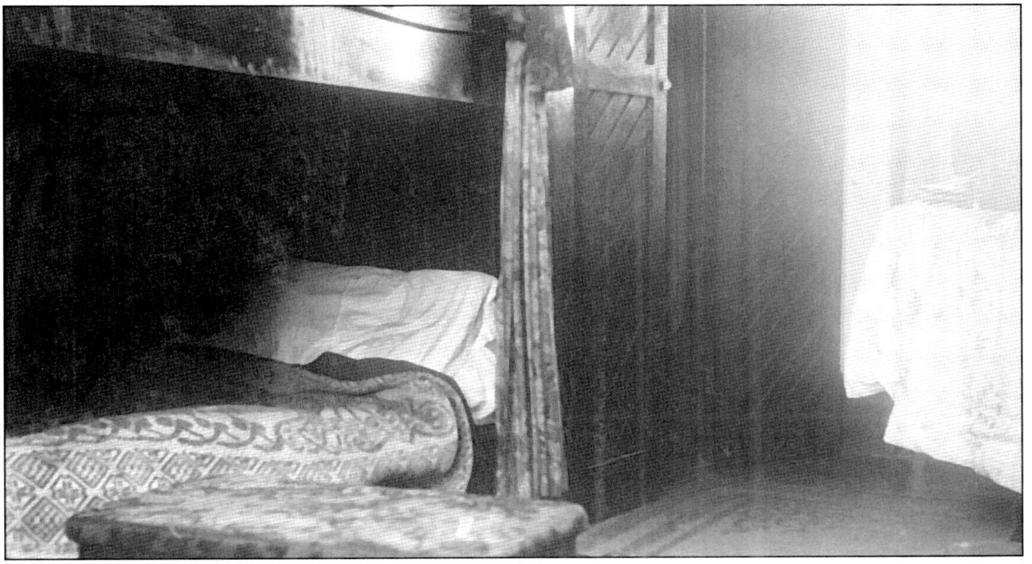

The number of keepers assigned at lighthouses typically varied between two and four, a head keeper and assistants. Due to the extreme danger and isolation at St. George, it was the only station in the service that allowed five. There were three keeper's rooms in the tower, and the usual arrangement was that the head keep slept in the top room nearest the lantern room and the assistants in lower levels. (Marhoffer Album.)

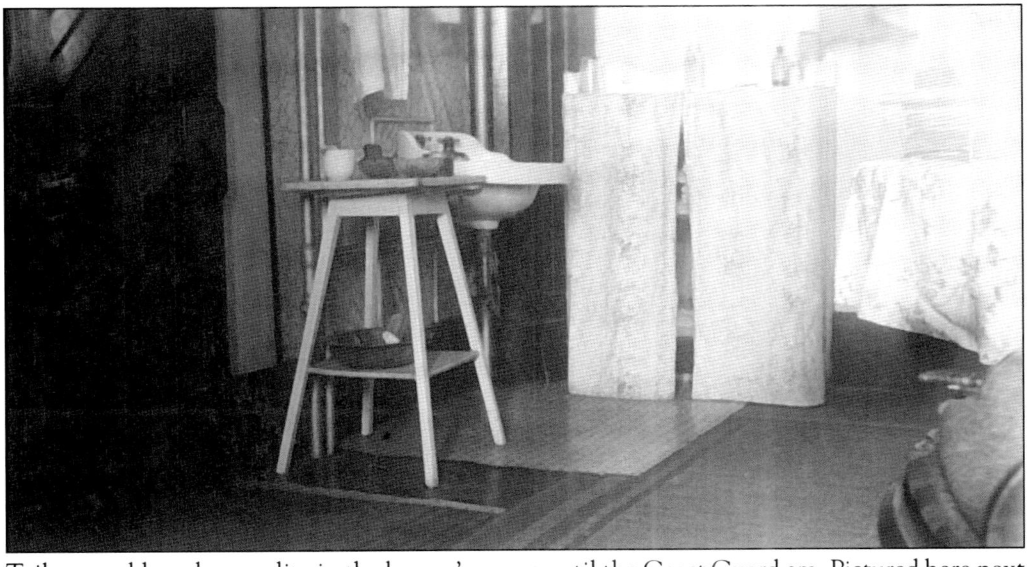

Toilets would not be a reality in the keeper's rooms until the Coast Guard era. Pictured here next to a sink with faucets is a humble stool serving as a washstand. Note the shaving mug on top; to the right, a curtained storage shelf and tablecloth add a bit of domesticity to the scene. In spite of comfortable accommodations, over a 40-year period, thirty-seven men resigned and twenty-six requested transfers. (Marhoffer Album.)

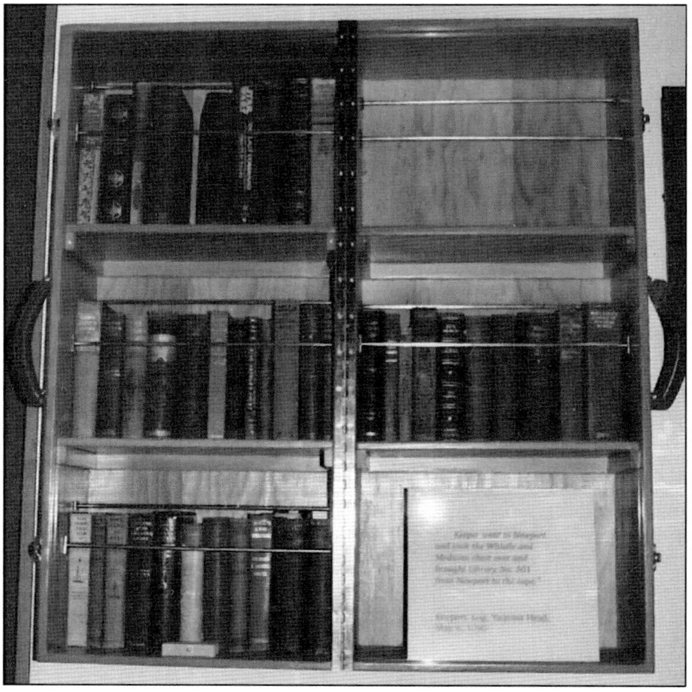

In between watches, there was time for leisure and recreation. No doubt St. George keepers enjoyed the time-tested standbys of checkers, chess, and cards. Among the efforts of lighthouse authorities to maintain literacy and provide for off-duty relaxation was a traveling library that circulated among district light stations. Strong and portable, the libraries looked like this one at the Yaquina Bay Interpretive Center in Newport, Oregon. (St. George Archives.)

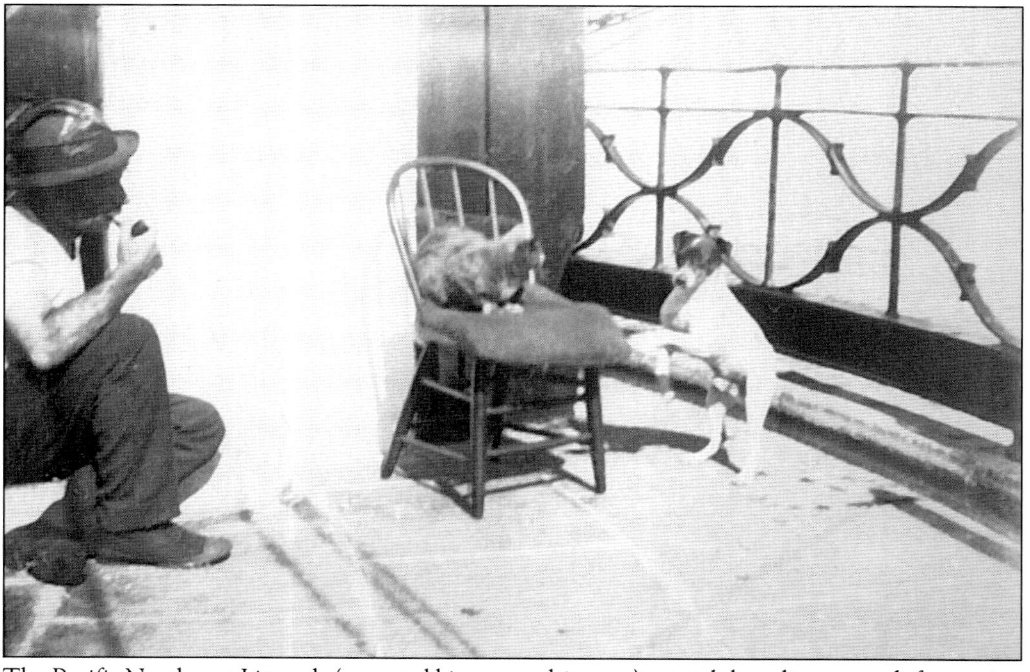

The Pacific Northwest Littorals (a coastal biogeographic zone) are rich breeding grounds for marine mammals, birds, fish, and mollusks. However, canines and felines of the landlubber variety also found their way onto the lighthouse. Shown here near the boom, keeper Georges Roux referees a confrontation between a terrier and a cat perched safely out of reach. Note the ornate handrail that guards the edge of caisson. (Marhoffer Album.)

The station cat stands in the tower entrance door, on guard, no doubt, for the canines that cohabit this little island in the sea. In the way of cats, the pose was probably of short duration with the feline exiting up the tower in hopes that the next supply tender would include some catnip among the coal sacks. (Marhoffer Album.)

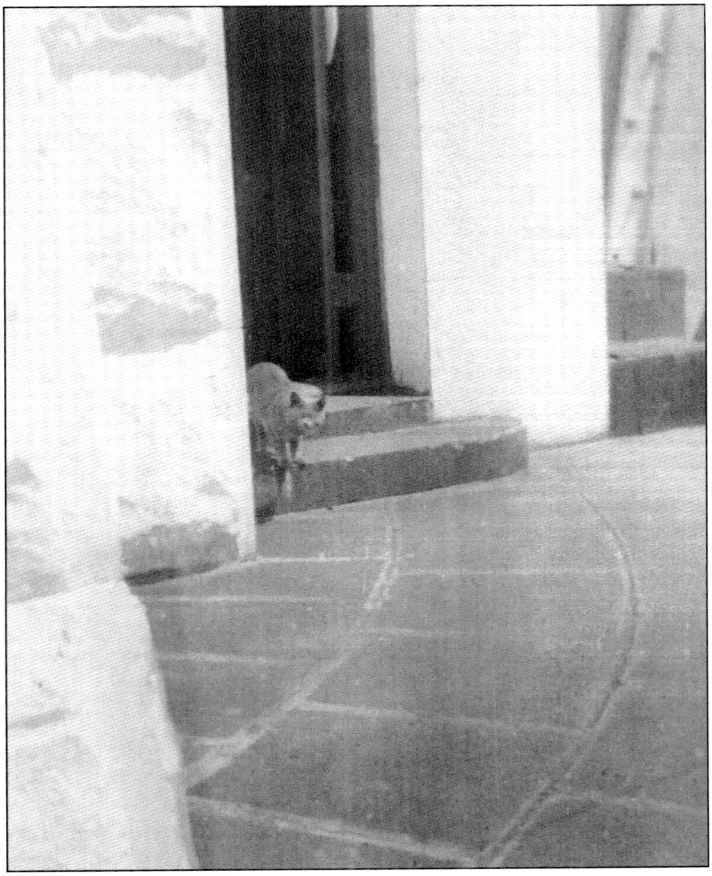

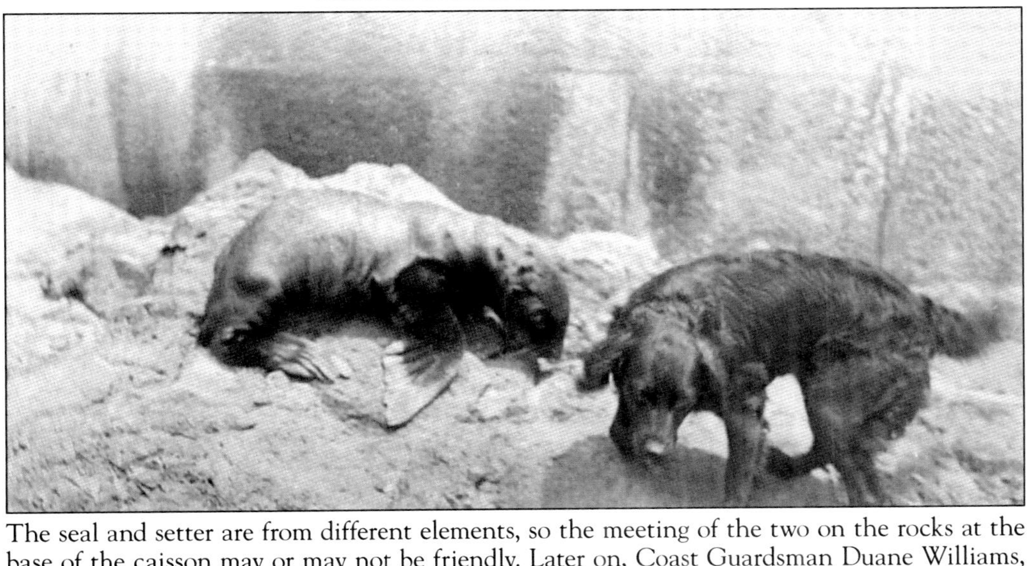

The seal and setter are from different elements, so the meeting of the two on the rocks at the base of the caisson may or may not be friendly. Later on, Coast Guardsman Duane Williams, attesting again to the power of the sea, recounted the time a sea lion was lifted by huge waves over the handrail onto the catch deck (caisson). (Marhoffer Album.)

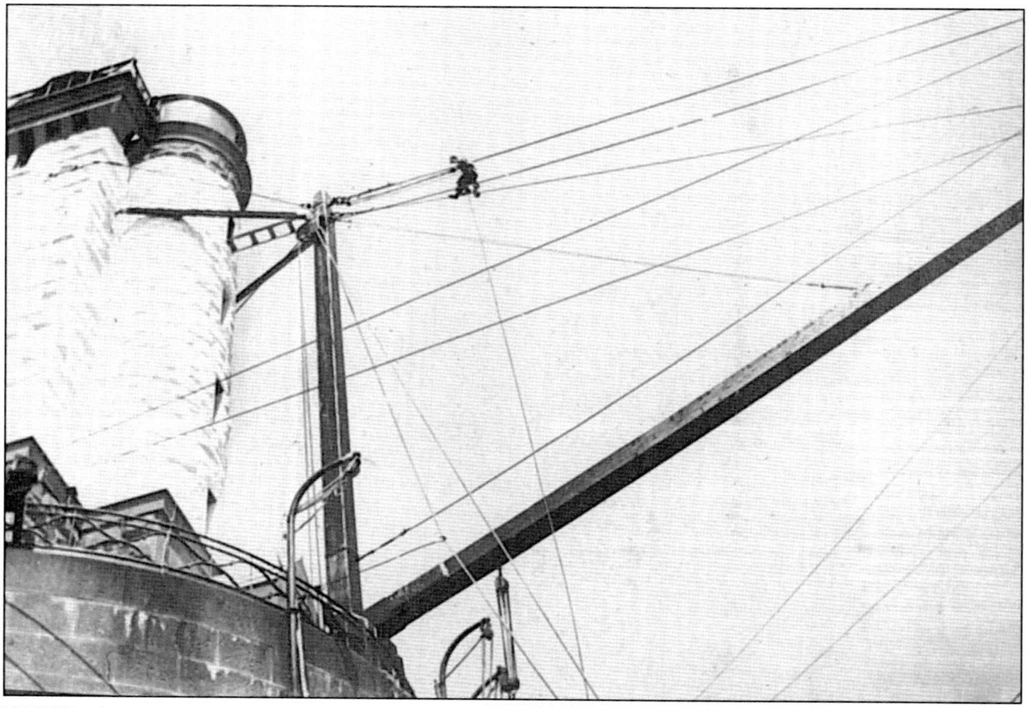

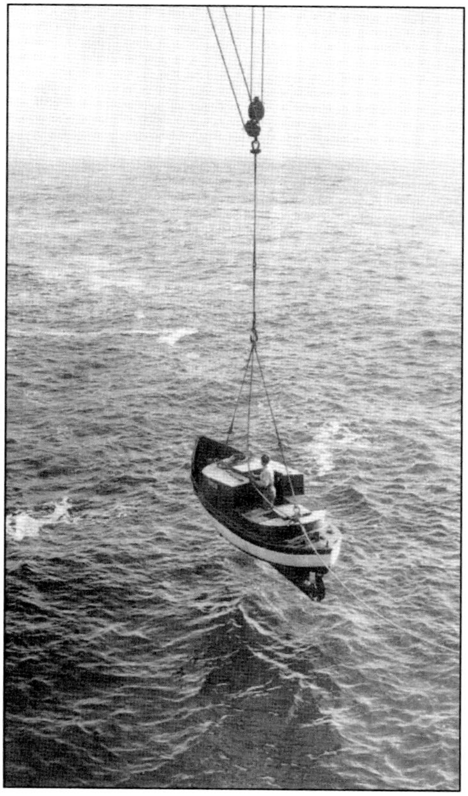

Perched high above, a keeper tends the network of cables that support the boom and are critical to its functioning. The boom does not lift but remains stationary. A system of pulleys attached to the mast (vertical part) moves a traveler back and forth in order to lower a line attached to a weight ball and hook. When the hook is attached, the pulleys and the traveler move the load to the lower landing. (Marhoffer Album.)

Most of the provisions needed to sustain operations at the station were brought by lighthouse tender from the supply depot at Yerba Buena Island, San Francisco, but there were occasions when small boats from Crescent City also paid a visit. Such an event is shown here in this image. A local craft is attached to the weight-and-hook assembly of the boom traveler. (Marhoffer Album.)

Black smoke belching from the smokestack of the hoist shack shows that coal is being shoveled into the hoist steam donkey in preparation for a lift in this 1920s image. The traveler ball and hook are secured to the lower landing just below the staircase. The dark stain on the northwest corner of the caisson reveals that the prevailing swell from that direction often approached 50 feet. (Marhoffer Album.)

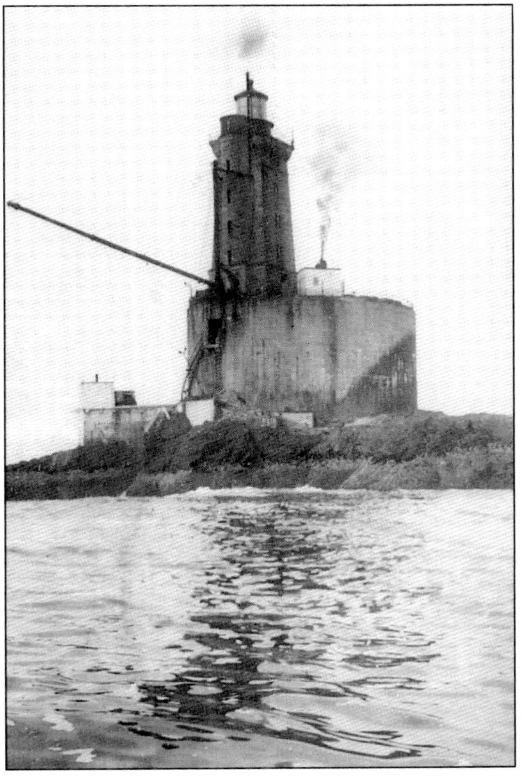

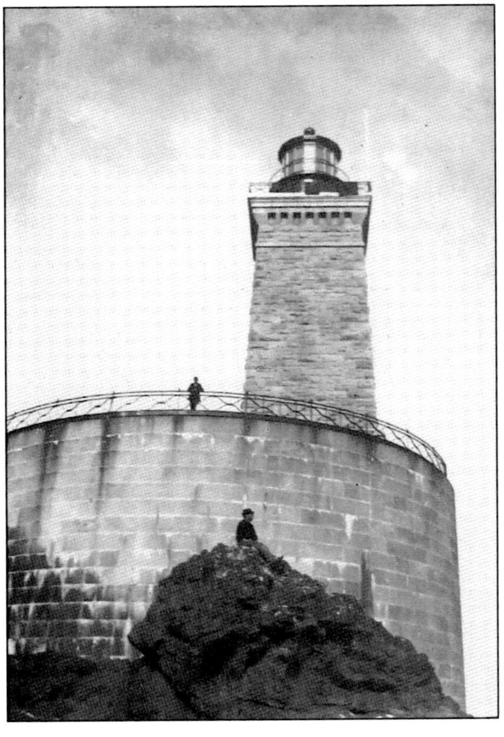

This view from the west side was obviously posed to show scale, contrasting the ant-like figures of the keepers to the mass of the rock, caisson, and tower. (Marhoffer Album.)

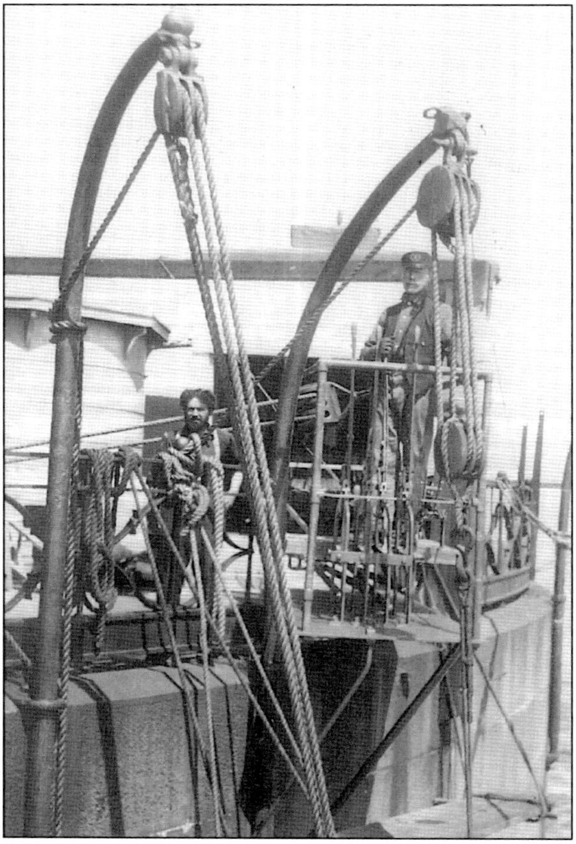

Two keepers watch a boat being lifted (or lowered) on the davits. Joseph Marhoffer looks on while an assistant is at the boom controls. The gooseneck apparatus with the rope and pulleys was used to bring craft such as the station boats from the lower landing and secure them above the threatening waves. A water tank to the left of Marhoffer is part of the gravity flow system. (Marhoffer Album.)

Pictured here is a daredevil keeper at the end of the boom. Also visible are the ornate caisson handrail, the davit, and to the far right, what appears to be a mounted pair of binoculars. Note the lines attaching the boom to the mast and masonry, called backstays. These lines secured the boom at six points; however, anchor points did not prevent accidents on the decay-prone wooden shaft. (Marhoffer Album.)

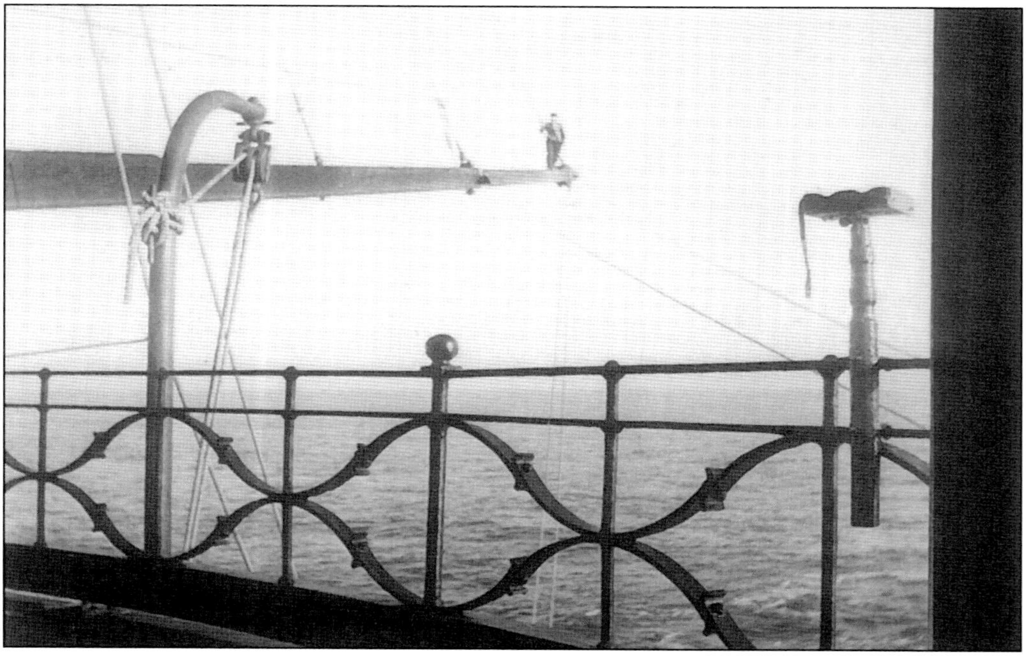

Most susceptible to decay in the marine environment at St. George was the wooden boom, which sometimes broke while in use and had to be replaced about every 10 years. To solve the problem, a metal replacement was proposed, and on August 8, 1929, the tender *Sequoia* delivered the new boom and a crew to replace it. Shown here is a view of the old boom. (Marhoffer Album.)

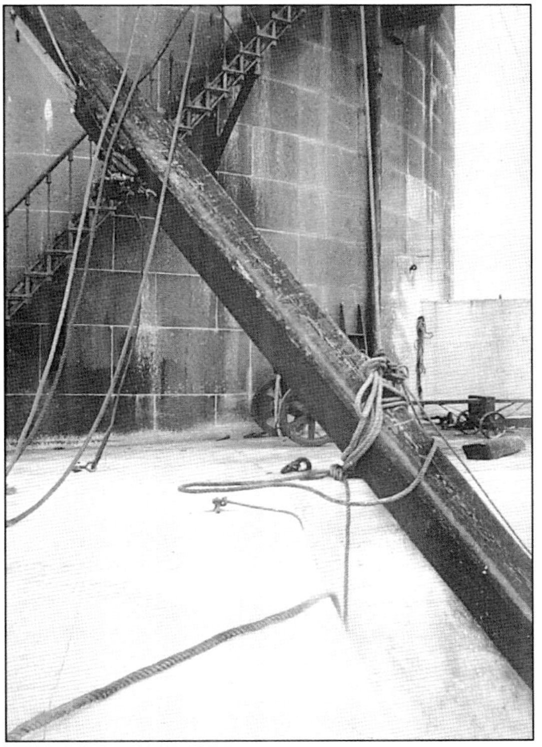

In this view, inspector Harry Rhodes sits on a boatswain chair on the boom traveler, preparatory to setting down on the lower landing. A boatswain chair is sometimes little more than a board supported by ropes attached to each corner. The oarsmen in the boat are from one of the tenders, and they are attempting to hold steady in a heavy sea. The photograph was taken from the staircase that descends from the engine room. (Coast Guard.)

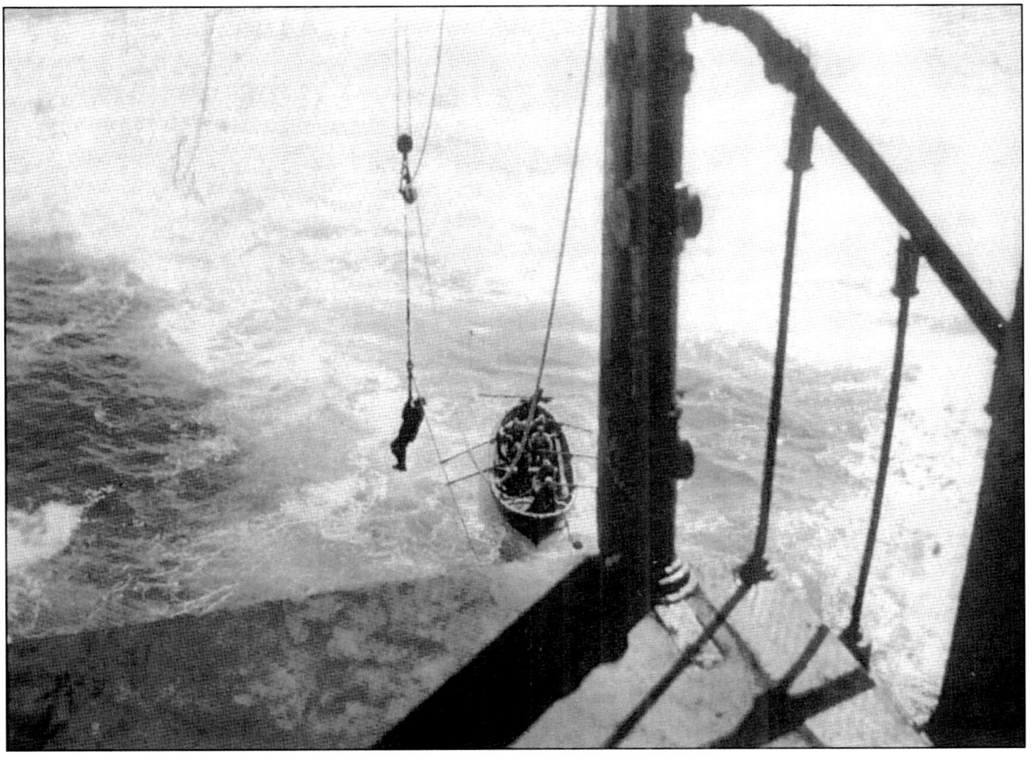

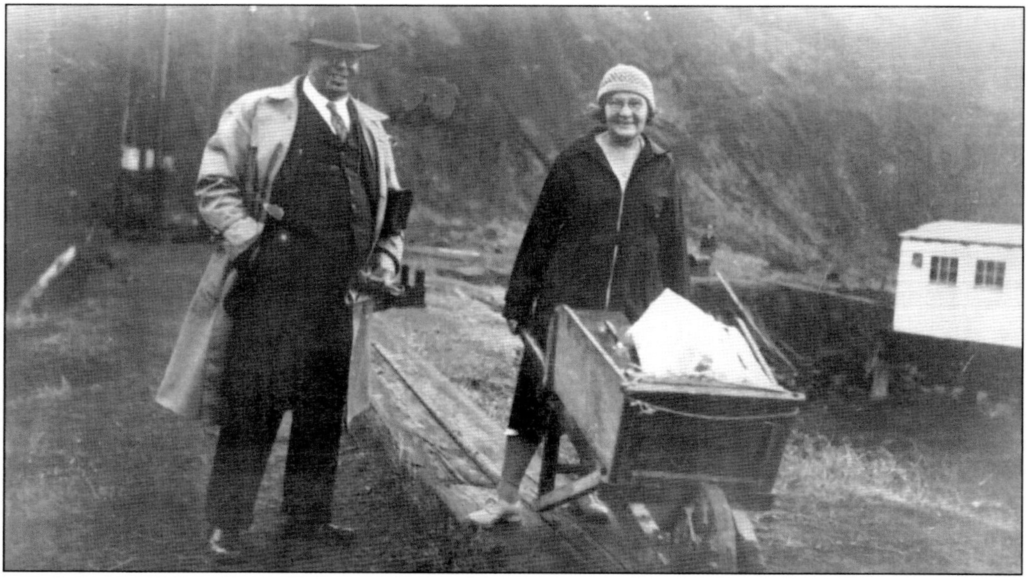

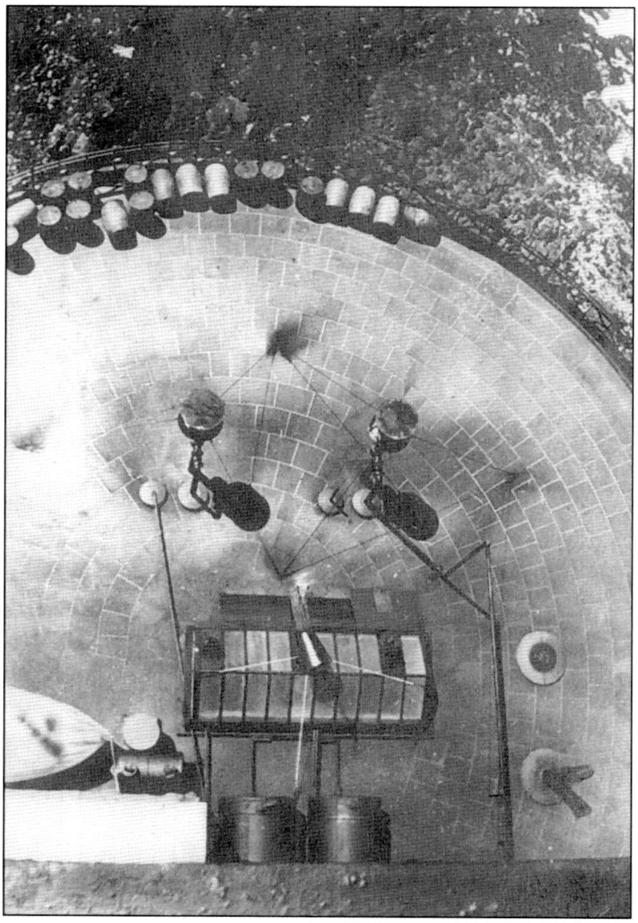

Periodic inspections were made of all aids to navigation to insure their proper maintenance. Here, Harry Rhodes, legendary superintendent and district inspector of the 12th Lighthouse District, is shown with a Mrs. Marhoffer at the Farallones Light Station. Known for his sternness and attention to detail, Rhodes began his career in the Coast and Geodetic Survey, transferring to the Lighthouse Service in 1912, and continuing until 1939. (Del Norte County Historical Society.)

"Our back yard" was how keeper Chester Johnson described this view of the caisson catch deck. It shows containers of distillate used as a fuel for the vapor lamps for the Fresnel lens, barrels of gas along the caisson handrail, the engine-room skylight, the twin air-siren fog signals, and the geometric stone flagging. One of the station boats is partly visible. (Photograph by Chester Johnson, courtesy of James Smallscreed.)

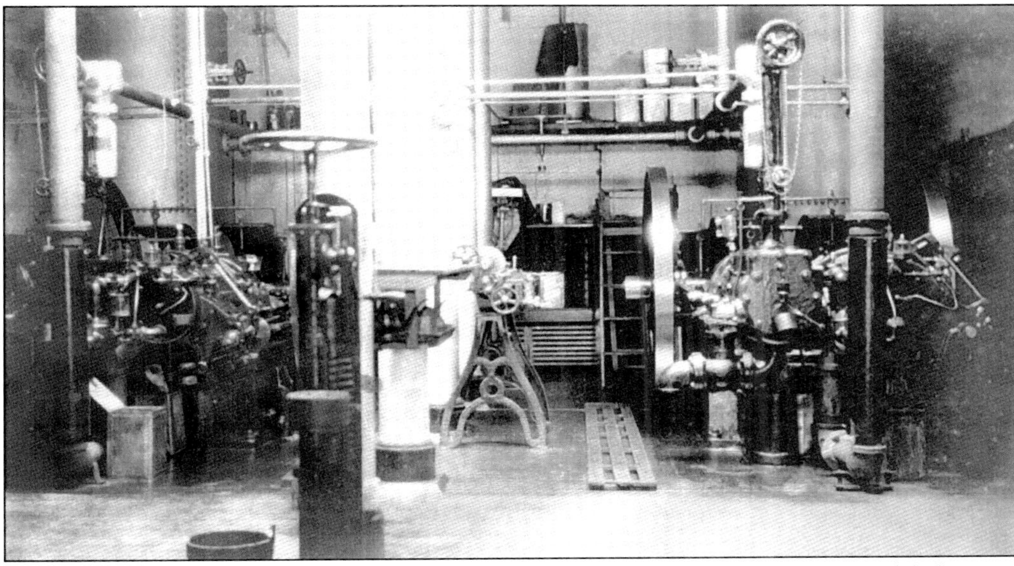

The balance wheel of a Doak gasoline-powered air compressor gleams in the remodeled engine room. By February 1913, the shift was made to compressed-air sirens, necessitating two compressors and compressed-air tanks as shown here. William H. Oliver of the Doak Gas Engine Corporation gave a quote of $3,425. The bid was accepted, and with a six-inch-diameter vertical trumpet for the fog horn, it completed the changeover. (St. George Archives.)

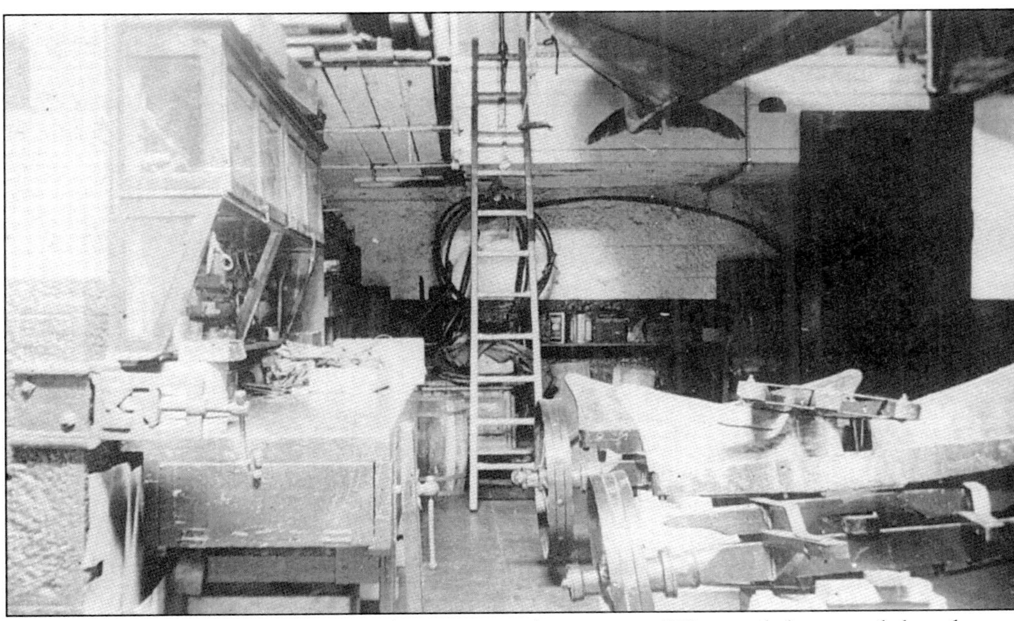

Keeper Chester Johnson describes this room in the caisson: "The workshop, work bench, tool locker, new wagon with cradle to set boat in when we leave it on the lower landing, eighteen foot row and sailboat hanging from the ceiling. Door leads to hallway outside and up in tower." (Photograph by Chester Johnson, courtesy of James Smallscreed.)

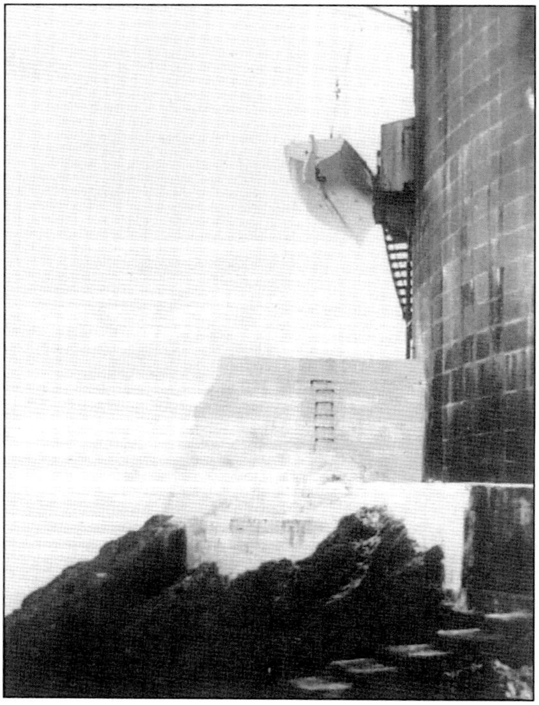

Shot from northeast, this photograph shows (from the top) the station launch abutting the caisson door and lower-landing stair case, precise courses of masonry, a lower landing "splash wall" installed after construction to ward off wave splash from a prevailing northwest running swell, and stairs in rock leading to sea level. Note the foot and hand rungs imbedded in the splash wall. (Photograph by Chester Johnson, courtesy of James Smallscreed.)

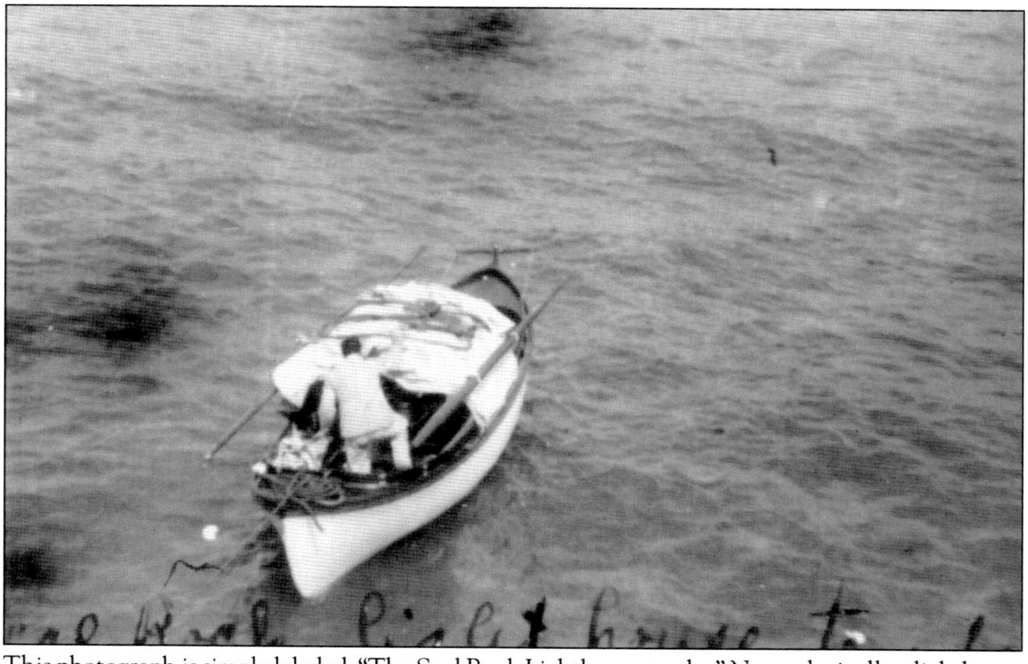

This photograph is simply labeled, "The Seal Rock Lighthouse tender." Not technically a lighthouse tender of the variety that serviced aids to navigation from Yerba Buena Island Depot, this smaller craft ran between Crescent City Harbor and the light station, ferrying supplies and transporting keepers. Given the conditions that often prevailed at St. George, one has to admire the courageous captain in his modest craft. (Private collection.)

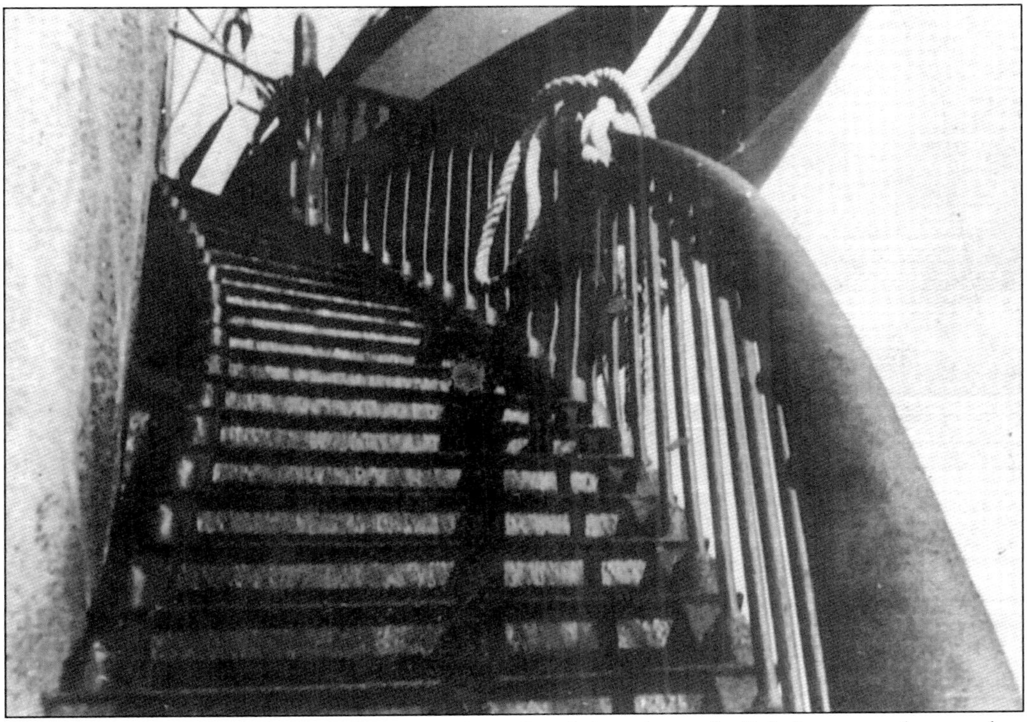

After someone pitched about in the station launch, a fishing boat, the lighthouse tender, or other craft, climbing the staircase from the lower landing to the engine room was the first introduction to solid footing. A quick-release knot secures the station launch to the staircase handrail in this scene from the 1920s or 1930s taken by former head keeper Chester Johnson. (James Smallscreed.)

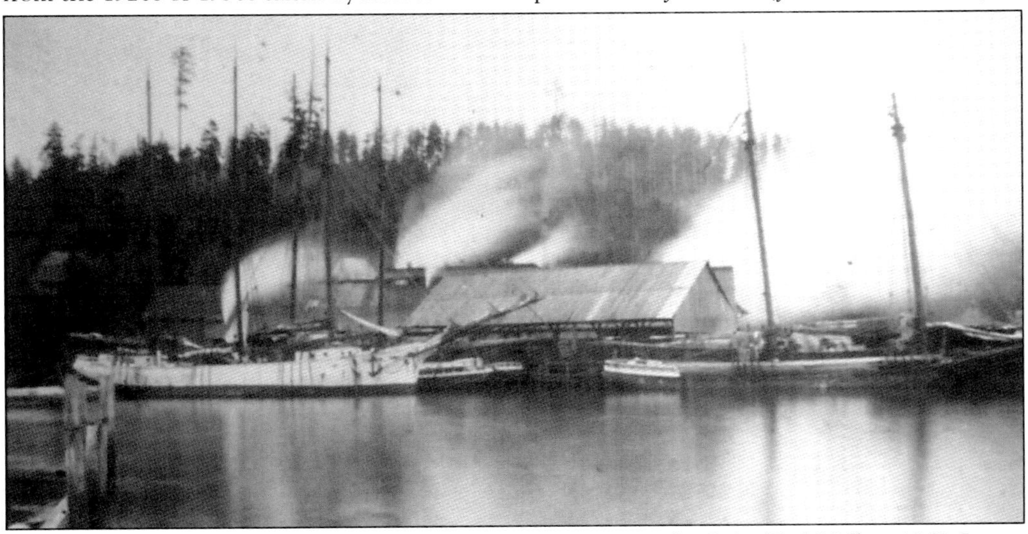

The first lumber produced in Del Norte County was sawn at the Lake Earl Mill in 1869. It was situated on a lagoon north of Crescent City and connected to the wharf in town by railroad. Logging dominated Pacific Northwest economies for many decades. Thousands of vessels such as these streamed past St. George, their decks loaded with lumber for ports all over the world. (Private collection.)

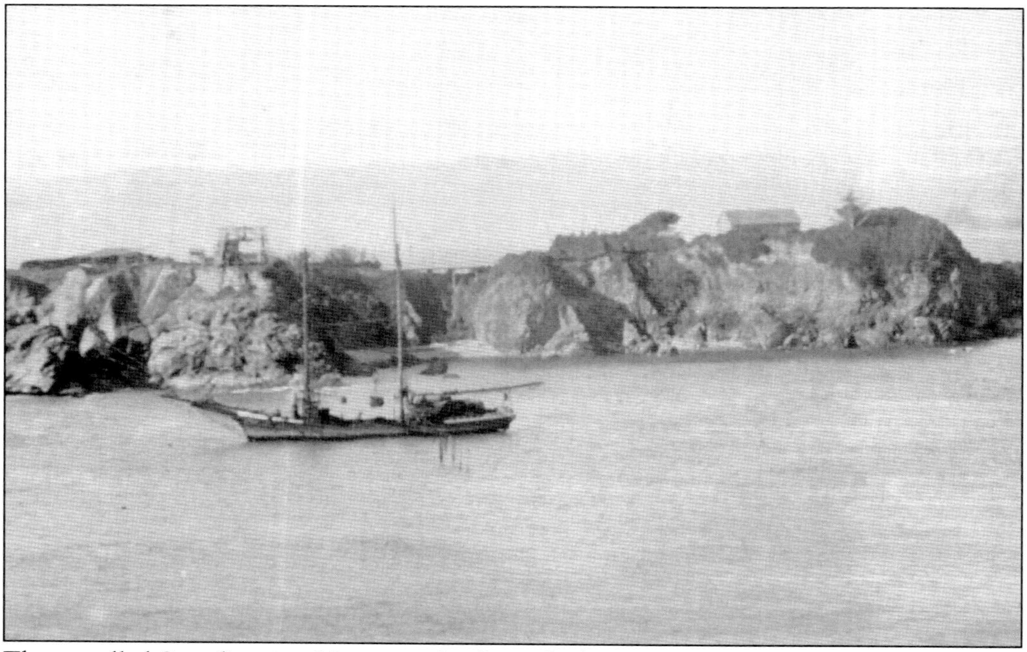

The so-called Scandinavian Navy was the fleet of schooners manned and operated mostly by Scandinavian immigrants who would deliver redwood as far away as the South Seas. A dockworker shares his memories in an issue of the *Humboldt Historian*: "When they left the dock you could see a big raft of lumber and a little bit of bow and stern." Pictured here is a lumber schooner. (Private collection.)

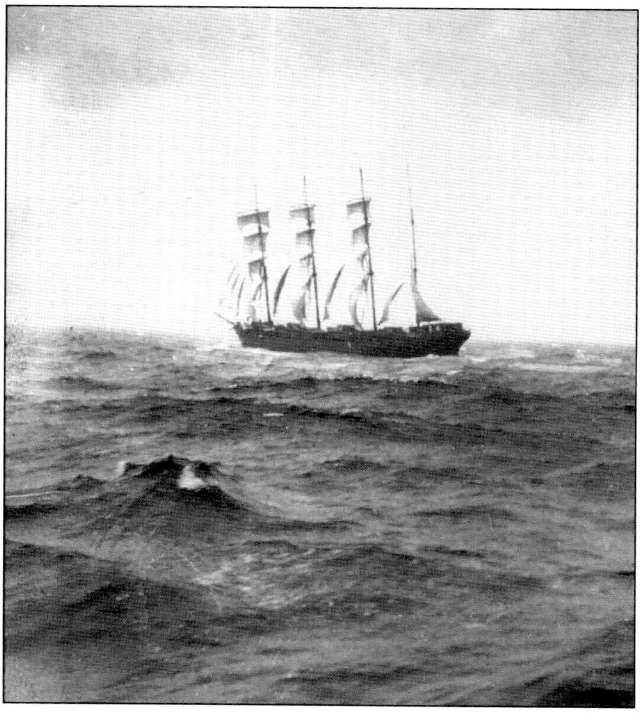

The ghostly figure of a four-master sails southward past St. George in this undated photograph, symbolic of the passing age of sail. First powered by steam, then by gas and diesel, the vessels no longer had to hug the coast for security, and they rarely sailed close to the lighthouse. Yet with its 20-mile range, the light was still visible, a still-vital, pre-technology aid. (Marhoffer Album.)

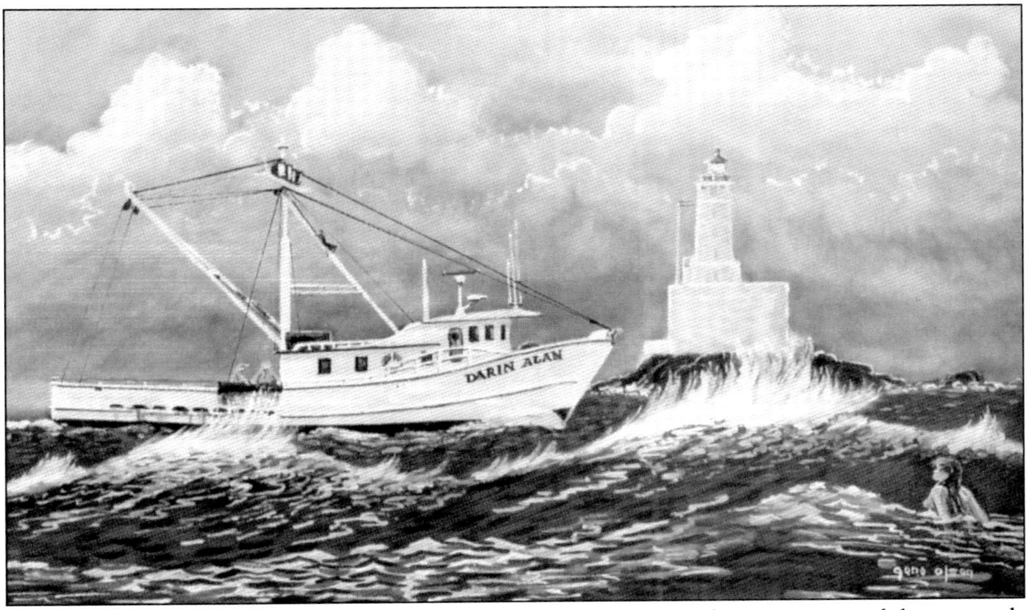

Among those still utilizing the lighthouse as a navigational aid at close range were fishing vessels in pursuit of salmon, crab, shrimp, and bottom fish. *FV* is an abbreviation used by the Coast Guard to designate a fishing vessel. In this painting by Gene Olson, the *Darin Alan* navigates choppy seas north of St. George. (Painting by and courtesy of Gene Olson.)

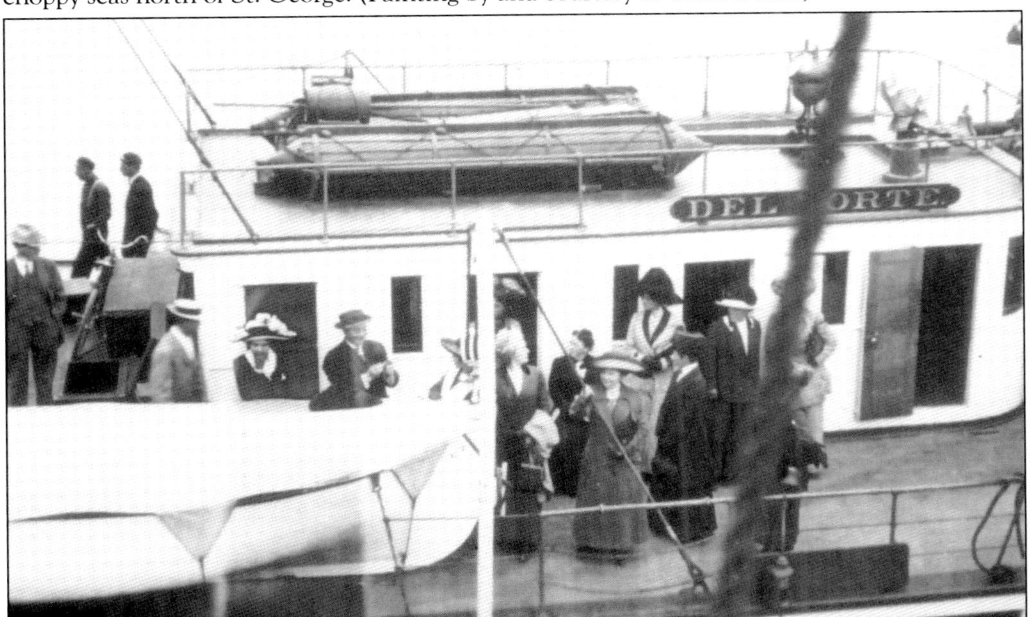

Still not venturing too far from shore were the coastal steamers such as the *Crescent City* and *Del Norte*, which figured so prominently in the construction of St. George. In a pre-railroad era (the railroad came to Humboldt County in 1914), steamers moved passengers and virtually every other item needed to sustain late 19th- and early 20th-century life. Shown here is the *Del Norte* loading or unloading passengers. (Private collection.)

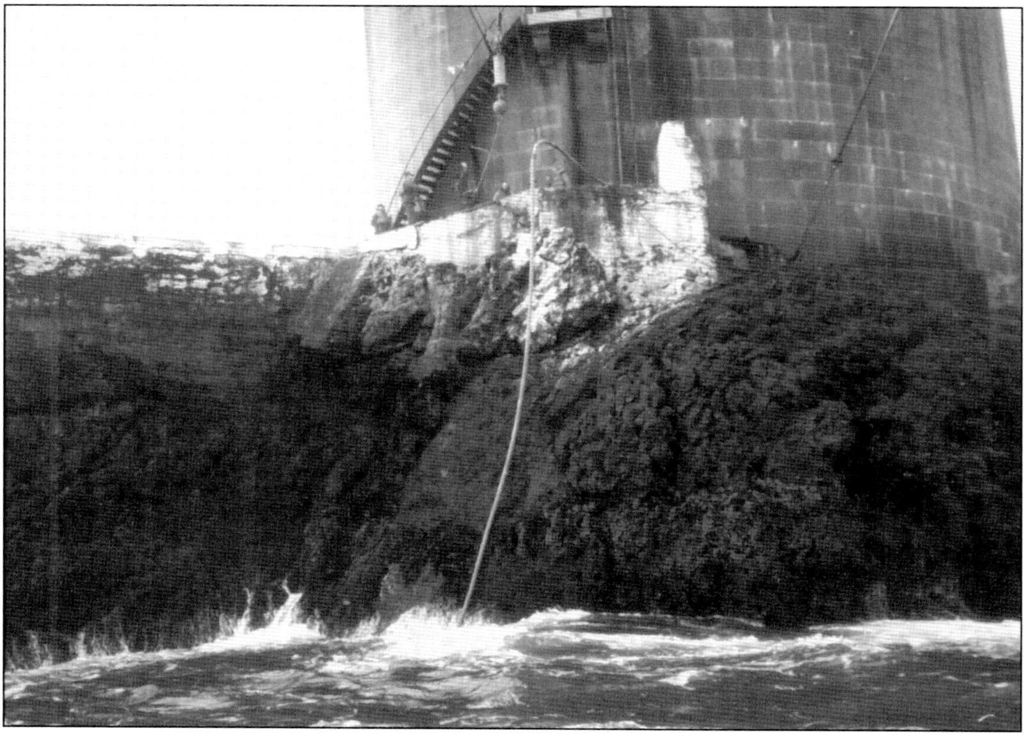

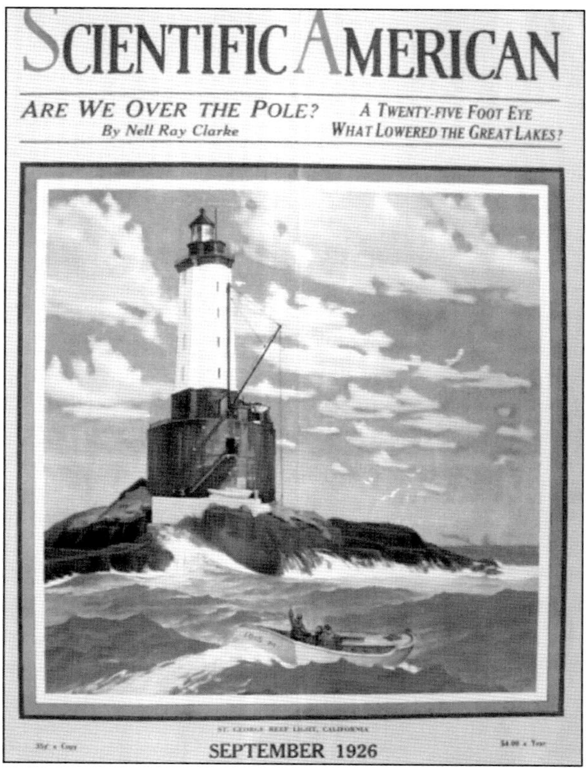

Following worldwide successes in underwater telephone communication, an attempt was made to lay a cable between St. George and Crescent City in the early 1920s. The tender *Manzanita* delivered the installation crew and the line, which was put in place between June 4 and June 13, 1920, but it broke several times due to chafing. It was replaced in 1926 by Army field radios. Above, a cable drops into the ocean from the lower landing. (Coast Guard Historian's Office.)

Highlighting its distinction as one of the greatest feats of American engineering, the whitewashed tower of St. George Reef Lighthouse soars above the friendly mariners in the *Lois* in this September 1926 issue of *Scientific American* magazine. Albeit 35 years after the fact, it is still a singular honor and testimony to its builders to be featured in America's premier scientific publication. (SGRLPS Archives.)

Four

THE COAST GUARD ERA

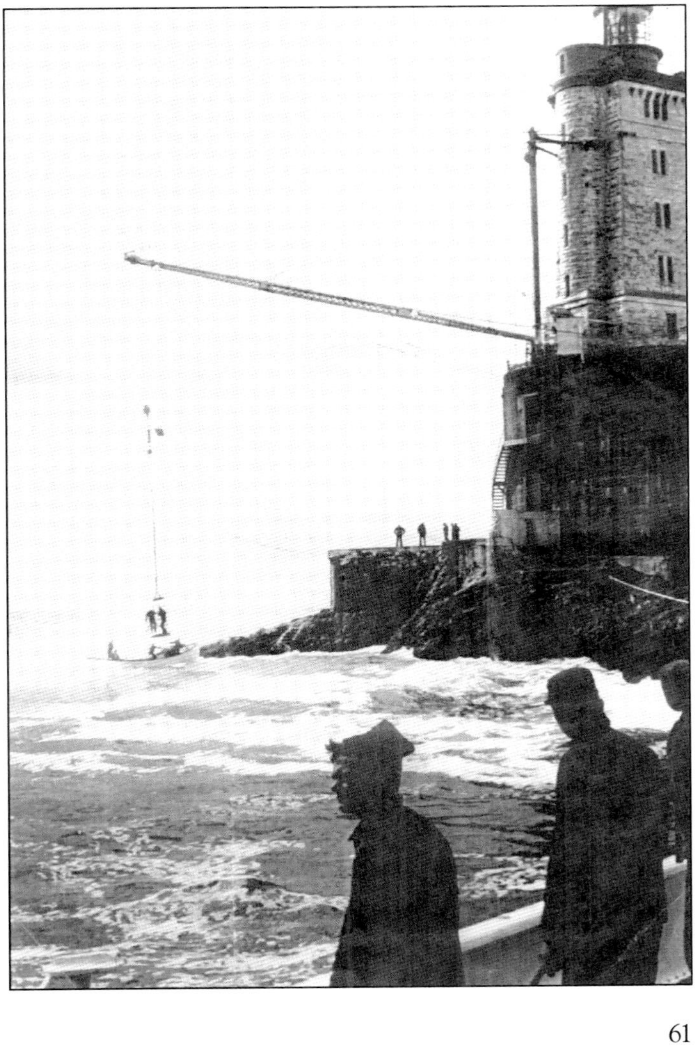

The Lighthouse Service merged with the Coast Guard on July 7, 1939, signaling a new era at St. George that would last for nearly four decades. The civilian casualness of former years was replaced by military discipline and order, shifting the identity of the station from a lighthouse to a ship underway. Reflecting that change, this Coast Guard cutter nestles in close to the lighthouse as the new caretakers perform a supply run. (Coast Guard.)

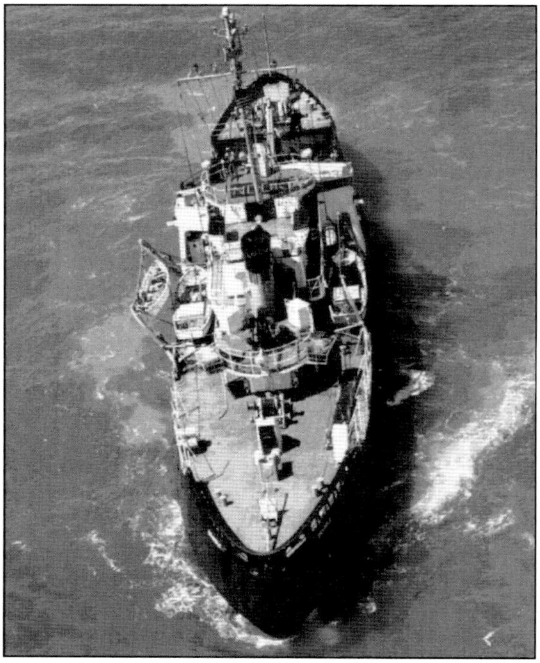

Without the supply ships from Yerba Buena, or "YBI" as the depot in the San Francisco Bay was listed in the log, the light at St. George would soon go out. Lighthouse tenders gave way to Coast Guard cutters around 1946. Pictured here is the *Bramble,* a cutter that began servicing the station after World War II. An aerial view shows the ship's deck configuration. (Coast Guard Historian's Office.)

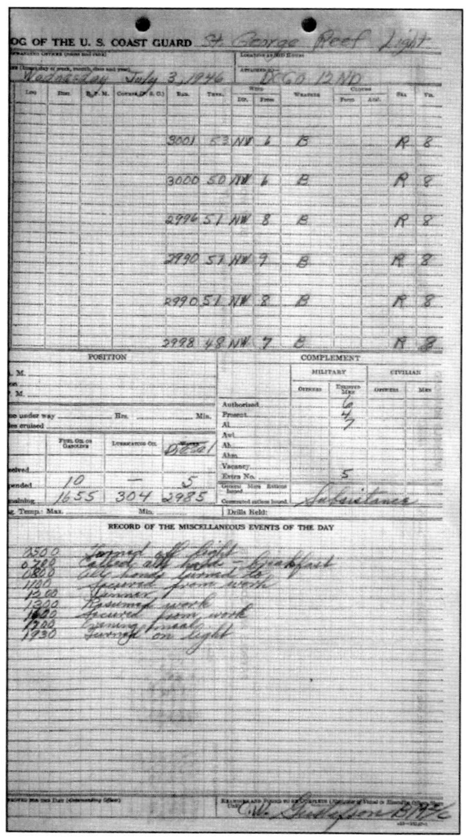

OG OF THE U. S. COAST GUARD St. George Reef Light

Wednesday July 3, 1946 — DCGO 12 ND

Bar.	Ther.	Wind Dir.	Force	Weather	Sea	Vis.
3001	53	NW	6	B	R	8
3000	50	NW	6	B	R	8
2996	51	NW	8	B	R	8
2990	51	NW	7	B	R	8
2990	51	NW	8	B	R	8
2998	48	NW	7	B	R	8

	Fuel Oil or Gasoline	Lubricating Oil	Diesel
Received			
Expended	10	—	5
Remaining	1655	304	2985

Commuted rations issued: Subsistance

RECORD OF THE MISCELLANEOUS EVENTS OF THE DAY

0500 Turned off light
0700 Called all hands—breakfast
0800 All hands turned to
1100 Secured from work
1200 Dinner
1300 Resumed work
1600 Secured from work
1700 Evening meal
1930 Turned on light

When the Coast Guard assumed command at St. George, the language of the sea entered the log. Doors became hatches, floors were now decks, walls turned into bulkheads, and the kitchen morphed into a galley. This log entry is from July 3, 1946, and it contains information about weather, sea conditions, fuel consumption, personnel authorized, and events of the day such as: "0700 Called all hands—breakfast" and "1600 Secured from work." (National Archives.)

In combination with the stations logs and photographs, the memories of men who served there offer a more intimate glimpse of duty at St. George. Robert Foltz, pictured here, served in the early 1940s and remembers Crescent City as a friendly place, but he also recalls close calls on the boom, lousy food, drinking water polluted with diesel, and waves that crashed outside his room near the top of the tower. (Robert Foltz and the SGRLPS Archives.)

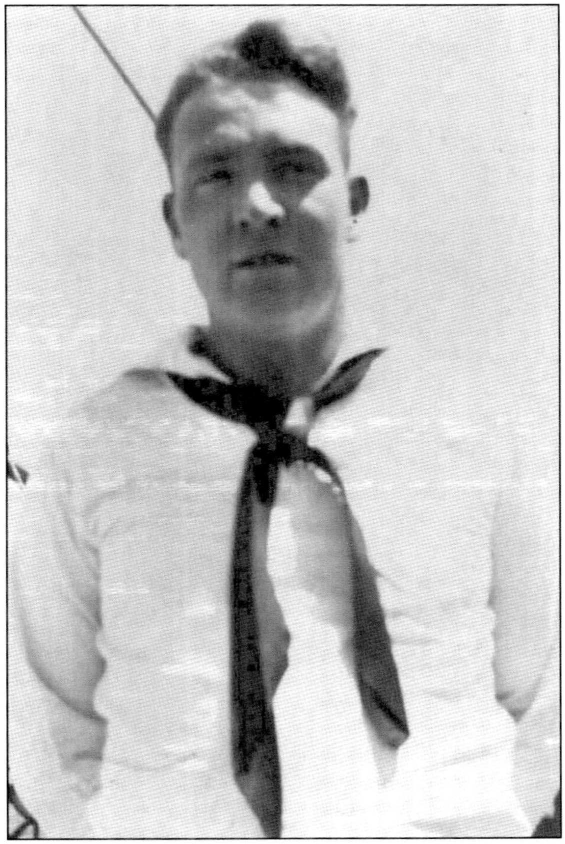

Roy Crockett, who served here in the 1940s, sent this annotated postcard featuring St. George to his family. His comments on the back read in part, "What do you think of my home? . . . The whole thing is made of granite . . . Waves sometimes break as high as where the boats are hanging." Roy also served at other California lighthouses. (Marjorie C. Crockett.)

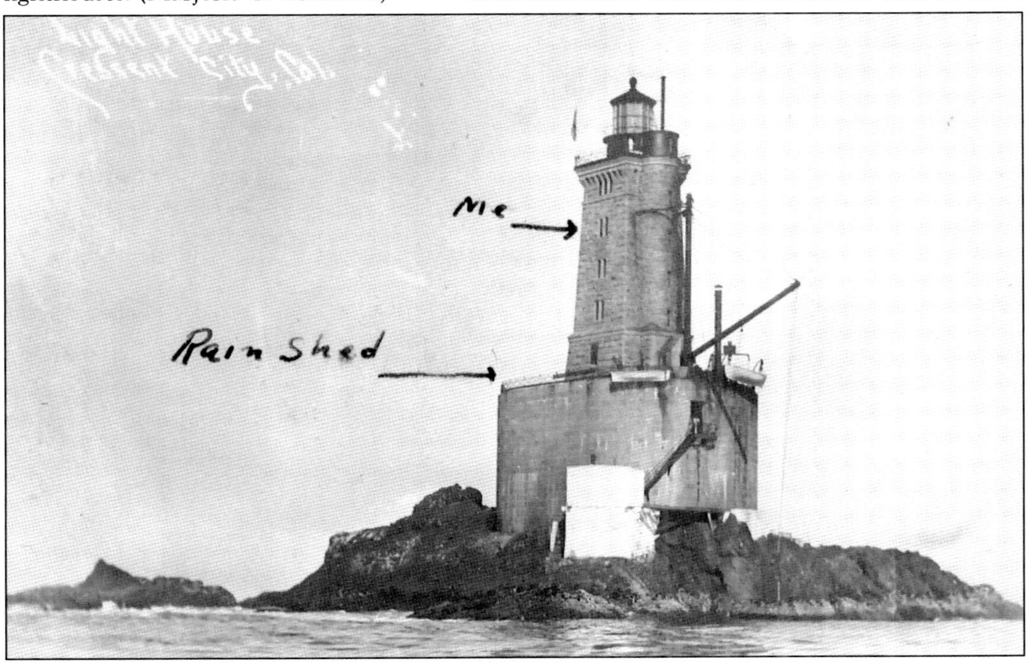

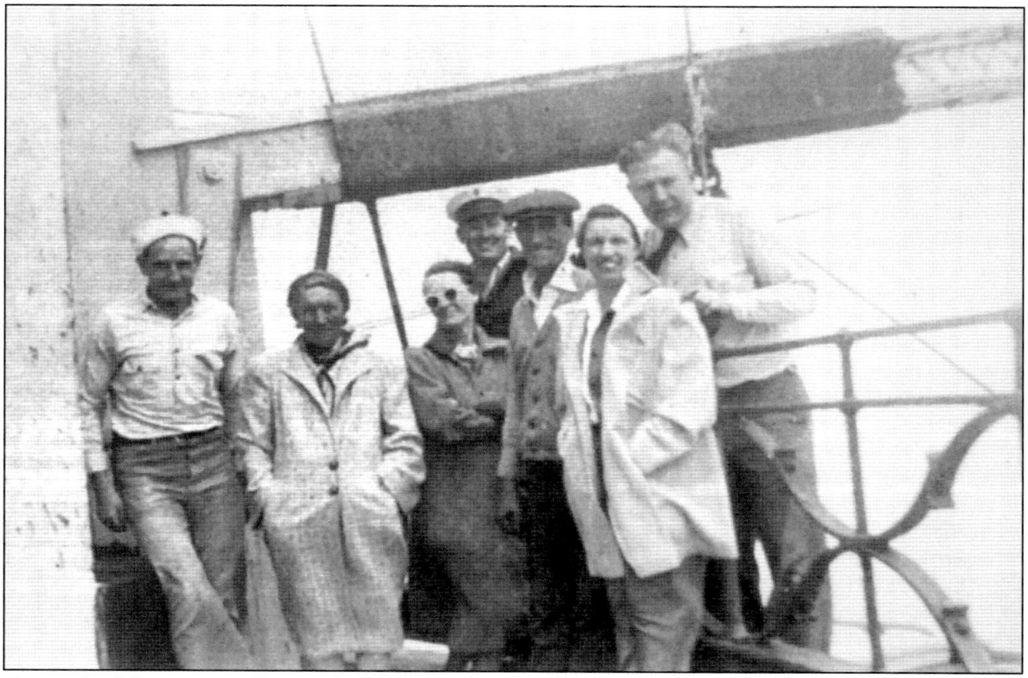

Guests huddle against the wind at the base of the boom in this photograph. Pictured here, from left to right, are Crockett and his wife, Elsie, an unidentified couple, Chester Johnson, and Marion and Jim Smallscreed. Smallscreed is standing behind the safety rail on the very narrow edge of the water catchment channel that circles the caisson. It is nearly 70 feet to the rocks below. (James Smallscreed and the SGRLPS Archives.)

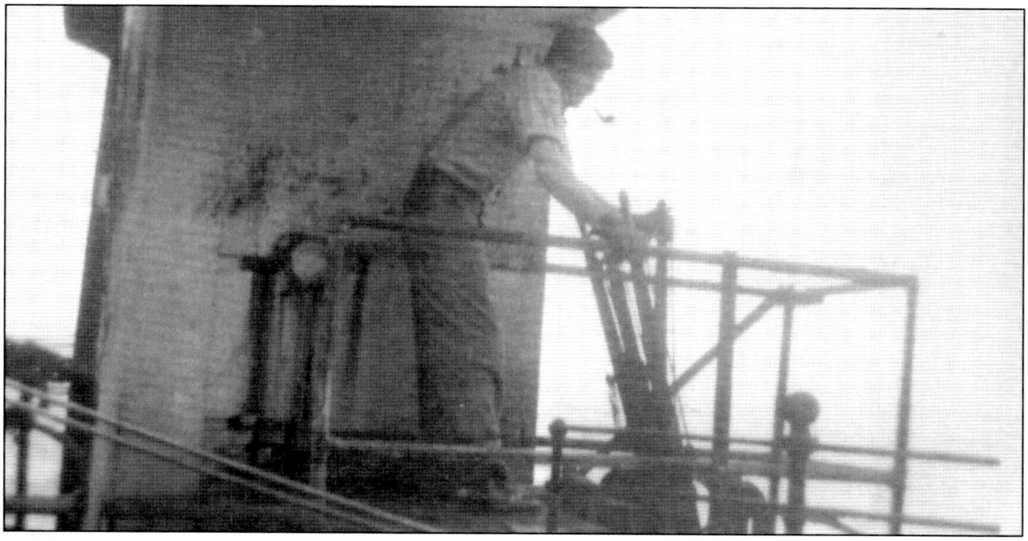

A 25-year-old Clair Shackleford stands at the boom-hoist controls. This interface between men, boat, and sea is the single most dangerous facet of operations at the lighthouse. Shackleford relates that the hoist controls were replaced sometime in 1947. A log entry reports that on September 9, 1949, the mechanism failed, and the station launch plunged, pulling a supporting cable loose from the tower. (Clair Shackleford and the SGRLPS Archives.)

George Hornbake was a career Coastguardsman (1938–1957) with assignments in New York, New Jersey, and the Philippines. He was at St. George in 1947–1948 and brought his wife, Ella Mae, and daughter, Georgia Carol, who lived in the shore station housing at Point St. George. While at the station, he saw some exciting changes to the fog signal and the driving mechanism for turning the lens, which was electrified. (Georgia Hornbake Spiess and the SGRLPS Archives.)

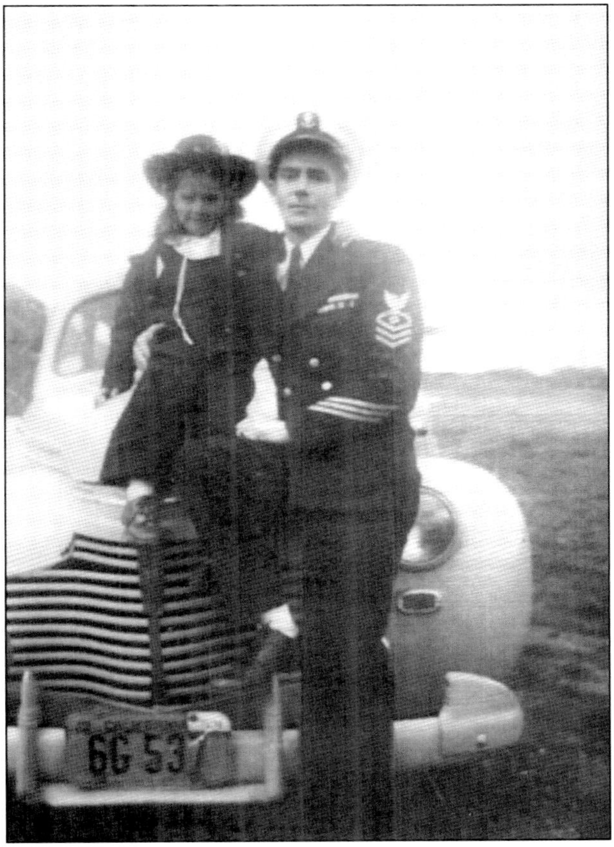

Norris Harpin was reassigned after World War II and also served in Korea and Vietnam. His most vivid memory was the time his wife, Mearl, paid an unexpected visit to the lighthouse, braving the 10-mile trip in the station launch and the dangerous ride on the boom. Norris (in uniform, top right) stands with his wife next to the Hornbakes. Kneeling are officer-in-charge Joe Richardson, his wife, Jackie, with daughter Tootie. (Norris Harpin and the SGRLPS Archives.)

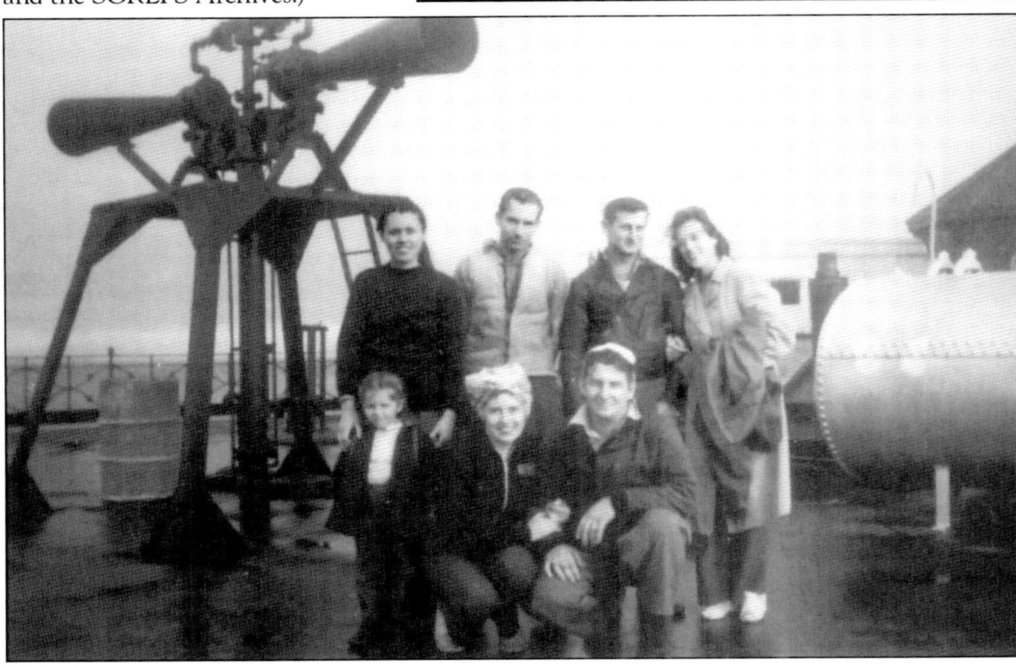

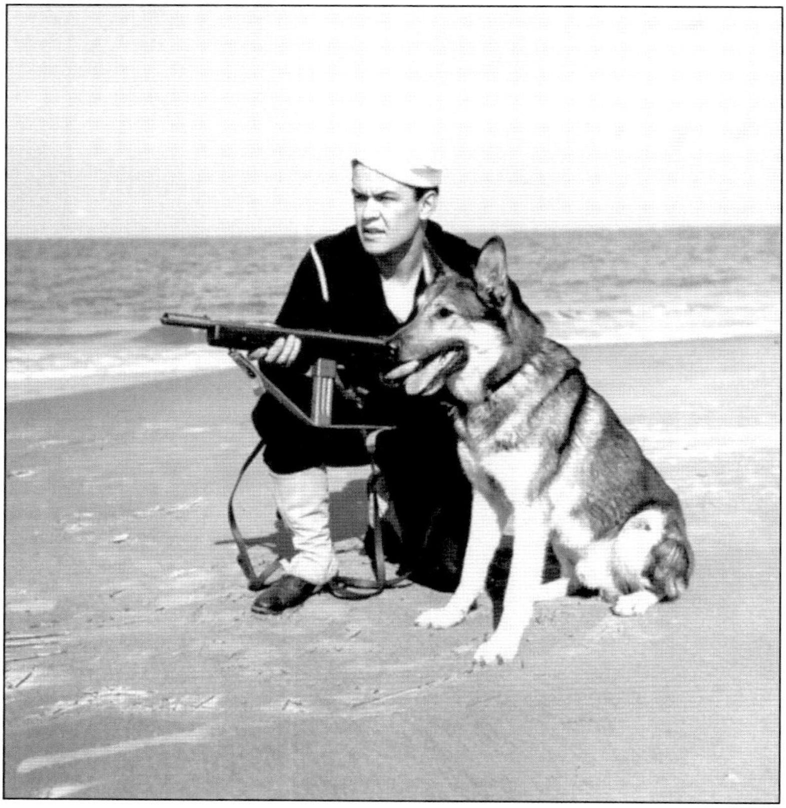

In reaction to threats of imminent invasion by the Japanese following Pearl Harbor, the Coast Guard formed the Shore Patrol, teams of men, dogs, and horses to guard hundreds of miles of isolated beaches on the Pacific coast and other threatened areas of the country. Local beaches were no exception, and the men on watch at St. George had the company of fellow servicemen, like the one pictured here. (Coast Guard Historian's Office.)

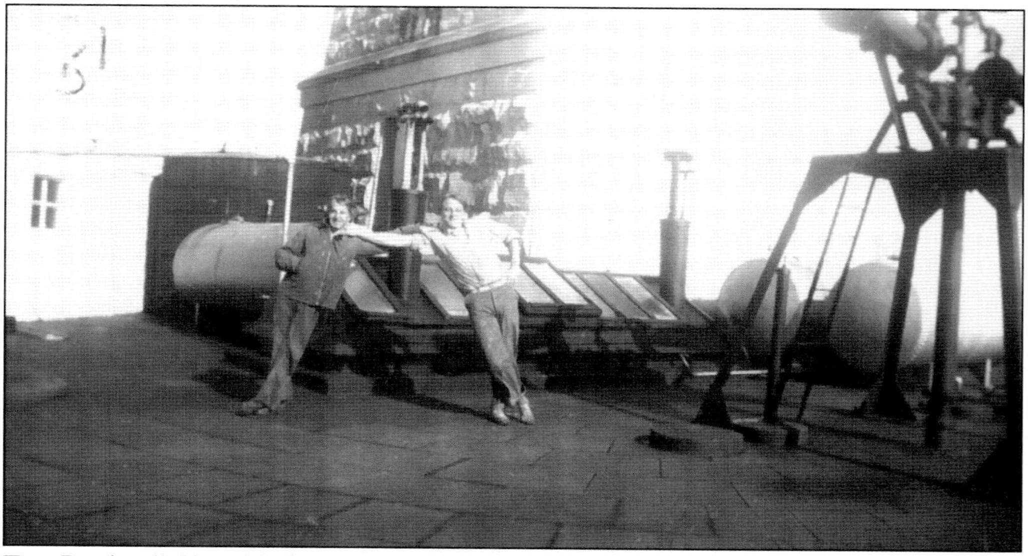

Tom Dunlap (left) and Robert Johnson clown around on the catch deck, providing a close-up look at the engine room skylight (so often broken by high seas) and the diaphone fog signal. Protruding through the skylight is the engine room exhaust, necessary because of carbon dioxide emissions from the generators. The white building in the background is the hoisting engine and boom-controller shed. (Tom Dunlap and the SGRLPS Archives.)

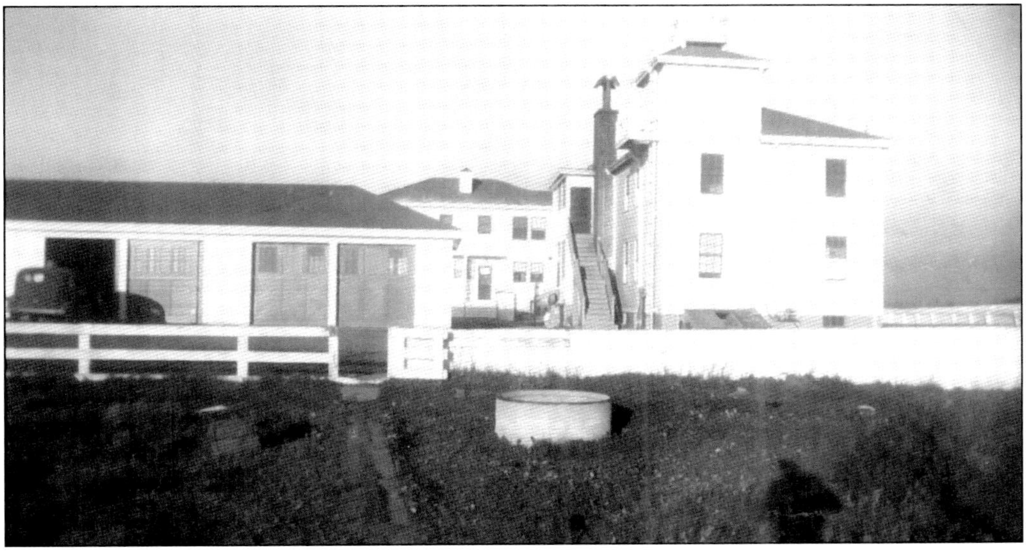

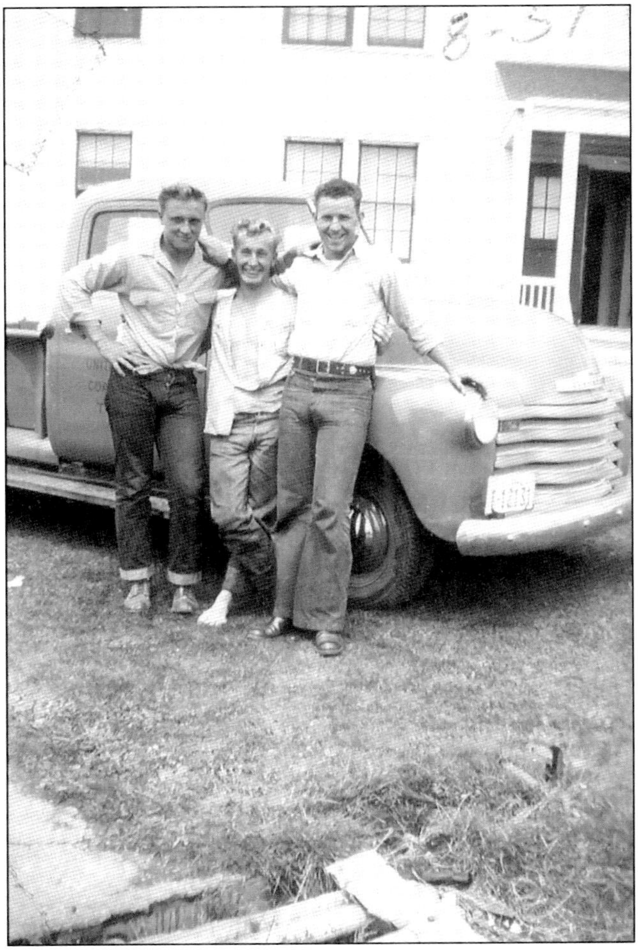

Tom Dunlap, who during his career in the Coast Guard saw duty at Anacapa Island and Yerba Buena, was just 19 years old when he received orders to proceed to the "Rock." Little did he know at the time that he would be witness to one of the most tragic events in the history of the Coast Guard Lighthouse Service. In a lighter vein, Dunlap offers a number of views of the lighthouse, the men with whom he served, and the shore quarters he called home when not on duty. Pictured here are views of the shore quarters, a former Navy radio facility located on Point St. George, and Dunlap (center) posing with his coworkers Richard Simmons (left) and Robert Johnston. (Both, Tom Dunlap and the SGRLPS Archives.)

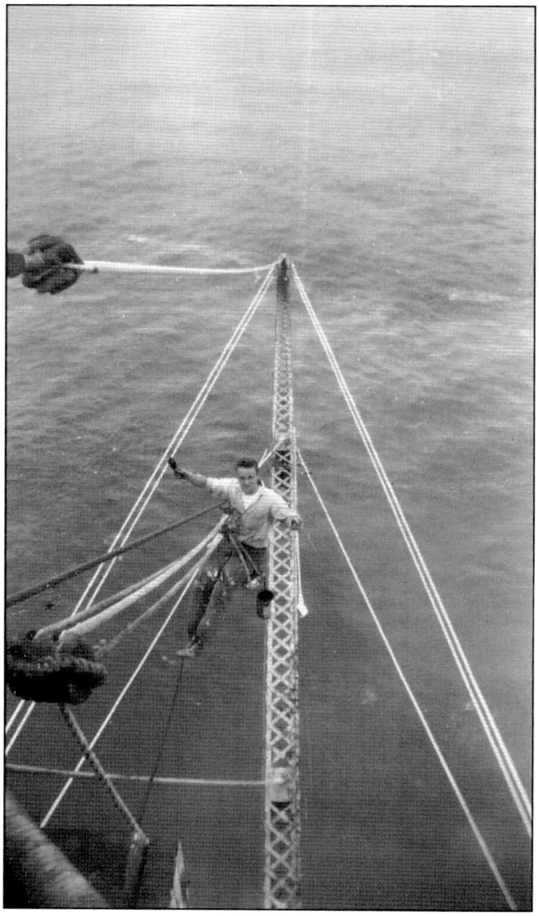

These two images reveal the risks taken by keepers on a daily basis to perform routine maintenance on the station. Richard Simmons (safety line attached) paints the cables that activate the boom traveler. Robert Johnston puts a protective coat on the cable encircling the tower that was put in place to secure the boom-mast assembly after the September 1949 accident. (Both, Tom Dunlap and the SGRLPS Archives.)

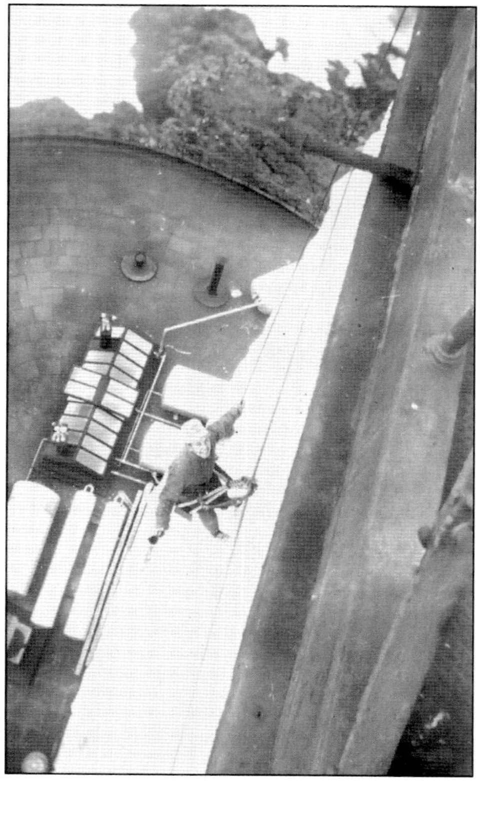

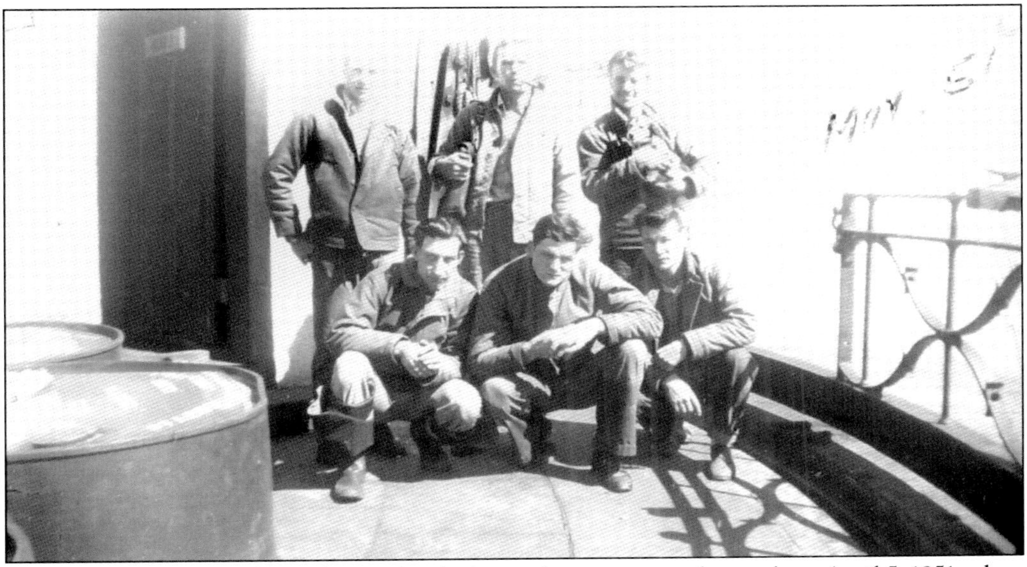

For decades, no lives had been lost under the boom; however, tragedy struck on April 5, 1951, when the station launch was being lowered by Tom Dunlap. Two of the men who lost their lives are in this photograph. Pictured here, from left to right, are (first row) Stanley Costello, Wilbur Walker, and Rollin Bechtel; (second row) Dunlap, Fred Permenter, and Ross Vandenberg holding his dog Jet. Costello and Walker were killed in the accident. (Tom Dunlap and the SGRLPS Archives.)

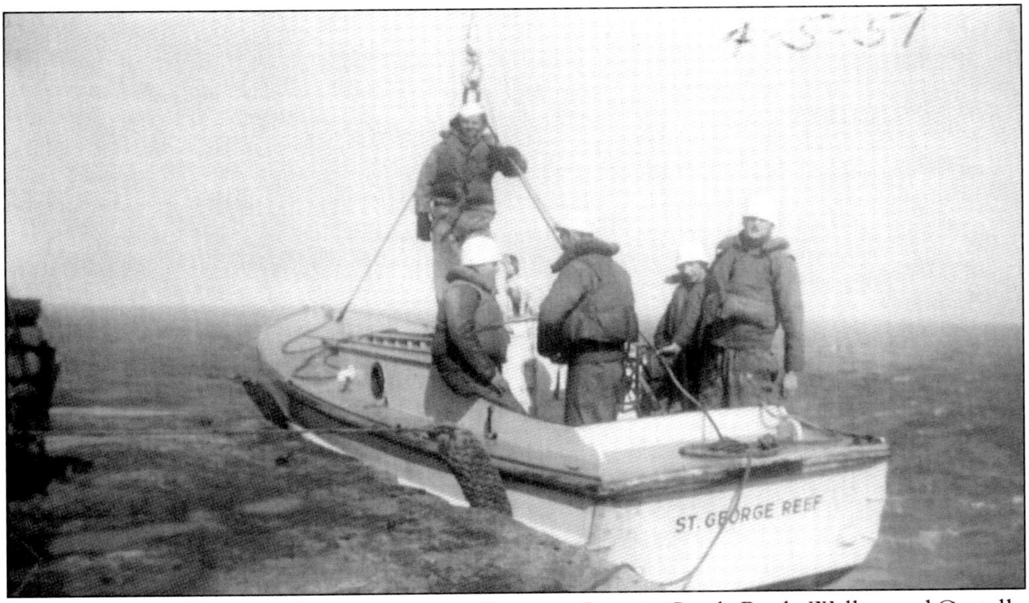

With thoughts of home and a routine run to Crescent City via Castle Rock, Walker and Costello glance at the camera from the stern of the launch while Beckett (sitting on rail) converses with Mulcahy, who is apparently securing his life vest. Vandenberg stands ready to unhook when they reach water. Inspector Harry Rhodes said, "Show me a man who has served at St. George, and I will show you a man and a lighthouse keeper." (Coast Guard and the SGRLPS Archives.)

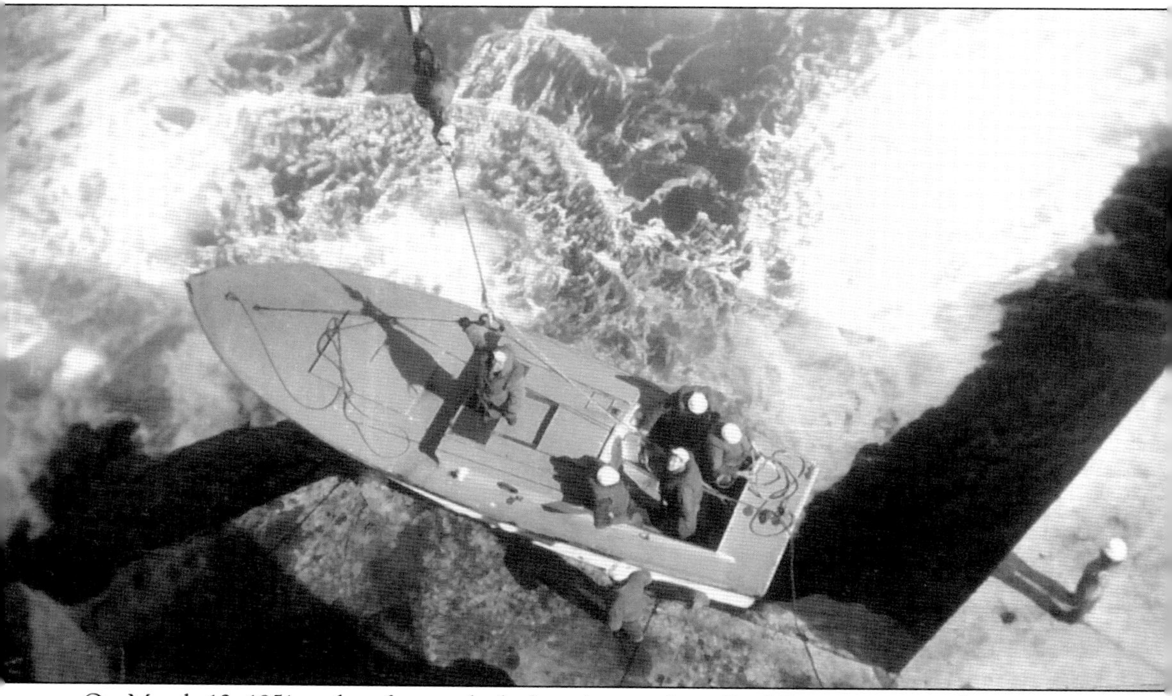

On March 13, 1951, only a few weeks before the accident, Fred Permenter signed in as officer in charge of St. George. When the tragedy occurred, there were five men in the boat. Lost in the accident were Stanley Costello, Wilbur Walker, and Bertram Beckett. Survivors were Ross Vandenberg and Thomas Mulcahy. Tom Dunlap offers this eyewitness account of the tragedy: "[I took this picture] from the main deck before I went to the winch controls and lowered boat about 1500 hours. Large swell caught and swamped [boat], knocked men into water. Two men looking up [in boat] Ross Vandenberg and Tom Mulcahy made it to mooring buoy approximately 100 yards out. Stanley Costello, Wilbur Walker, Bertram Beckett died from exposure. Fred Permenter and Rollin Bechtel standing on deck. Wayne Piland, keeper at Crescent City Light heard our radio transmission and got fishing vessel *Winga* to come out, picked up Vandenberg and Mulcahy." [signed] Tom Dunlap. Sadly, Vandenberg's pet dog Jet was also aboard and became a fourth victim. (Tom Dunlap and the SGRLPS Archives.)

Wilbur Walker was a married veteran of World War II and was making a career in the Coast Guard when he was assigned to St. George on temporary duty to work on the radio compass system called LORAN (long range navigation). He was buried at Ocean View Cemetery in Eureka on April 10, 1951. Bertram Beckett received military rites at Arroyo Grande, California, and Stanley Costello was interred at Golden Gate National Cemetery at San Bruno, California. (SGRLPS Archives.)

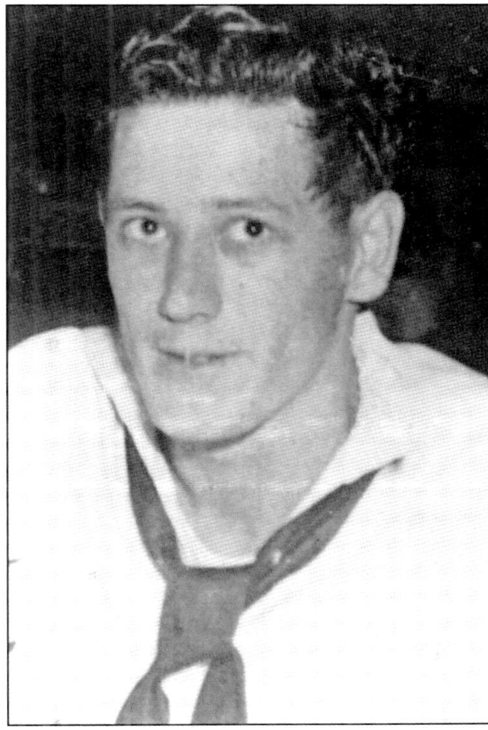

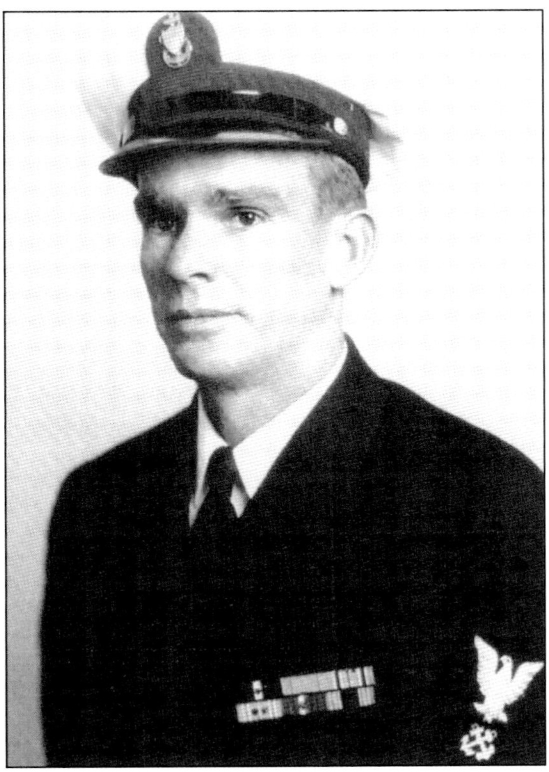

Fred Permenter is credited with saving the lives of the two survivors and was given the Treasury Department Gold Lifesaving Medal and the American Legion Gold Medal of Valor. His official citation reads, in part, "For extreme and heroic action on April 5, 1951 . . . Sent out a distress radio call . . . retrieved a life raft from the vessel . . . threw out the raft and jumped into the water . . . picked up a third unconscious man and lashed a fourth to the raft." (SGRLPS Archives.)

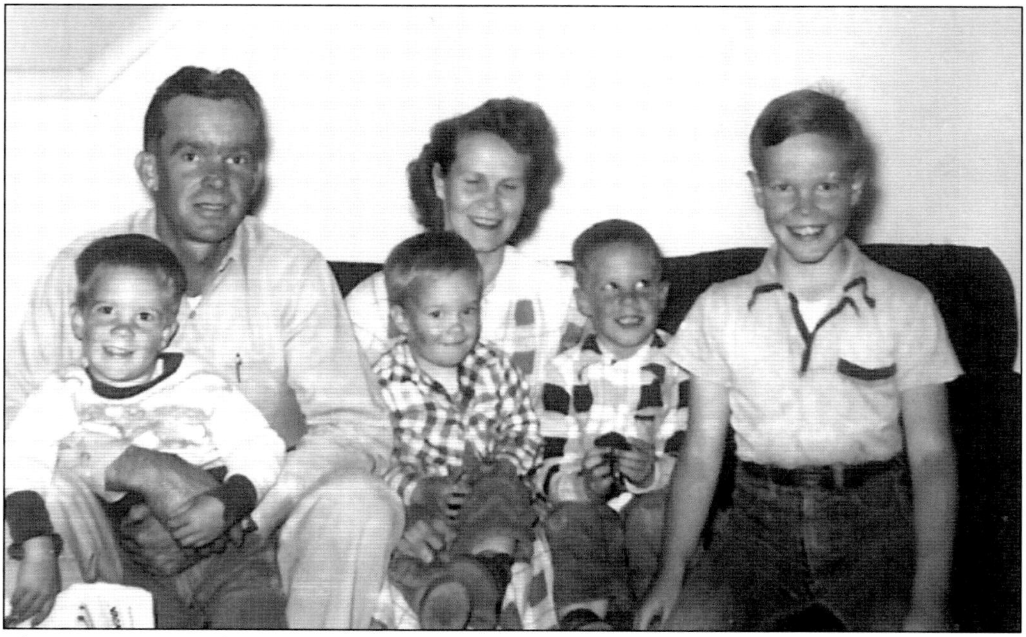

The Permenters pose here in happier times at the shore station housing complex. "Bennie" Permenter shared some memories of the accident with the author. She remembered the kindness of Dr. Vipond, a local physician who comforted Costello's wife, Fred's anxiety when called to testify at an inquest, and his relief when he was exonerated. (Permenter family and the SGRLPS Archives.)

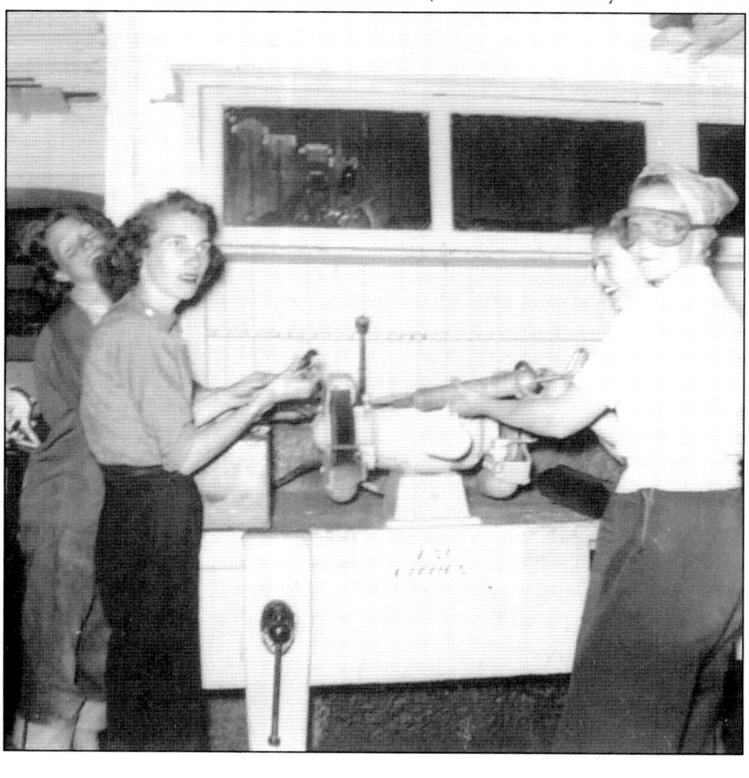

From left to right, Ginger Griffin, Marcia Harden, Mary Duck, and Bennie Permenter visited on a calm day in the 1950s and toured the site. Here, they ham it up in the engine room workshop. Bennie's goggles are a reminder of the dangers their husbands faced on a daily basis. Aside from accidents on the boom, very few injuries or sicknesses are noted in the log. If treatment were required, it would be done locally, in Eureka, or at the Marine Hospital in Alameda. (Mel Harden and the SGRLPS Archives.)

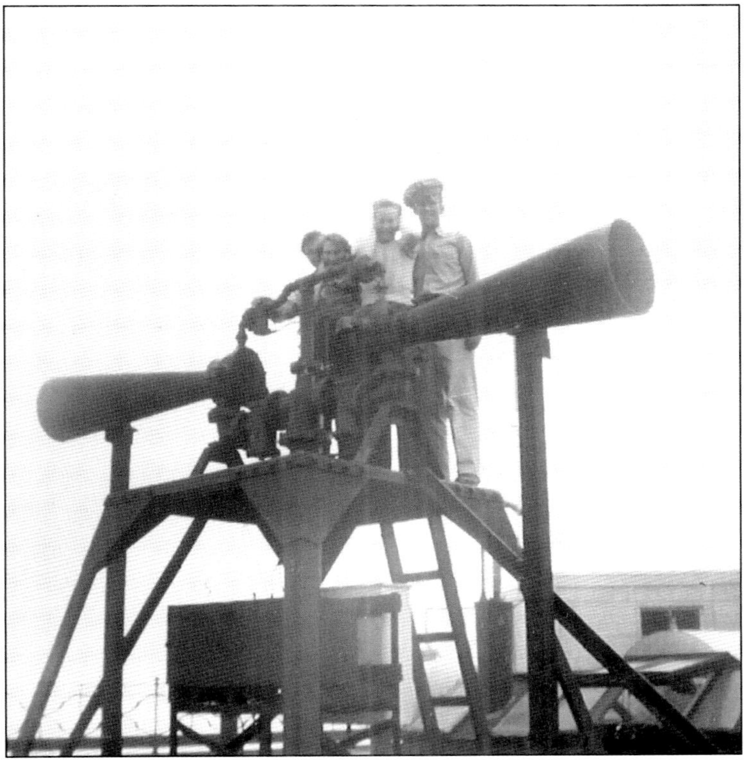

Hosts and guests stand on top of the heavy metal stanchion that supports the superpowerful fog signal on the main deck. Beware the decibels of this monster. Seagulls that use it as a convenient perch have been known to fall over dead after a blast. New keepers lost sleep, even with earplugs, and have put wooden shims between bedspring coils to prevent them from vibrating. (Permenter/Harden and the SGRLPS Archives.)

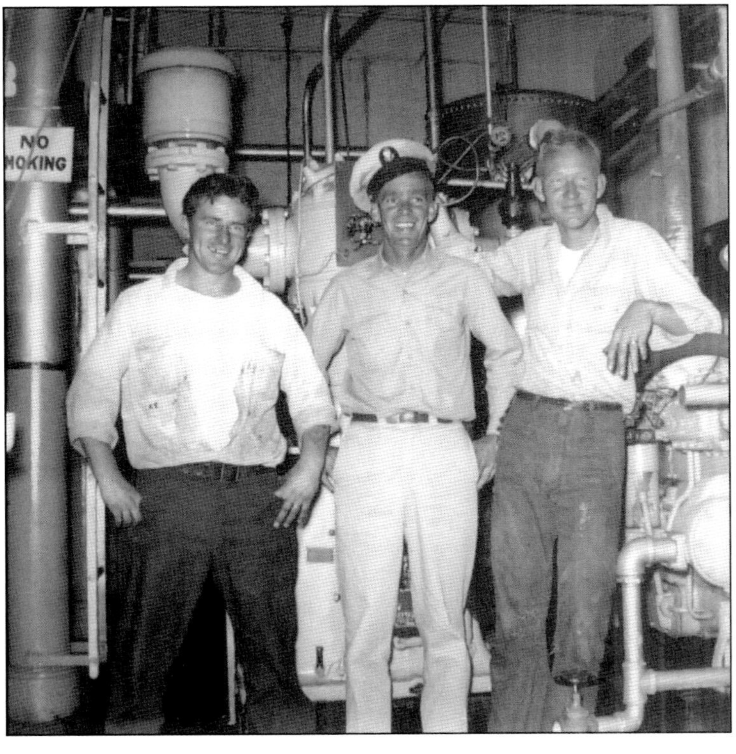

Mel Harden (left), Fred Permenter (center), and Gene Duck stand in front of a generator in the engine room. Here are the sights, sounds, and smells dear to the heart of a machinist or electrician's mate. Protected by the thick walls of caisson, the engine room was the heart and brains of the station, providing power for domestic use and the main operations, including the light, hoist, and fog signal. (Mel Harden and the SGRLPS Archives.)

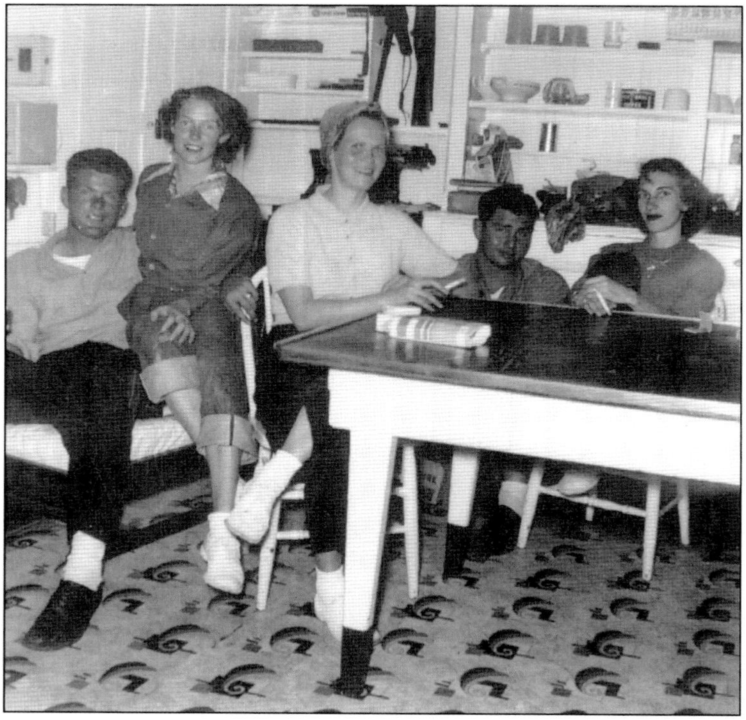

Up one flight of the spiraling granite staircase brings them to the galley, the social and recreational center. Although it is not shown in this photograph, at various times the galley was also used as a radio room. With frequent supply runs, the galley was usually well stocked, but in 1953, when savage storms prevented relief, the crew was down to canned meat and World War II rations before the weather broke. (Permenter/Harden and the SGRLPS Archives.)

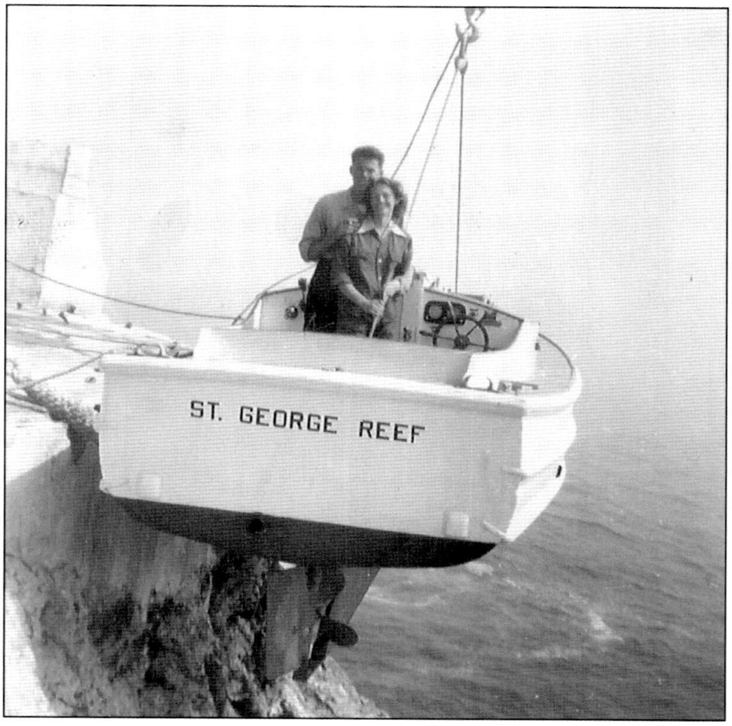

Here, the Griffins pose in the station launch hanging from davits on the lower landing. Vital for shore communications, crew transfers, and emergency evacuations, the 25-footer made hundreds of runs to Crescent City. The craft was originally designed for freshwater use and did not have a gas tank large enough to make the trip. Several log entries read, "Out of gas, water in gas, mechanical trouble, or abeam Castle Rock." (Mel Harden and the SGRLPS Archives.)

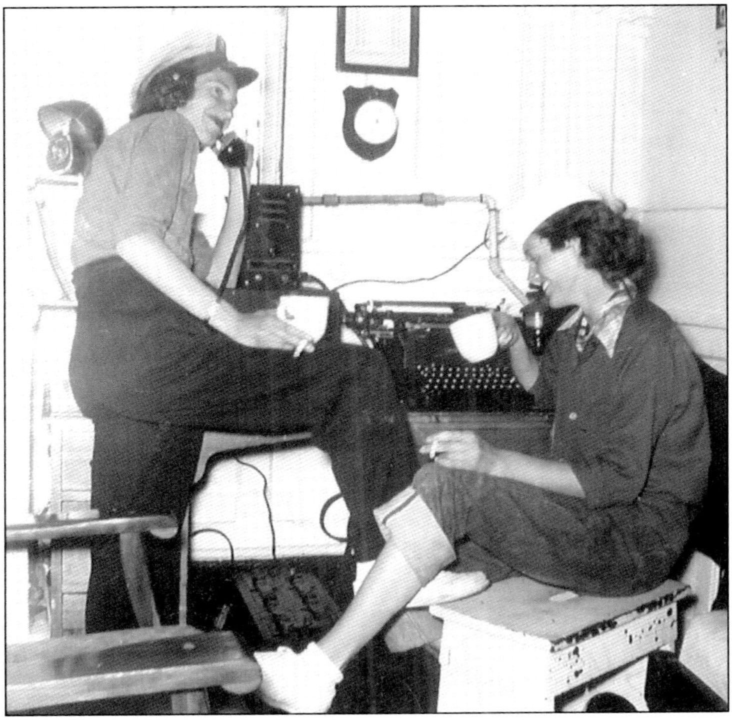

Marcia Harden dons the chief's hat and Ginger Griffin acts the seaman in this pantomime of a busy day in the command and administrative center of the station, the office of the officer in charge (OIC). Routine matters such as leave requests are handled here as well as serious matters requiring disciplinary action. The log reports an incident in which three men were AWOL at one time. (Permenter/Harden and the SGRLPS Archives.)

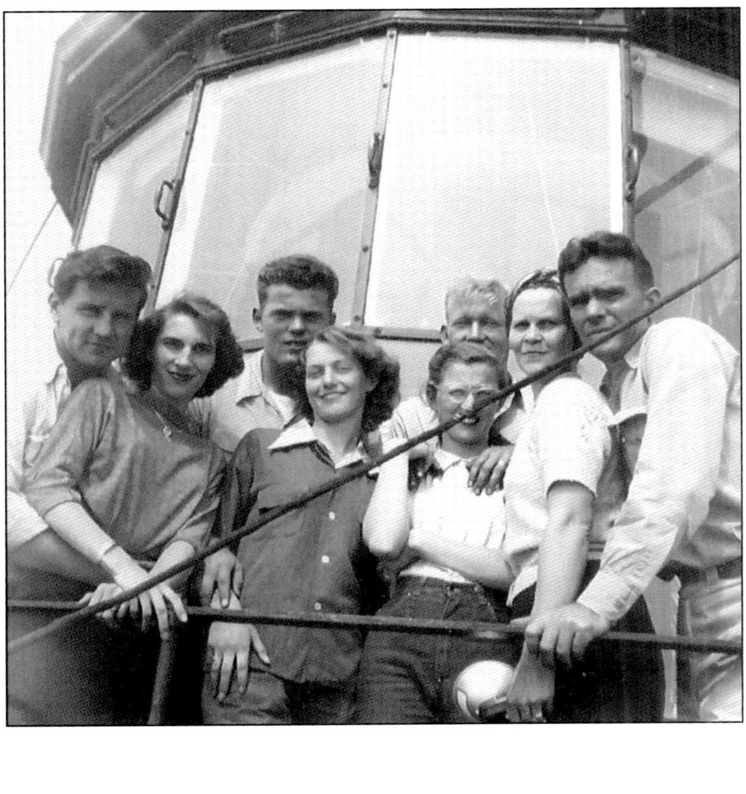

Keepers and spouses have their portraits taken outside the lantern room; pictured here, from left to right, are Mel and Marcia Harden, Pat and Ginger Griffin, Gene and Mary Duck, and Bennie and Fred Permenter. Usually, a protective curtain covered the windows in the daytime to prevent fires that can start when the temperature of the sun's rays, magnified by the thick glass optics, reaches combustible levels. (Permenter/Harden and the SGRLPS Archives.)

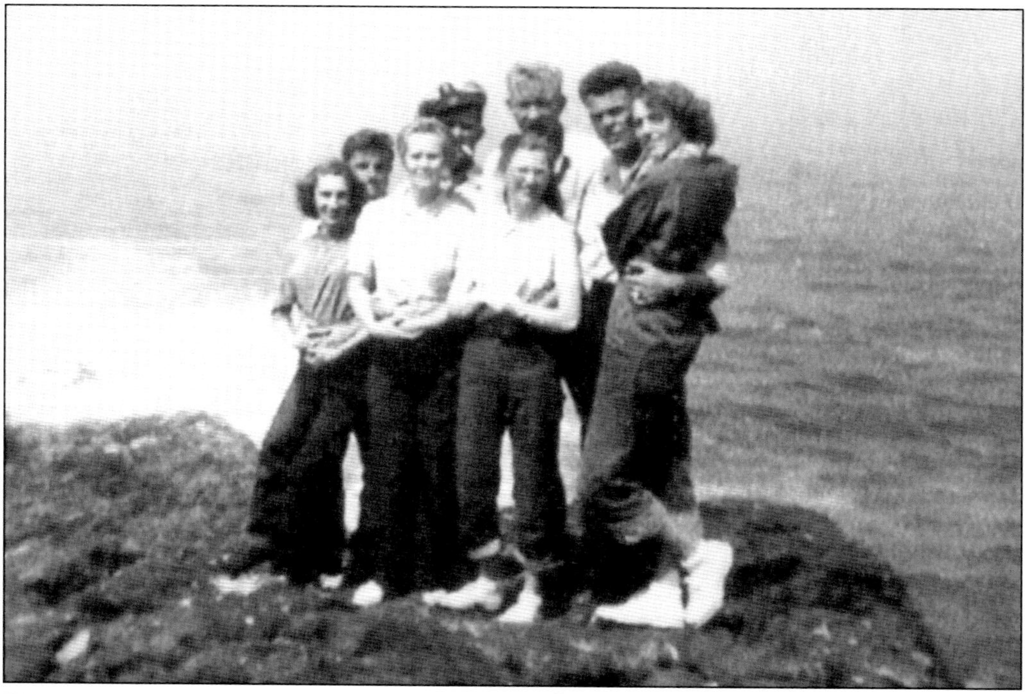

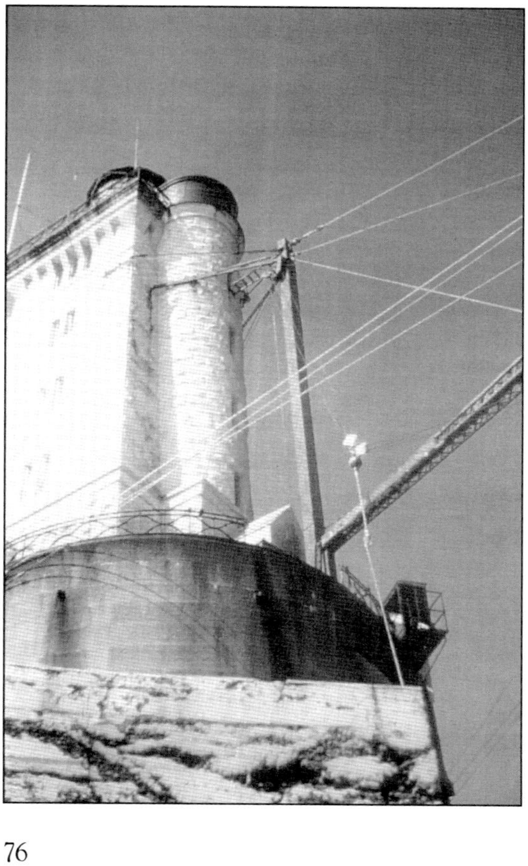

Permenter, Harden, and Griffin served together at St. George in the early to latter part of the 1950s. Bennie Permenter remembers: "The day Fred took Mary Duck, Marcia Harden, Ginger Griffin [and me] out to St. George's Reef Lighthouse, Gene Duck and Mel Harden were spending their ten days [watch] at the light." The happy adventurers pose here on the rocks at the base of the tower at a low tide. Pictured, from left to right, are Mel and Marcia Harden, Fred and Bennie Permenter, Gene and Mary Duck, and Pat and Ginger Griffin. (Permenter/Harden and the SGRLPS Archives.)

James Patrick "Pat" Griffin joined the Coast Guard following a stint in ROTC at college. Before his passing in 2000, he contacted the St. George Reef Lighthouse Preservation Society and contributed much historically significant information about his stay there. Griffin was unable to visit his old haunt, but he did enjoy watching a video of the last crew at the station the day before he died. Pictured here is the station as Griffin knew it. (Pat Griffin and the SGRLPS Archives.)

Pat Griffin, shown here on board a cutter, was witness to a near-fatal accident that occurred when water was being pumped to the station from a cutter. Griffin and a fellow keeper were transferring a large-diameter hose from the ship through the caisson door when the line was pressurized while the men were still holding it, causing it to flay about, striking Pat's companion, lacerating his skull. (Pat Griffin and the SGRLPS Archives.)

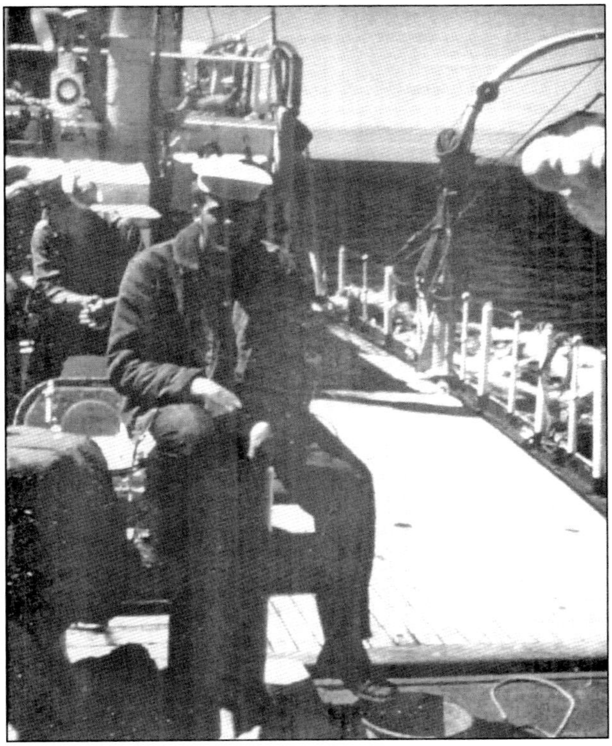

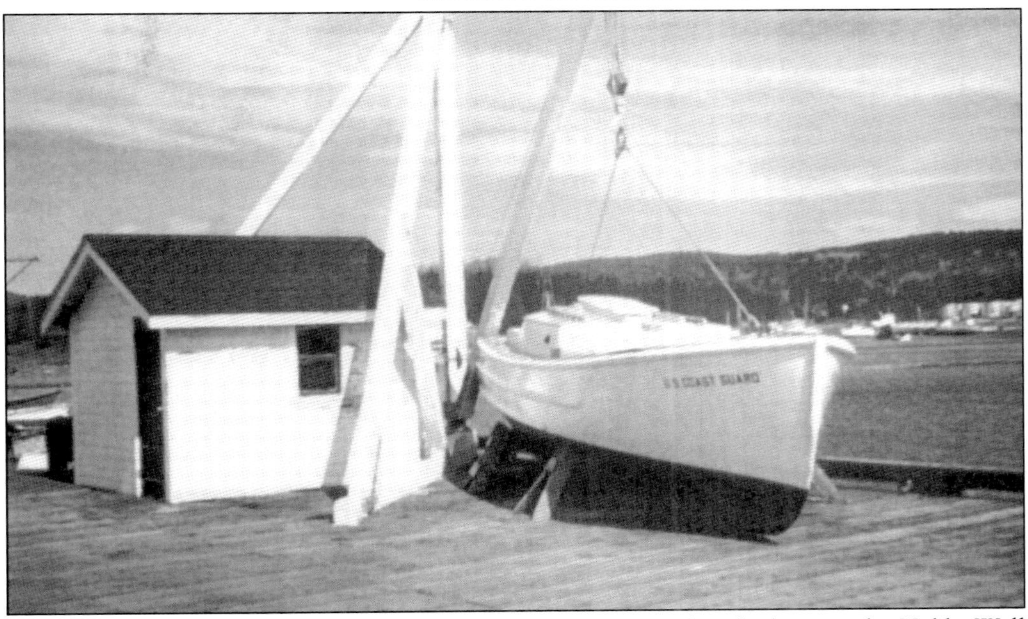

After a journey through the reef, the station launch was secured to the hoist at the Hobbs Wall Dock in Crescent City Harbor. Judging by the gleaming white paint on the hull, Griffin and friends may have just applied a fresh coat. Note the gasoline storage tanks to the right of the vessel. Prior to the 1964 tsunami, when they were destroyed by fire, the tanks held gasoline hauled into the port by tankers. (Pat Griffin and the SGRLPS Archives.)

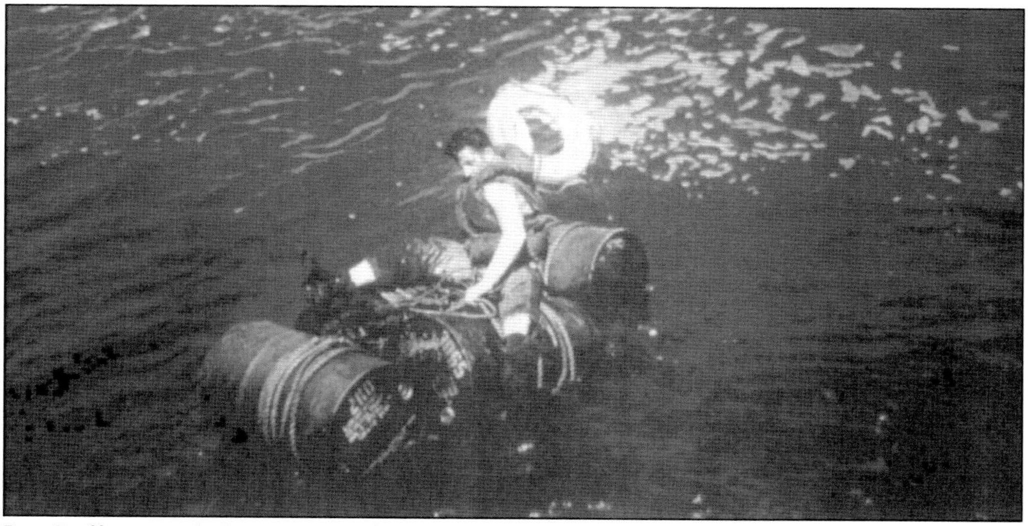

Pat Griffin records for posterity the only voyage of the SS *St. George Dragon*. He and Daryl Swanson concocted the craft and launched it on a very calm day at the reef. Swanson is shown here, no doubt wearing a Coast Guard–certified life jacket and doubly protected with an approved life ring. The shakedown cruise only lasted a few minutes, and the *Dragon* was hoisted aboard on the boom. (Pat Griffin and the SGRLPS Archives.)

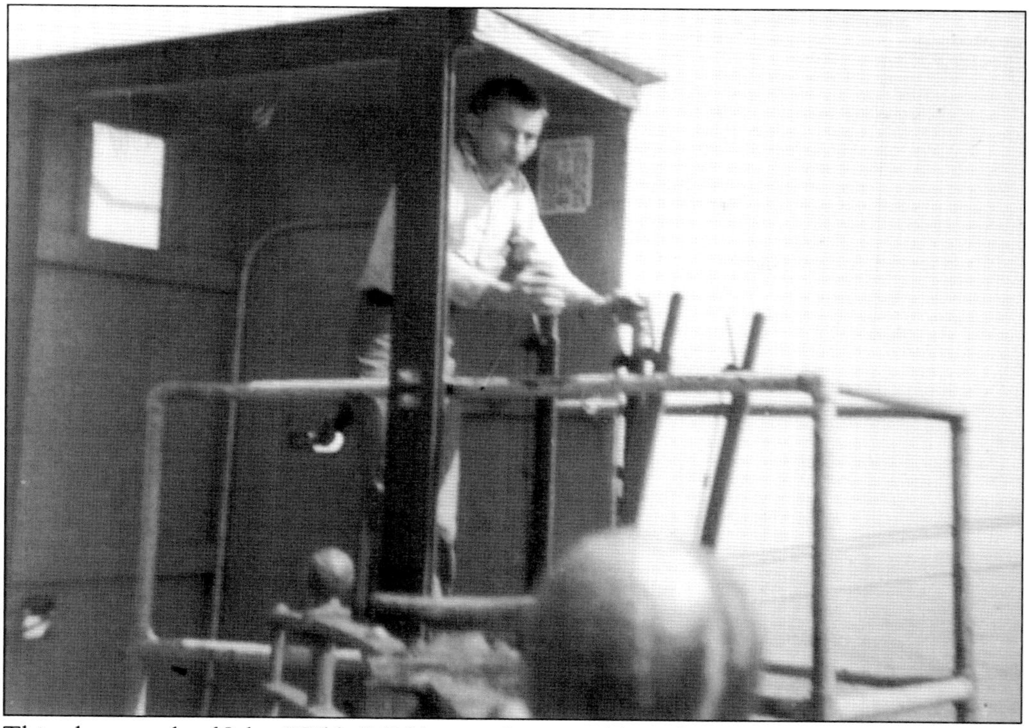

This photograph of John "Gibby" Gibbons, who served here from 1952 to 1956, at the boom controls begs the question, who or what is coming or going? Could it be the station launch, a crew of technicians from YBI to repair the LORAN, a district inspector, delivery of fuel, food, water, or best of all, mail out of Humboldt Bay? (John Gibbons and the SGRLPS Archives.)

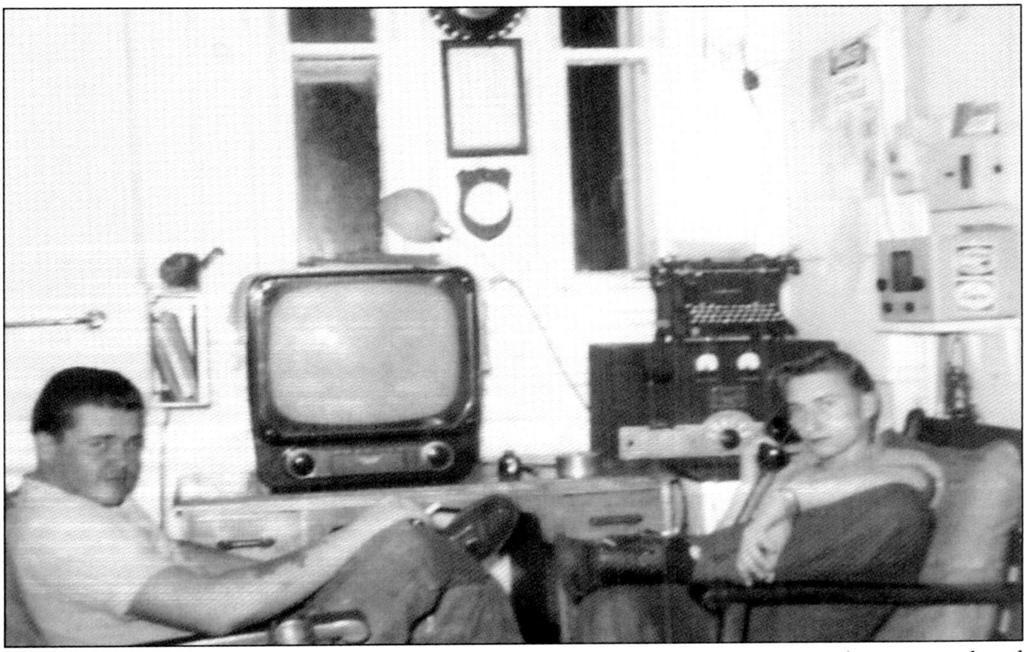

Gibby said, "I thought I was a dead man when I realized where I was going to be stationed and I saw the lighthouse emerge out of the fog like Dracula's castle." He had an engineman's rating, and cooking had never been his forte; but using memories of Grandma's meals, he soon became the main chef. The crewmen pooled their money and purchased a television. Here, Gibby (right) relaxes with Ron Postman. (John Gibbons and the SGRLPS Archives.)

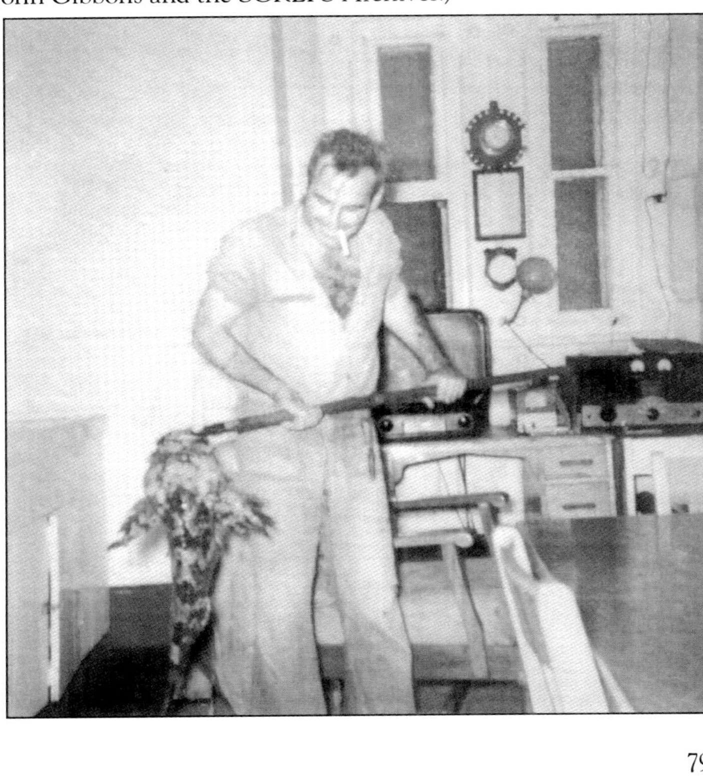

Chief "Chuck" Carroll holds a giant lingcod, rock cod, or other rockfish that Gibbons had just caught. Sadly, Gibbons relates that the chief thought the fish was a type of sea monster, so he threw it back. Fishing was done at every opportunity, sometimes from the rocks, but usually from the boom. (John Gibbons and the SGRLPS Archives.)

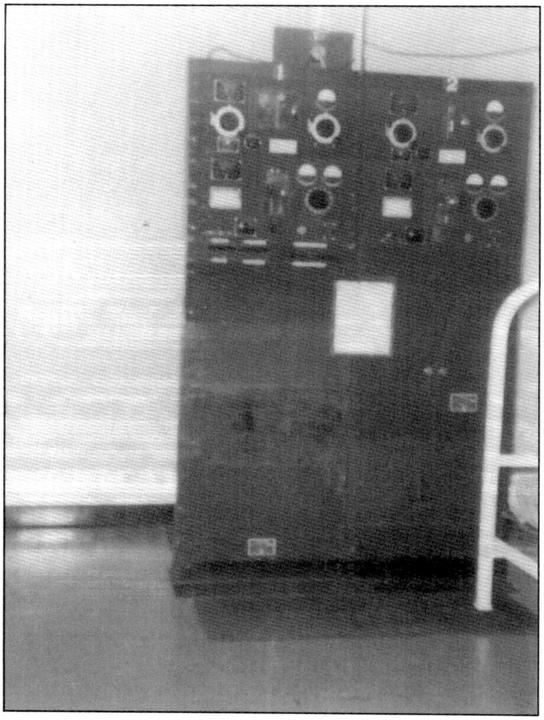

Until satellite navigation was perfected, the electronic marvel that was LORAN (long range navigation) was the latest tool to guide mariners and aircraft. What it meant for St. George was that a radio signal emanating from the station could be picked up by a cutter's radio, allowing it, with technical adjustments, to follow the beam to its destination. A LORAN system is shown here. (John Gibbons and the SGRLPS Archives.)

This scene, which shows a boom transfer being attempted in hurricane-like wind and sea conditions, was captured by *Humboldt Times* photographer Doug Wilson, who was a guest on board the Coast Guard cutter *Avoyel* out of Humboldt Bay, when it made a logistical run to the Rock on November 7, 1961. The men in the boat are Evans; Lt. Comdr. Walter Shafran, 12th Coast Guard District; and Raymond C. Burke, commanding officer, Group Humboldt Bay. (Doug Wilson, *Humboldt Times*.)

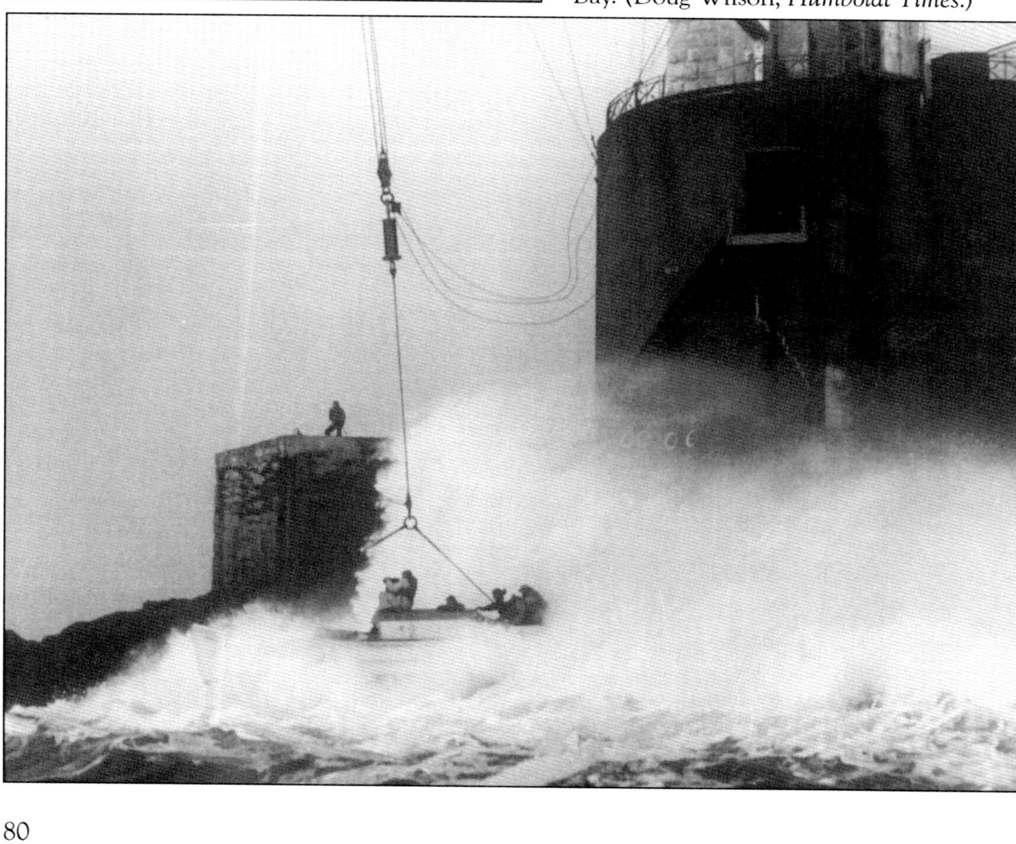

Duane "Fergie" Ferguson had several tours at St. George between 1955 and 1963. As an engineman, he tended the compressors, batteries, and generators that powered the station. Although duty rotations varied over time at the lighthouse, there was a six-man crew when he came aboard, three serving at a time, with 14-day rotations. Ferguson (center, holding plaque) receives an award for a deepwater mooring technique he developed. (Duane Ferguson.)

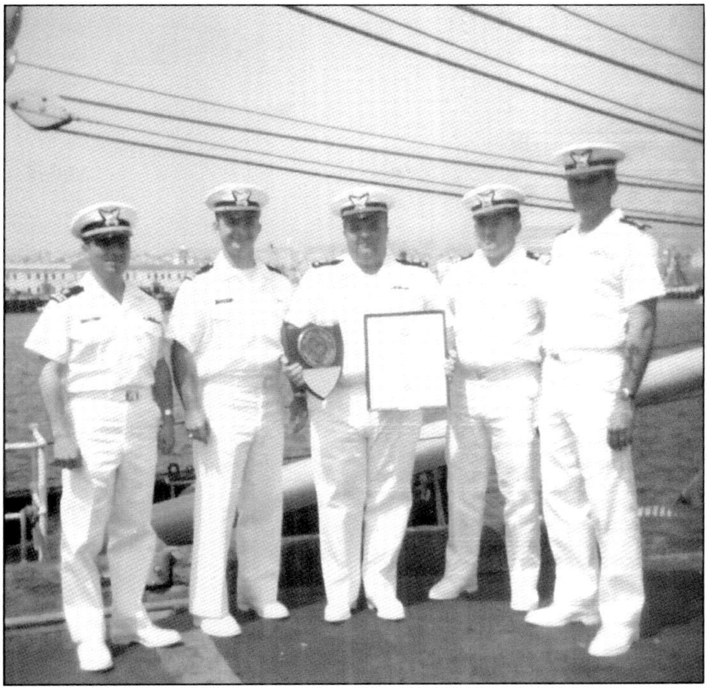

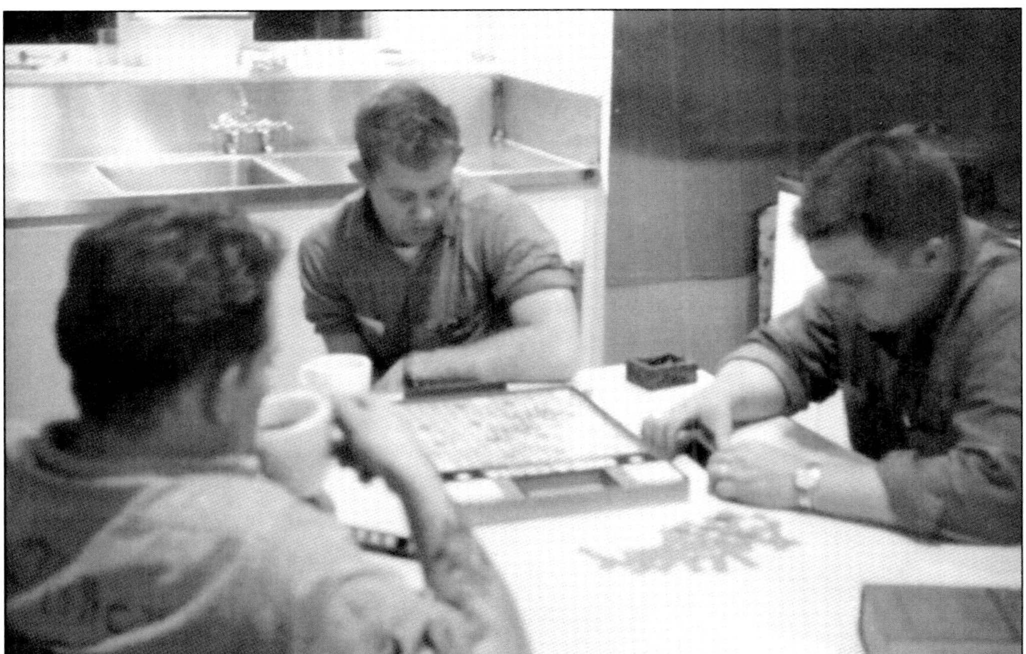

Here, Fergie records a moment of relaxation in the galley. He remembers the night he and other crewmen were sitting there and suddenly heard a loud crash above them. Investigating, they traced the noise to the drop tube for the old clockwork-lens-turning mechanism, hidden behind a wall. Made of lead, and quite heavy, the weights were sold and used to purchase recreational equipment. (Duane Ferguson and the SGRLPS Archives.)

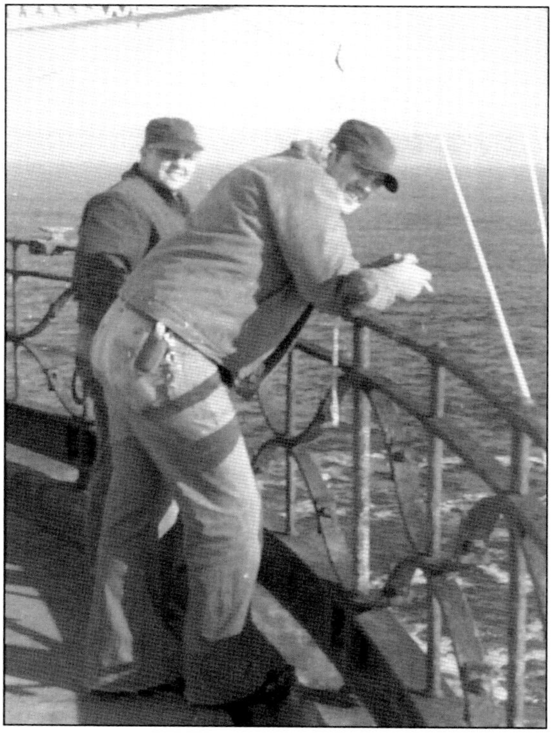

Fergie, standing in front of fellow keeper William Hoffman, experienced both the pleasures and perils of duty on the Rock. He loved the fishing available on the reef but was twice dumped into the brine on boom transfers. He also had some bad duty assignments; the one he most hated was cleaning the 50,000-gallon water storage cistern beneath the engine room floor. (Duane Ferguson and the SGRLPS Archives.)

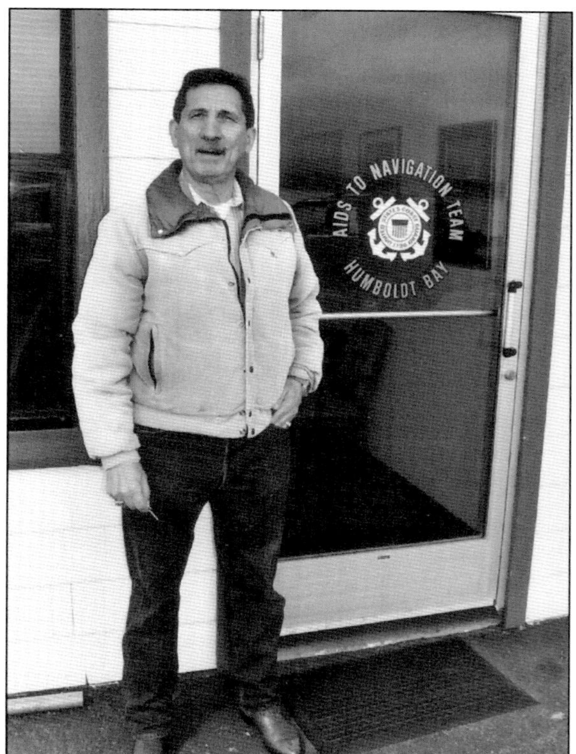

After the tutelage of the California Cadet Corps, a three-year hitch in the US Navy, and 17 years' service as a cutter man with the US Coast Guard, Dwayne Paul Evans (shown here) produced a three-volume history of the Coast Guard cutter *Avoyel* titled *On Call for Humanity,* in which he chronicles the resupply missions to the Rock from the perspective at sea level. (Author's collection.)

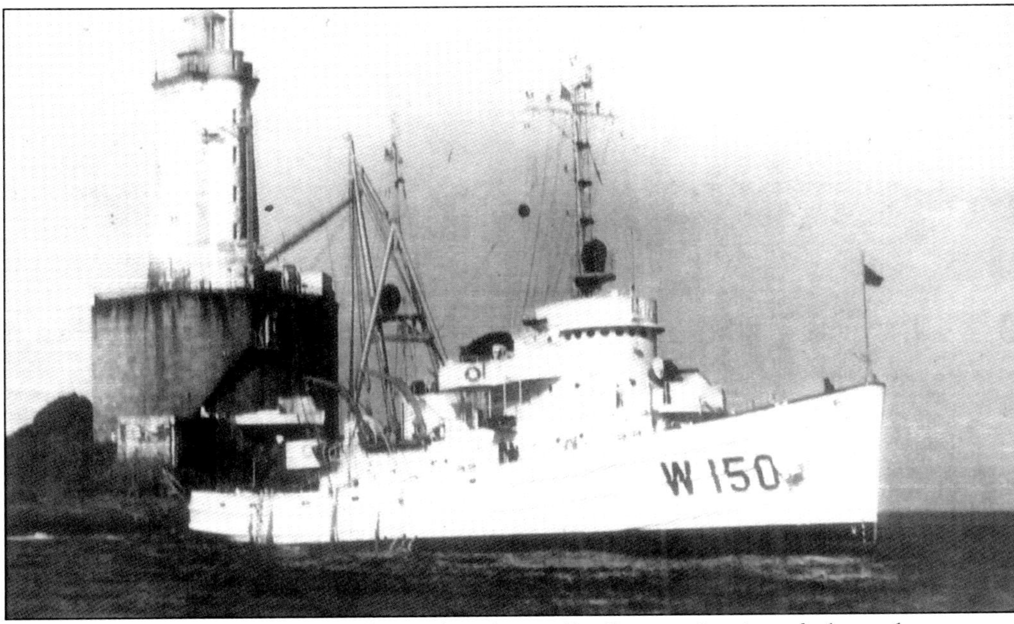

Of the Coast Guard vessels that dropped anchor at St. George, the *Avoyel*, shown here, served the longest. Dwayne records that the first logistical run to the Rock was on December 19, 1956. "The ship was anchored near the rock . . . and the [ship's small boat] shuttling water and fuel hose lines . . . for replenishment." Three men were transferred to the station to relieve three others. (Duane Ferguson and the SGRLPS Archives.)

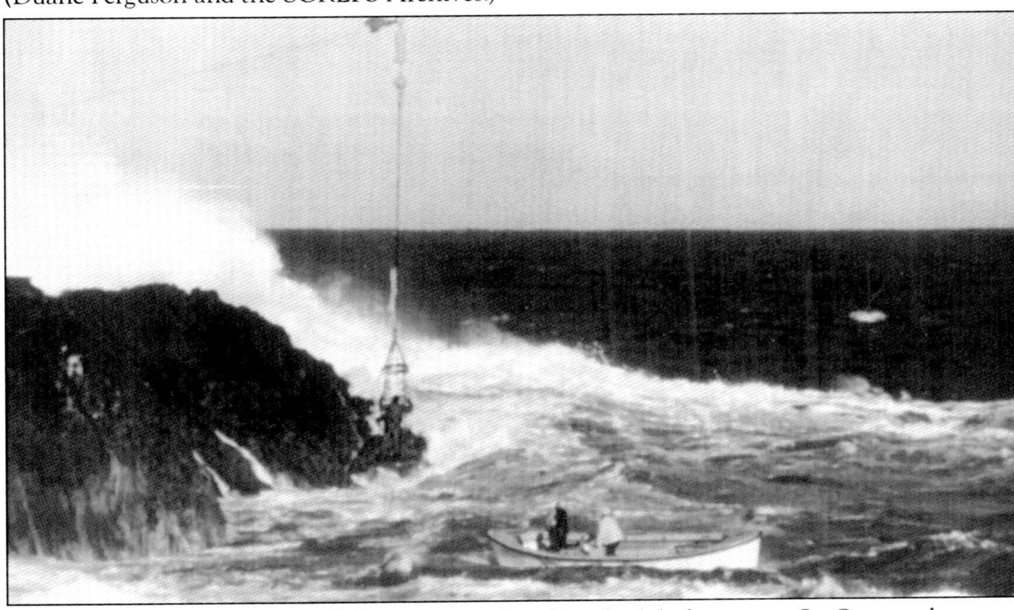

Dwayne tells readers in *On Call for Humanity* that the schedule for runs to St. George alternated Tuesdays and Thursdays, and crew transfers were sometimes attempted in very hazardous sea conditions. At times, men were thrown into the ocean. Ferguson is the coxswain in this spray-shrouded scene of a transfer. The departing crewman is wearing a wet suit and clinging to a Billy Pugh net. (Duane Ferguson and the SGRLPS Archives.)

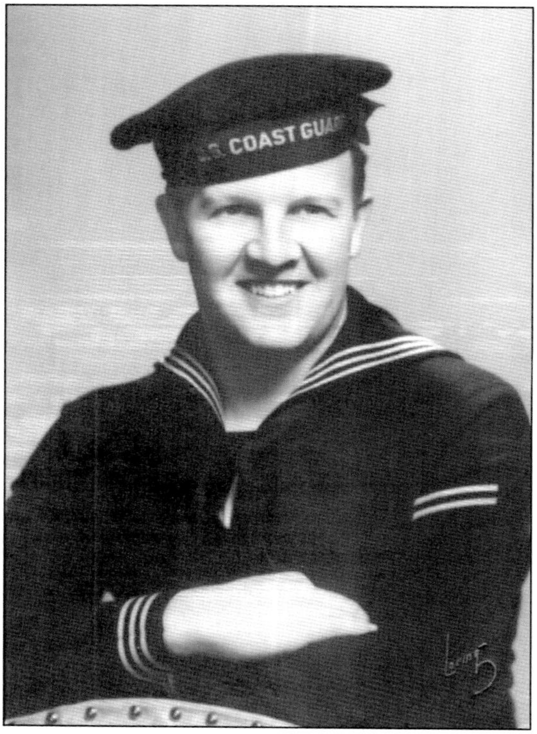

Byron Horrocks remembers Gibby and other roommates from the early 1950s enjoying pleasant off-duty times playing cards and watching television. He enjoyed his walks around the caisson on clear nights with the moonlight shimmering on the water and the lights of Brookings and Crescent City twinkling in the distance. One of the more tense times on duty was when it took three men to wrestle the water line into the cistern connection. (Byron Horrocks and the SGRLPS Archives.)

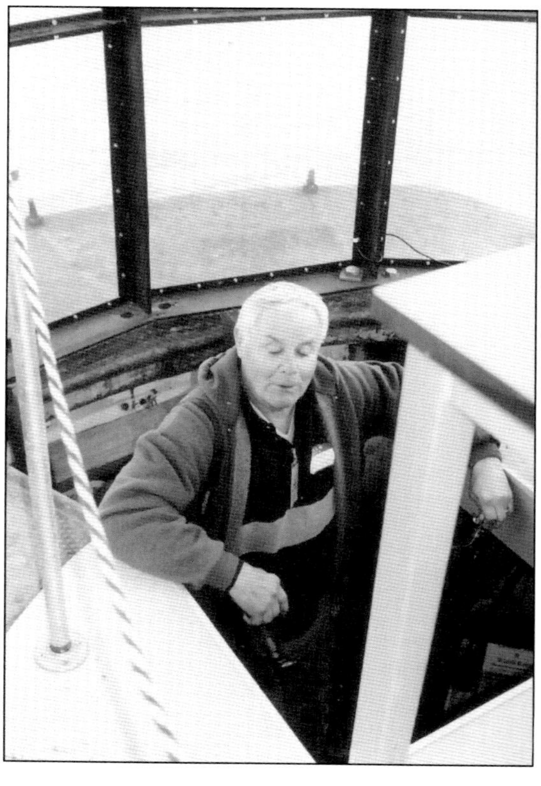

In exchange for a stint on the Rock in 1958, Lee Kollorz was promoted to second class engineman. He arrived at the lighthouse greeted by fog and Category 8 waves. He said, "I had 20 seconds to secure the ball and hook to the boat harness." On one occasion, he had to run out a confused sea lion that had wandered into the engine room. Here, he revisits some of his old haunts on a tour. (Author's collection.)

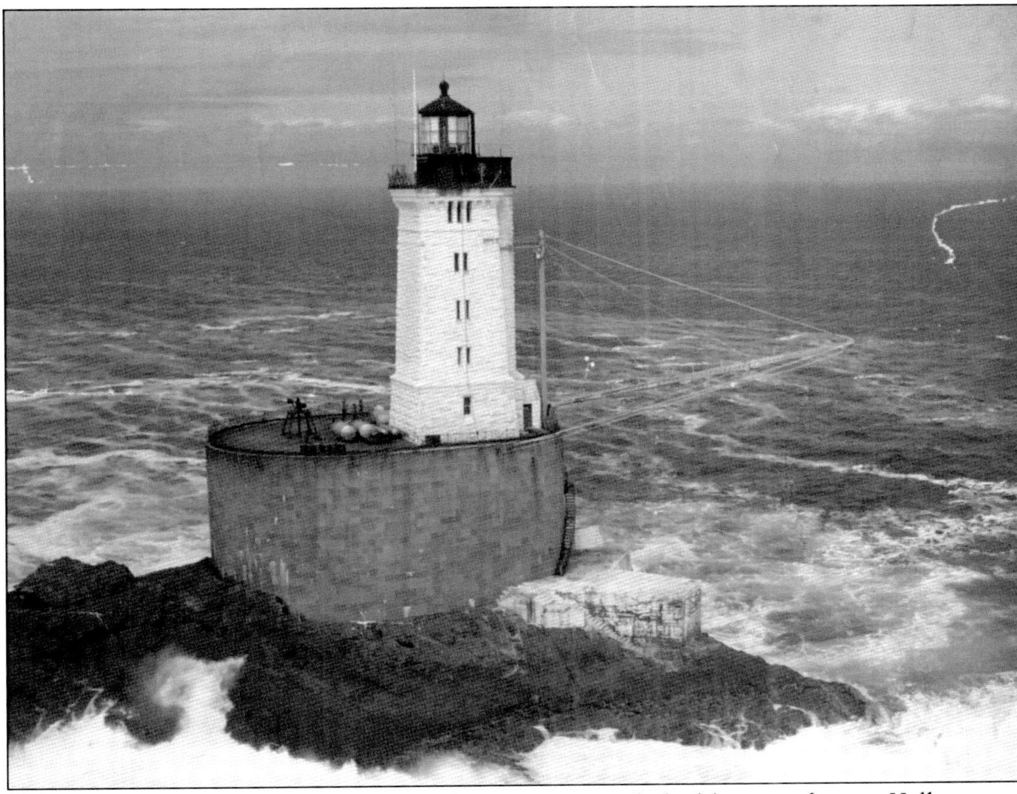

This aerial view submitted by Lee Kollorz shows an apparently freshly painted tower. Kollorz spent many spine-tingling hours painting the boom or climbing out the top window of the stairwell to replace cable sheaves (pulleys) at the peak of the mast. Once a year, the boom was weight-tested by dropping 9,000 pounds of dead weight. Lee also turned out lampstands and other items from scrap brass, using a lathe. (Coast Guard.)

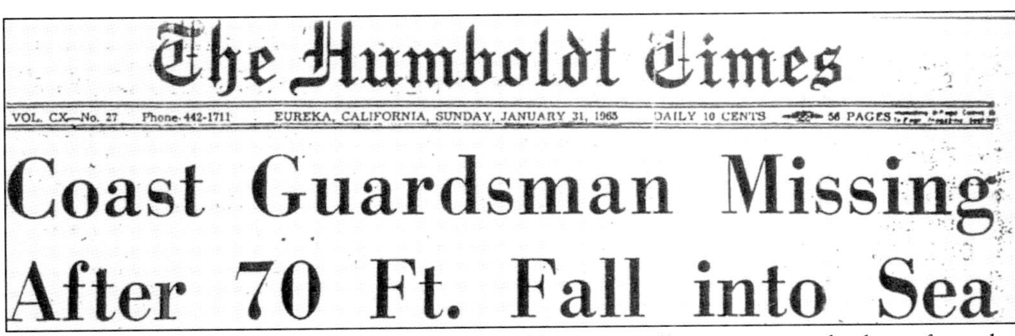

The Humboldt Times

VOL. CX—No. 27 Phone 442-1711 EUREKA, CALIFORNIA, SUNDAY, JANUARY 31, 1965 DAILY 10 CENTS 56 PAGES

Coast Guardsman Missing After 70 Ft. Fall into Sea

The front page of the January 31, 1965, *Humboldt Times* sadly announces the loss of another life at St. George. Donald C. Hale, of Central Valley, California, fell from the structure and was last seen struggling in the water 400 yards northeast of the station. Ships and planes launched a five-hour search, but the effort was called off due to fog, and Hale's body was never found. The 22-year-old fireman's apprentice had previously served aboard the *Avoyel* and was assigned to the lighthouse on December 26. (*Times-Standard*.)

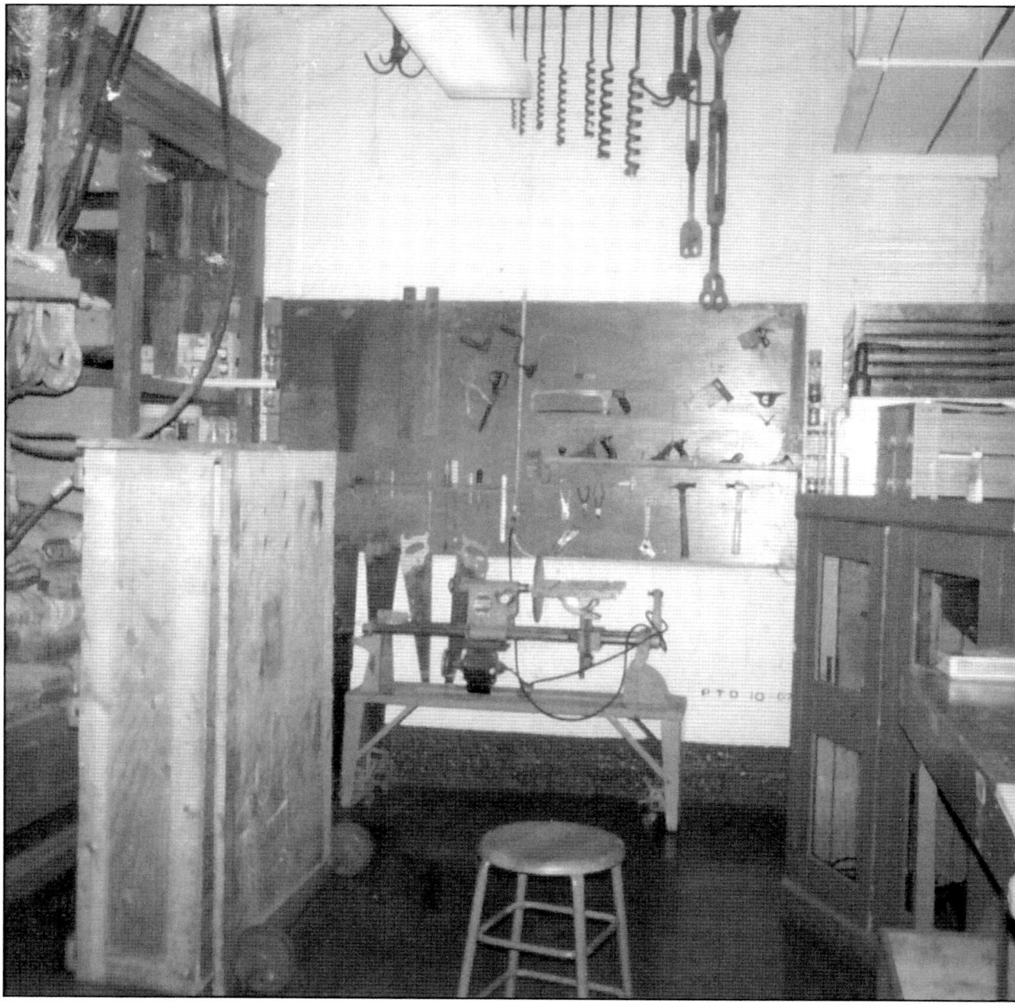

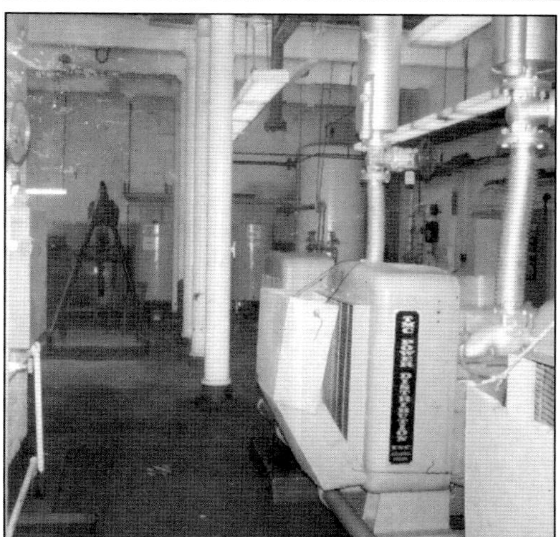

Ron Markuson, who served at the lighthouse in the late 1960s, and his wife provided these photographs that show upgrades in equipment and the results of modernization plans implemented by the Coast Guard since assuming control in 1939. Except for the watch room, which still retains its redwood tongue-and-groove wainscoting, all the walls are plastered and painted. The built-in bunk beds are removed, and the floors in the living quarters are covered with linoleum. This is a spartan, immaculate facility. These two views show sections of the engine room: the bos'n locker with its lathe and neatly organized tools on the wall and the row of three generators. (Both, Ron Markuson and the SGRLPS Archives.)

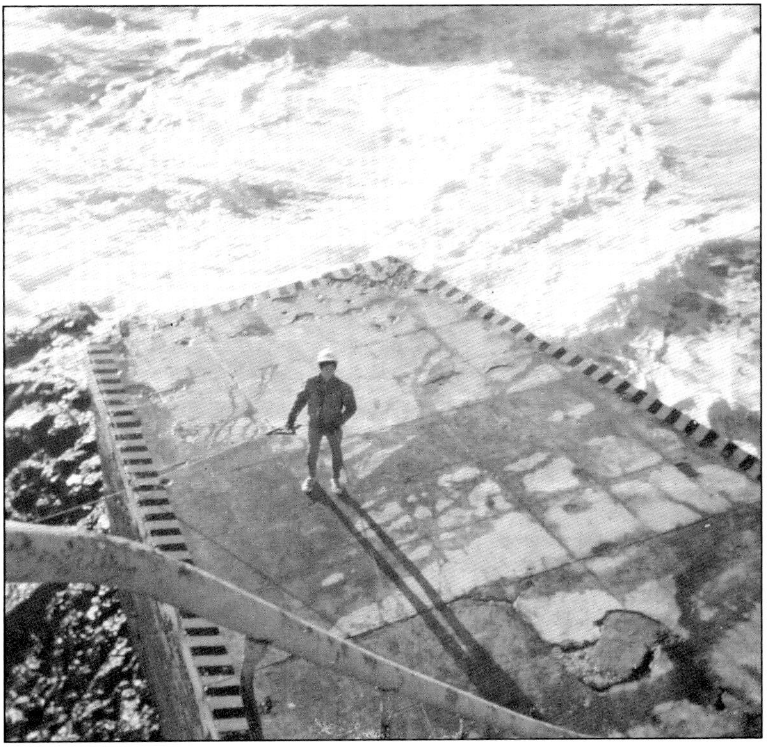

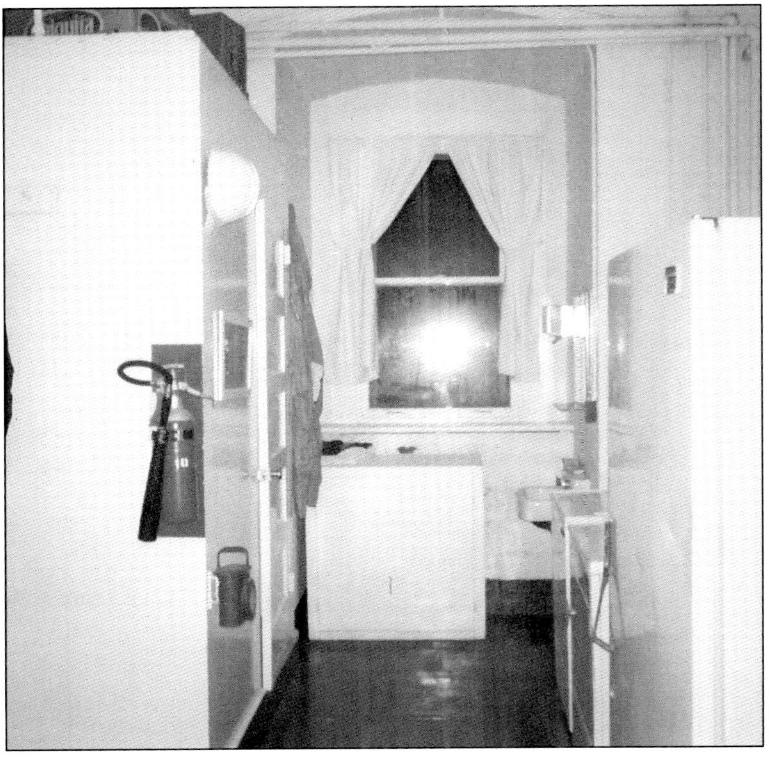

Safety perimeter markings neatly frame a fellow crewman on the lower landing, scene of so much drama. Workmen who built the lighthouse were housed here and endured seas crashing through walls, which soaked and terrified them. William Erickson, Wilbur Walker, Stanley Costello, and Bertram Beckett departed from here and never returned. Station launches and the blacksmith shop formerly located there were endlessly in danger. Every crew transfer from ship to landing was an adrenalin-pumping experience. In view of this history, these perimeter safety markings seem inadequate. The other photograph shows the utility room with a washer, dryer, refrigerator or freezer, and a fire extinguisher on the cabinet. Not shown is the doorway into the head (toilet). This space functioned as a pantry in the remote past. (Both, Ron Markuson and the SGRLPS Archives.)

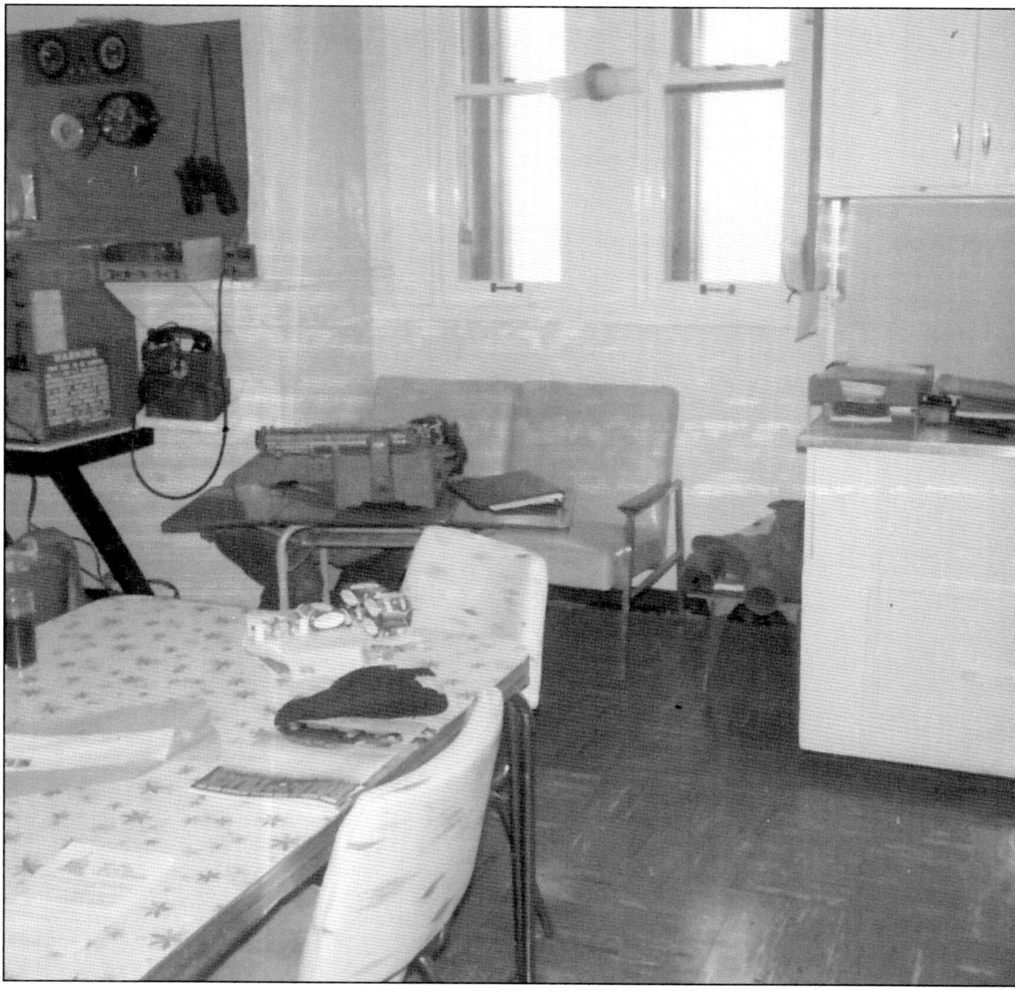

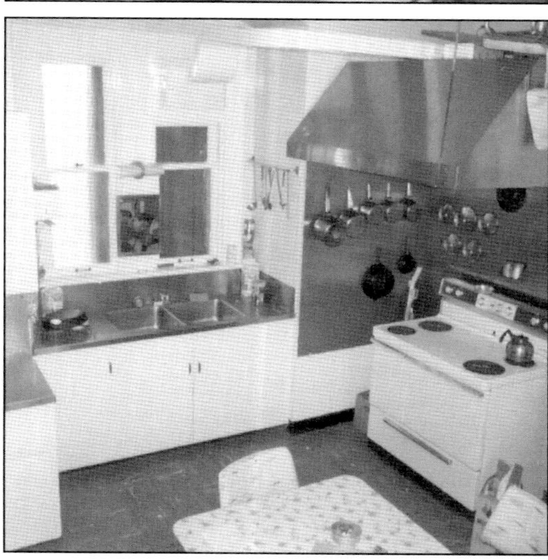

Welcome to the galley, the kitchen and social center of the station. Except for sounds of waves crashing and the radio phone (at upper left in the above image), one might think this scene belonged in any apartment complex of the 1960s. This view, looking south, shows the windowpanes uncovered. In southwest storms, in spite of shutters, the glass was frequently broken or completely blown out. The north side of the room shows the modern cabinetry, stainless steel sink, range exhaust hood, and restaurant-like orderliness of the hanging pots and pans. Pat Griffin remembers the time the crew from YBI spent an entire day installing the stainless-steel sink and hood for the stove. (Both, Ron Markuson and the SGRLPS Archives.)

A protective curtain was usually in place in daylight hours, but it was removed for the photograph. By this date, of course, an electric bulb provided the illumination source, and the clockwork-timing mechanism was also electric. Aside from the oft-lamented polishing of brass work in the lantern room and cleaning the windows, little else was needed to keep the light functioning. (Ron Markuson and the SGRLPS Archives.)

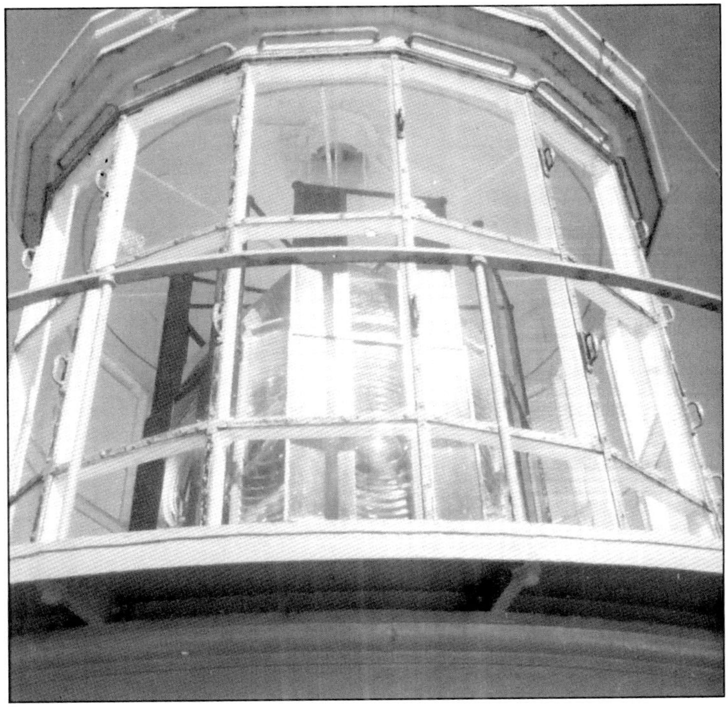

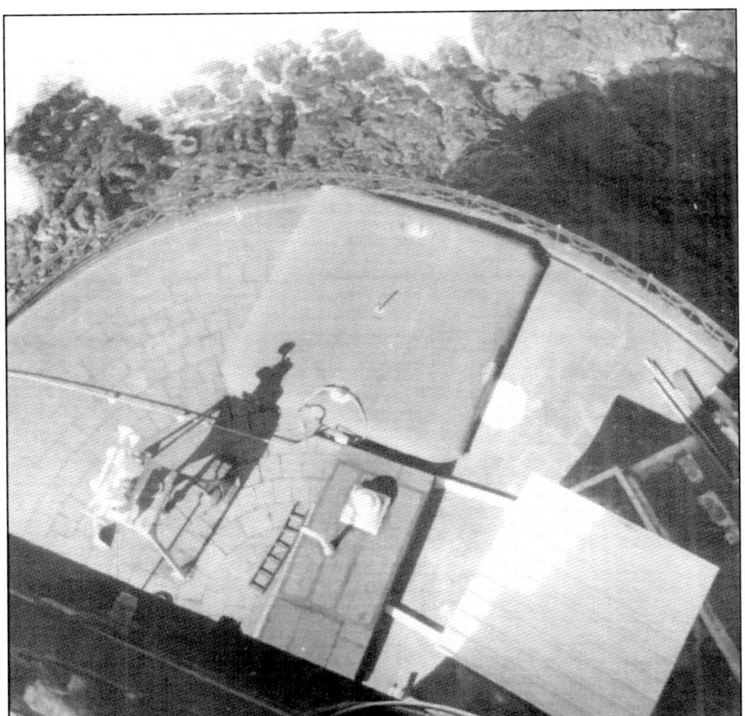

Compared with the photograph on page 54, this image reveals a catch deck configuration very different from the 1950s. The new fog signal is in place, and the engine room skylight, so frequently broken by high seas, is now a solid roof. The hoisting engine and boom-controller shed is under the white roof. Instead of gasoline drums stacked around the handrail is a 42-by-42-foot, 10,000-gallon rubber-pillow fuel-storage tank. (Ron Markuson and the SGRLPS Archives.)

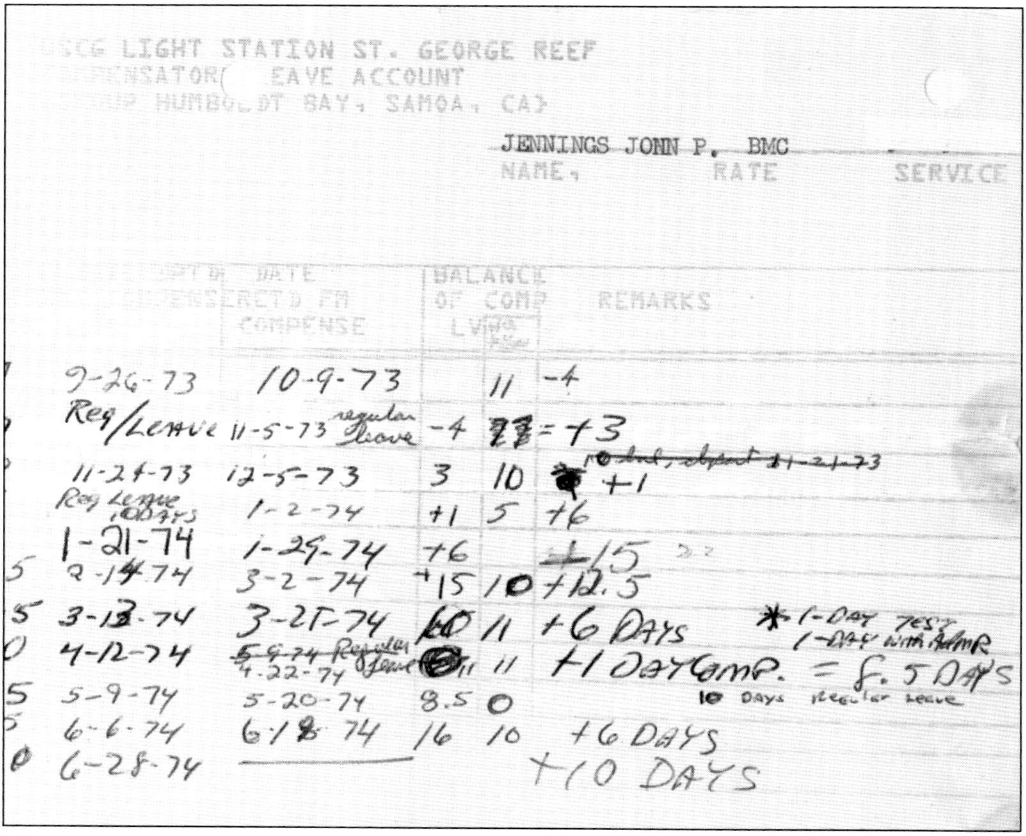
USCG LIGHT STATION ST. GEORGE REEF
COMPENSATORY LEAVE ACCOUNT
GROUP HUMBOLDT BAY, SAMOA, CA

JENNINGS JOHN P, BMC
NAME, RATE SERVICE

DATE DEPT ON COMPENSATORY	DATE RETD FM COMPENSE	BALANCE OF COMP LV		REMARKS
9-26-73	10-9-73		11	-4
Reg/Leave	11-5-73 regular leave	-4	7	= +3
11-24-73	12-5-73	3	10	+1
Reg Leave 10 Days	1-2-74	+1	5	+6
1-21-74	1-29-74	+6		15
2-14-74	3-2-74	+15	10	+12.5
3-13-74	3-27-74	60	11	+6 DAYS * 1-DAY TEST 1-DAY WITH ADMR
4-12-74	5-9-74 Regular Leave 4-22-74		11	+1 DAY COMP. = 8.5 DAYS
5-9-74	5-20-74	8.5	0	10 DAYS Regular Leave
6-6-74	6-18-74	16	10	+6 DAYS
6-28-74				+10 DAYS

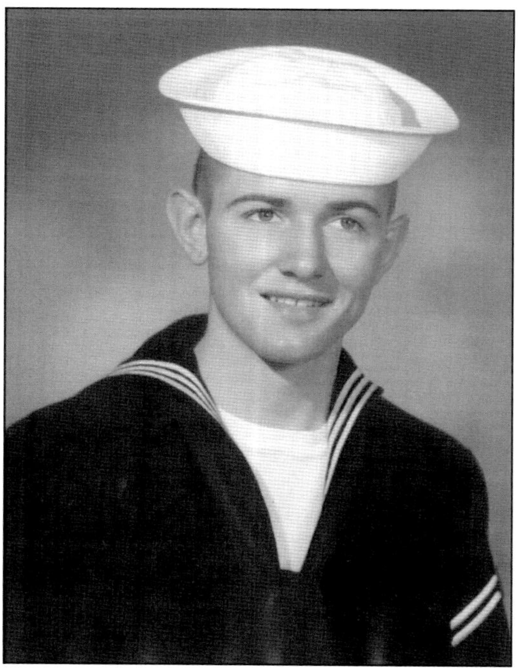

John Jennings, one of the last OICs at St. George, recalled an incident when the boom cable became entangled while two men were being lowered in a Billy Pugh net. The men hung in midair for over an hour before repairs were made. Another time, the pillow tank was blocked, forcing Jennings and crew to fuel the engine room by hand, carrying buckets through a windstorm. Pictured here is a document showing Jennings's leave record, found at the lighthouse. (SGRLPS Archives.)

When he said, "Call me Dr. Doolittle," Duane Williams was referring to experiences he had with animals while serving at St. George in 1963–1964. The young man was sympathetic to the plight of the many birds that collided with the glass panes in the lantern room. He and the crew played nursemaid to an injured bat; even the OIC posted a "Quiet, Bat Sleeping" sign on the critter's abode. (Duane Williams and the SGRLPS Archives.)

Duane Williams is pictured here near the tower entrance door with part of the day's catch of fish. Williams shudders when he tells of nearly being swept away one day when he was testing his ability to stand in waist-deep water coursing over rocks on the south side of the lighthouse. Quick action by companions saved him from a terrible fate. (Duane Williams and the SGRLPS Archives.)

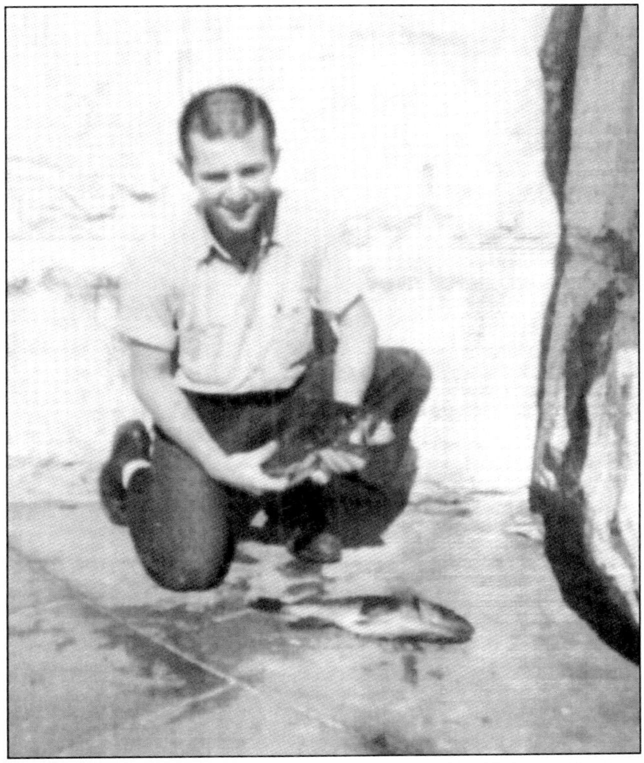

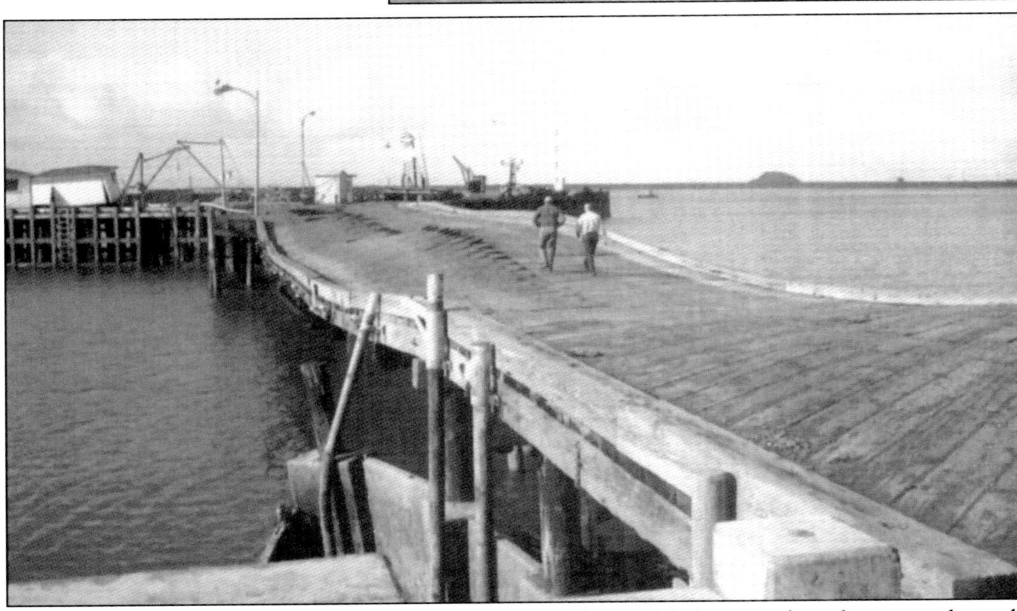

On March 27, 1964, a devastating tsunami generated by an Alaskan earthquake swept through Crescent City in a series of waves that left much of the town in ruins. Crescent City was called the "Comeback Town" for its efforts to rebuild but is still plagued by tsunamis, the most recent of which hit on March 11, 2011, causing millions of dollars in damages. St. George was unaffected. Shown here is the main dock at the harbor in 1964. (Del Norte County Historical Society.)

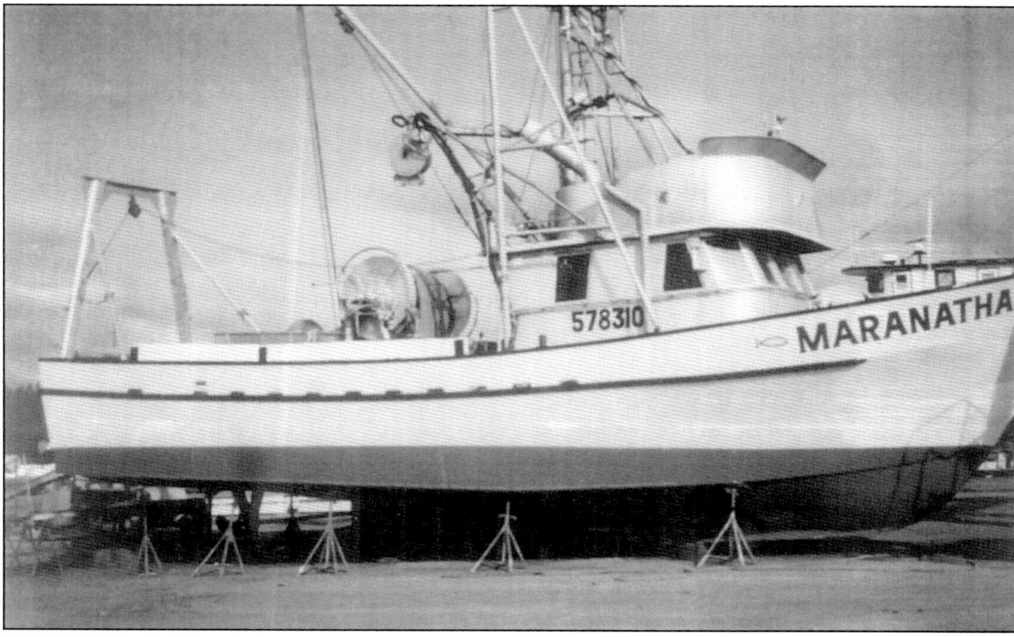

Representative of the local fishing fleet that relied, at least in part, upon a light at St. George until its closing days is the *Marantha,* translated "Come, Lord Jesus," shown on it way in the final phase of construction. Owned and managed by Dale and Florence Miller, the *Marantha* succeeded other craft, such as the *Arney P,* operated by Miller, a long-term resident of Crescent City and career fisherman. (Dale Miller.)

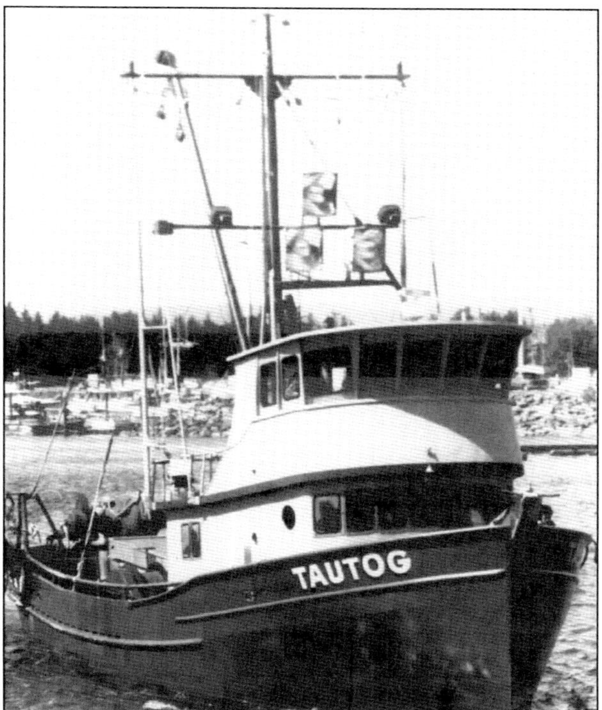

Named for a bottom fish, the *Tautog* is shown here in Crescent City Harbor. The steel-hulled vessel, built by Fashion Blacksmith Inc. of Crescent City for local fisherman Richard Evanow, was subsequently owned and operated by Gene and Martha Varner. St. George keepers report that local fishermen often shared their catches in appreciation for the service of the light. (Gene and Martha Varner.)

Mark Miller served aboard the *Cape Carter*, which first began operations out of Crescent City Harbor in September 1969. He is shown here on the deck of the *Carter*, which is keeping a watchful eye on a Soviet trawler that has been caught fishing within the territorial waters of the United States. (Mark Miller and the SGRLPS Archives.)

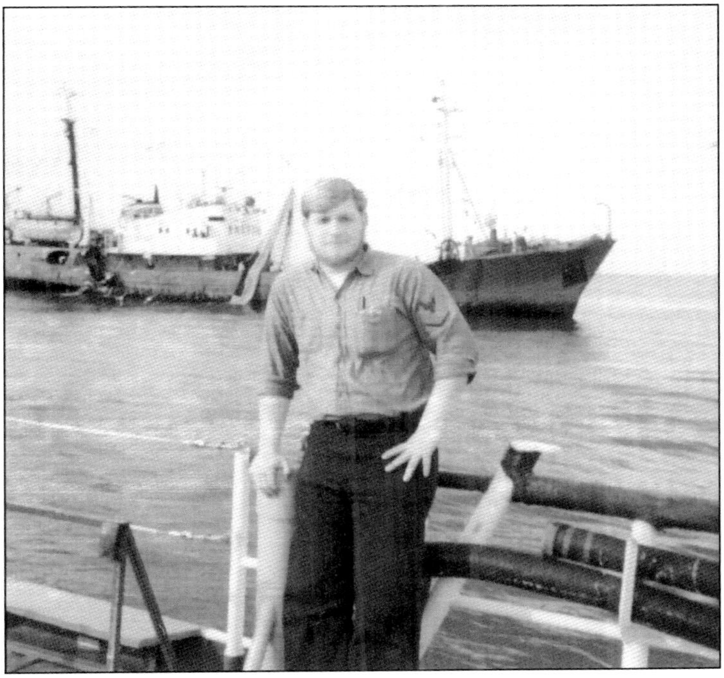

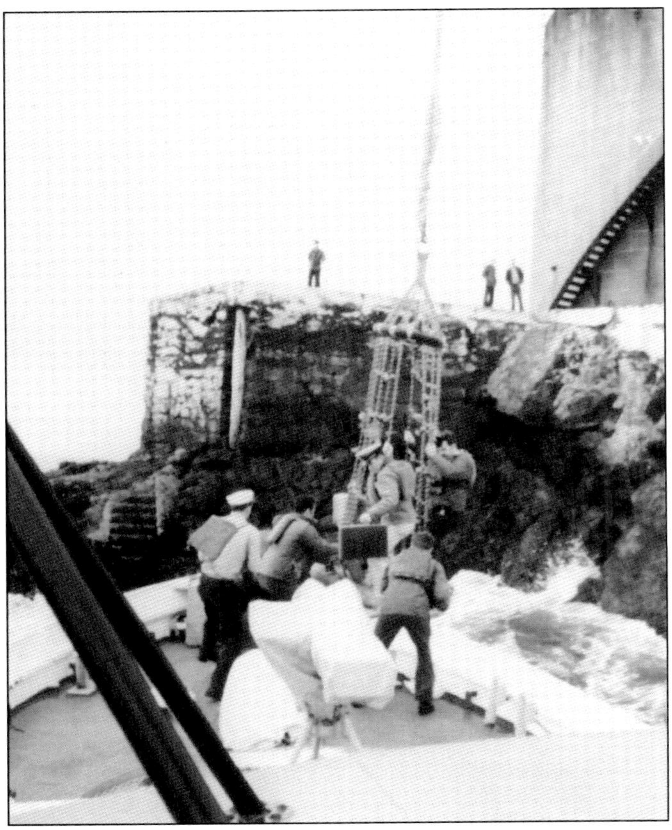

Captured here is the tense moment when the *Carter* receives two men on its bow who are departing St. George in the Billy Pugh net. The ship is mere feet from the sharp edge of the rock, and the cutter's helmsman must take into consideration wave height and direction, wind, currents, and the ship's drift, in addition to watching the split-second ballet performed by the five men scrambling to keep their feet. (Mark Miller and the SGRLPS Archives.)

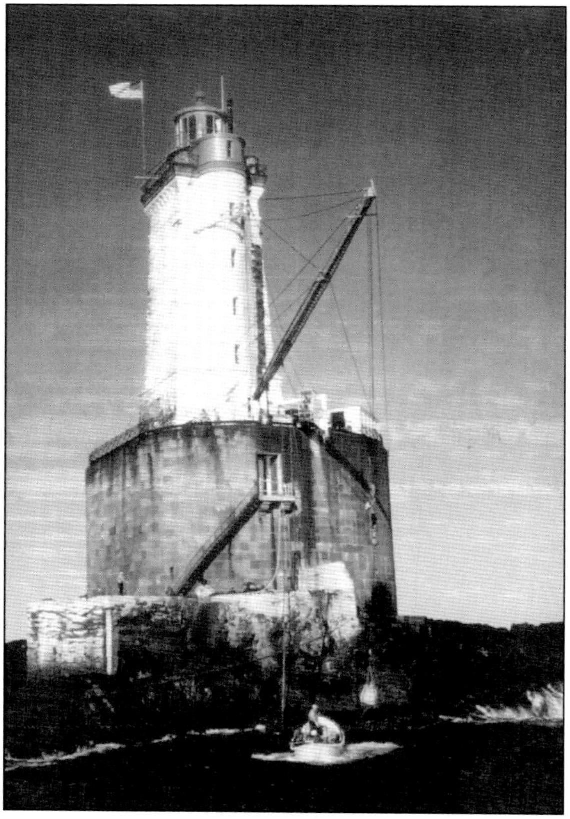

Keepers report that the national flag was not raised daily; it was hoisted only when a regional or district inspector made a tour of the station. Here, the National Ensign, suspended from the watch-room handrail, flutters in a northwest breeze above what looks like freshly painted metalwork at the top of the tower. The boom appears to be in a "present arms" posture as it lifts a bundle of supplies from the *Cape Carter*'s small boat, which is maneuvering in the deceptively calm water. The commander of the *Carter* (and photographer) on this inspection and supply run is Lt. Larry Munhall, around 1964–1965, who showed in photographs that the small boat with the inspector aboard was transferred almost kite-like to the lower landing in Force 8 seas. (Both, Larry Munhall and Phil Cox.)

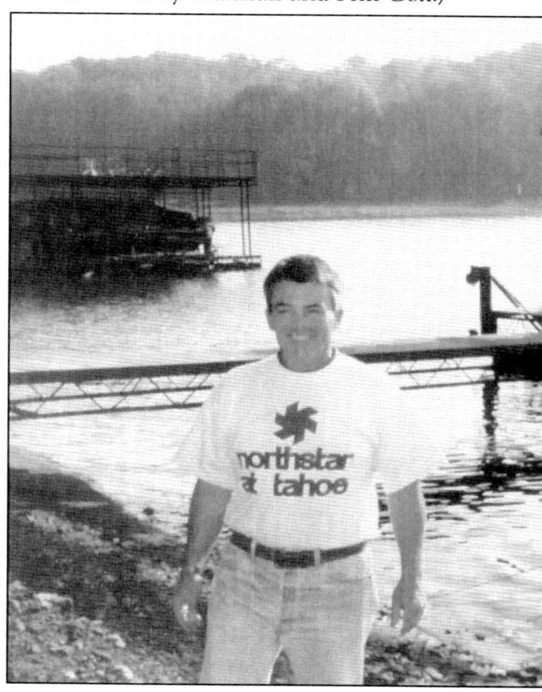

Dennis Streng served at the lighthouse from 1962 to 1963. Streng, who at the time was historian of the Coast Guard Sea Veterans Organization, contacted the society in 1998. He sent a number of annotated photographs, which provide additional perspectives of St. George in the 1960s. He is shown here in the galley writing a letter home. (Dennis Streng and the SGRLPS Archives.)

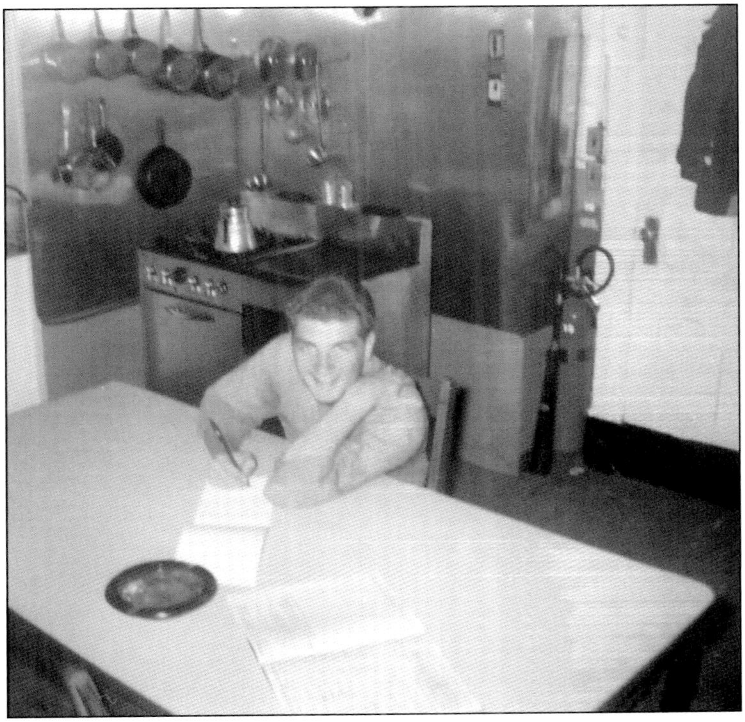

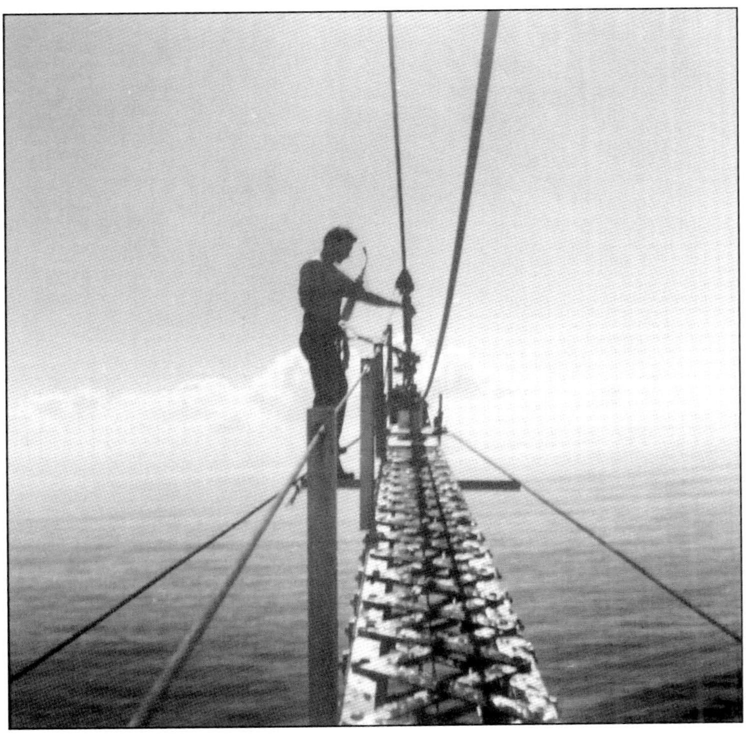

Streng annotated this photograph: "Ken Davick at the end of boom—90 feet out and 90 feet up. On a clear, calm day was the only opportunity to perform routine maintenance. Out on that boom we had to use a hand-held grease-gun to lubricate wire rigging." Note a safety cable has been added. Later, the boom will be extended to over 100 feet. (Dennis Streng and the SGRLPS Archives.)

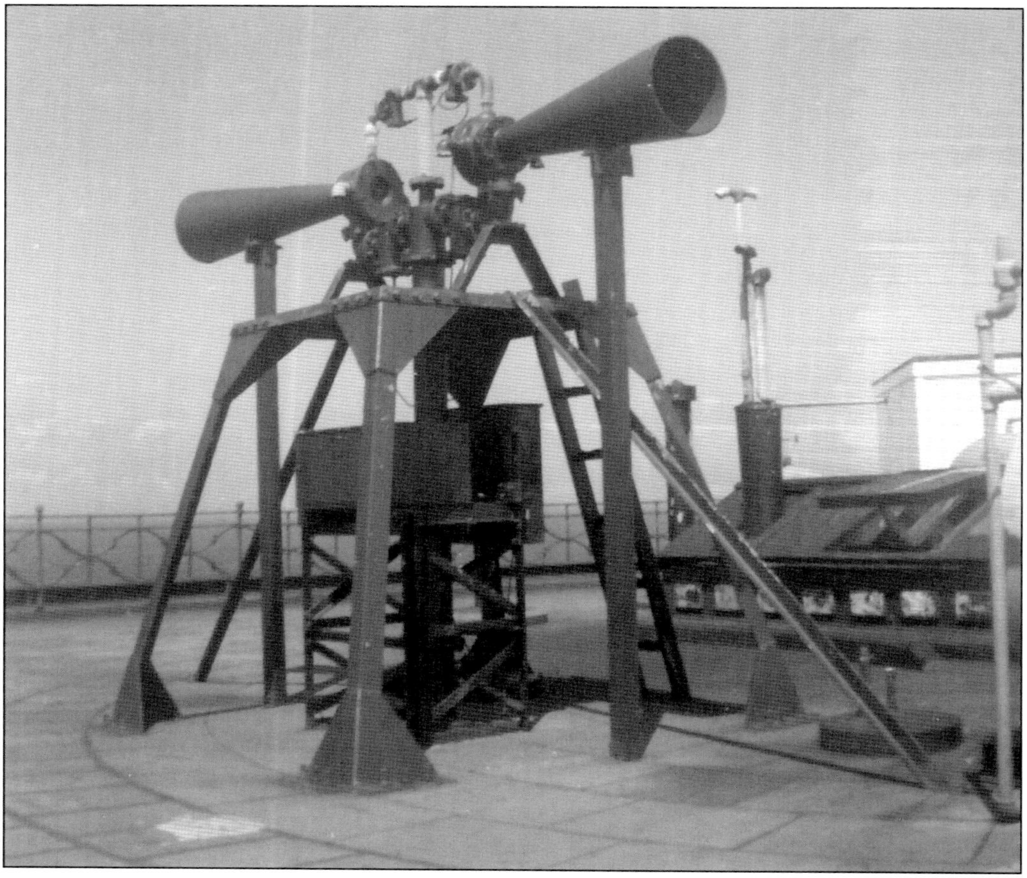

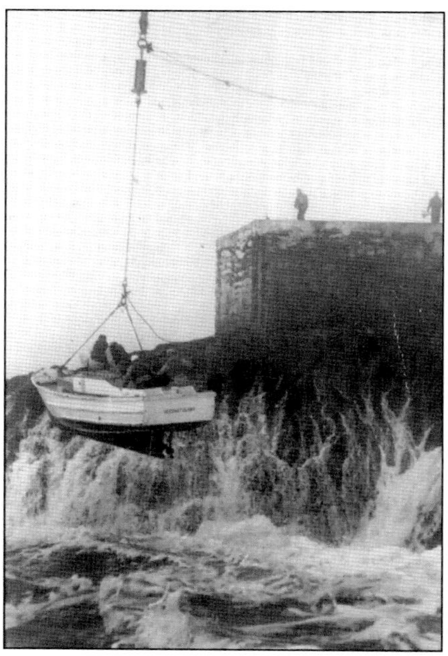

Here is an excellent view of the powerful diaphone fog signal. True, it is a slayer of birds, disturber of sleep, and enemy of the eardrums, but its deep-throated bass is a sound sweeter than an angelic choir to a ship's helmsman inching his way through cotton-thick curtains of disorienting mist. The trumpets are complex instruments, and multiple log entries tell of near-disastrous failures. (Dennis Streng and the SGRLPS Archives.)

This shot marks the end of an era that witnessed death and injury when crew transfers were made by lifting boat and personnel from unpredictable seas. Dennis Streng notes, "1962 – Boat relief – I'm one of the seamen on boat deck. This was the last time the boat was used. It was just too dangerous." (Dennis Streng and the SGRLPS Archives.)

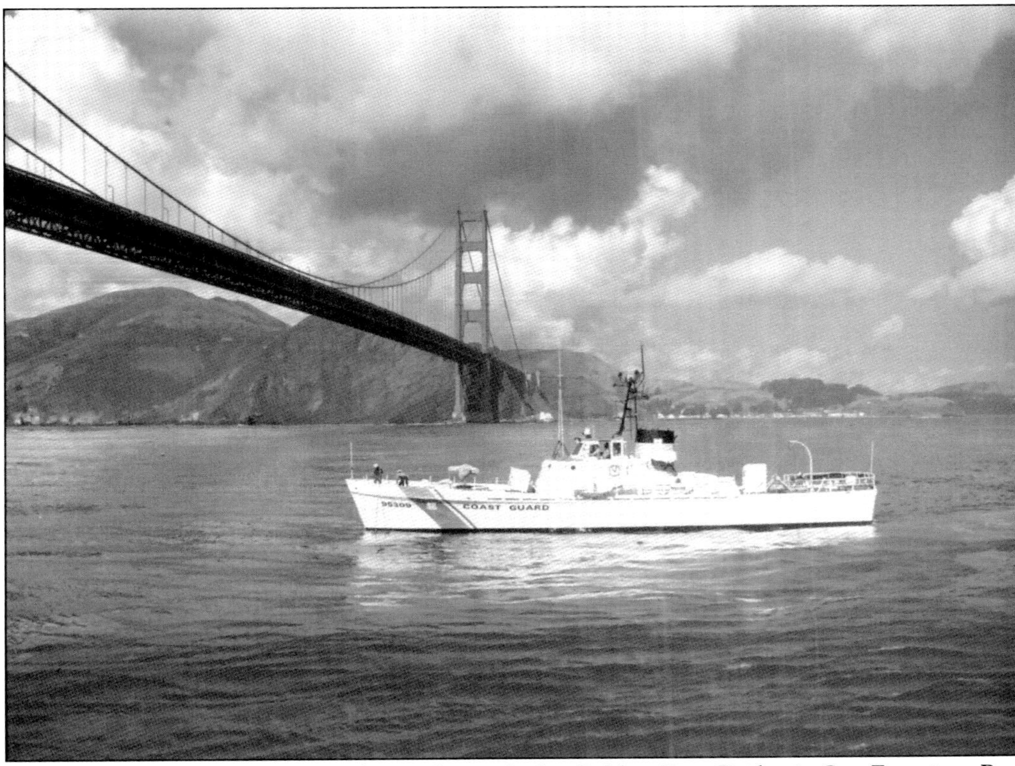

The *Cape Carter*, shown here underway beneath the Golden Gate Bridge in San Francisco Bay, was the last of her kind to moor off St. George. Other vessels that plied the waters from Yerba Buena Island and Humboldt Bay to ensure smooth operations on the Rock were *Ironwood*, *Yacona* (1951), *Balsom* (1953–1955), *Avoyel* (1956–1969), *Magnolia* (1954–1971), *Comanche*, and *Willow* (1968). (Coast Guard.)

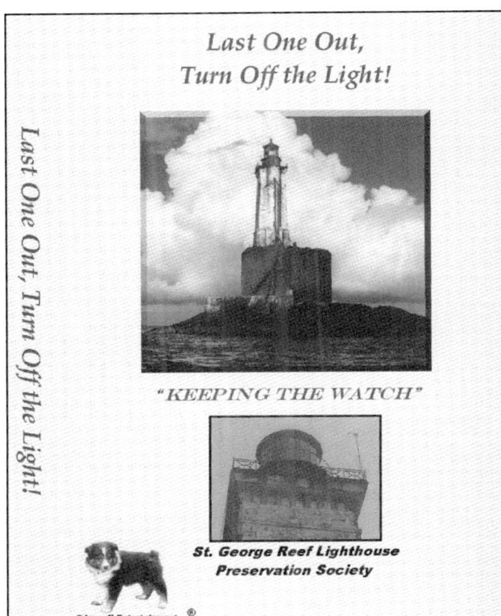

With the advances of technology, the automation of the country's lighthouses was inevitable. In the 1960s, the Coast Guard launched the Lighthouse Automation and Modernization Program, which greatly reduced the number of manned stations. Sensing the historical significance of the closure, in 1974 Humboldt State University produced a documentary called *Last One Out, Turn Off the Light!* (Humboldt State University Media Department and Odonnell Entertainment.)

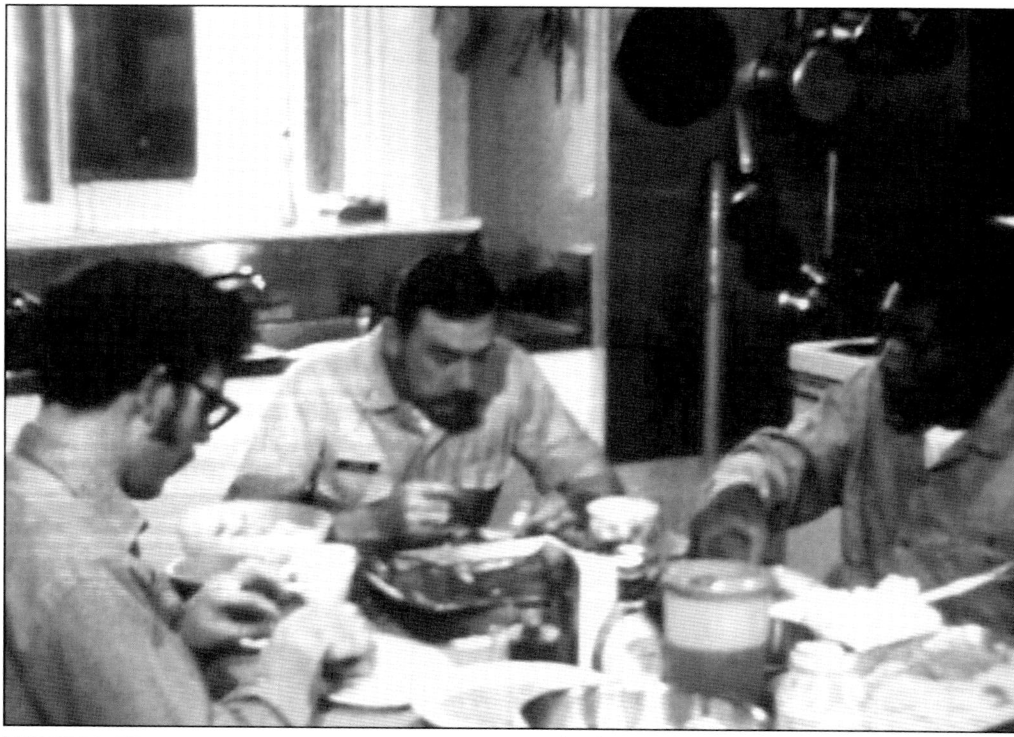

As depicted in *Last One Out, Turn Off the Light!*, here are three of the four crewmen who have been designated to "turn out the light"—Chief James Sebastian facing MK2 Rusty Woodward and SA Garry Newberry across the table. Sebastian laments the passing of an era, while the other two have mixed emotions. (Humboldt State University Media Department and Odonnell Entertainment.)

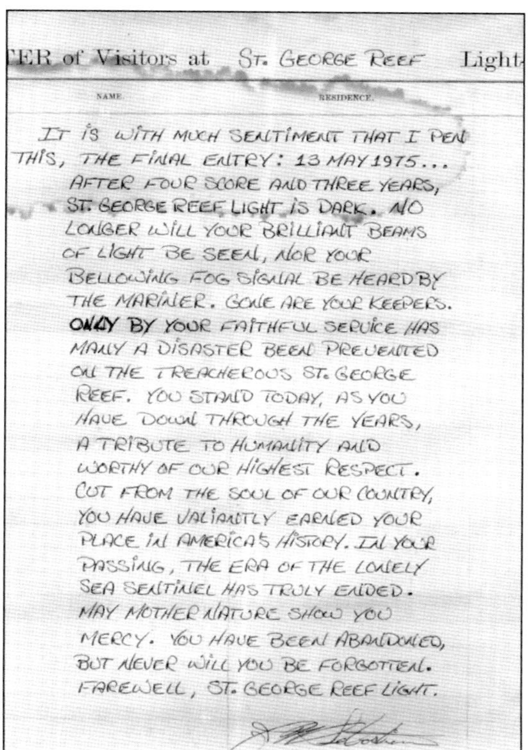

ER of Visitors at ST. GEORGE REEF Light

NAME. RESIDENCE.

IT IS WITH MUCH SENTIMENT THAT I PEN THIS, THE FINAL ENTRY: 13 MAY 1975... AFTER FOUR SCORE AND THREE YEARS, ST. GEORGE REEF LIGHT IS DARK. NO LONGER WILL YOUR BRILLIANT BEAMS OF LIGHT BE SEEN, NOR YOUR BELLOWING FOG SIGNAL BE HEARD BY THE MARINER. GONE ARE YOUR KEEPERS. ONLY BY YOUR FAITHFUL SERVICE HAS MANY A DISASTER BEEN PREVENTED ON THE TREACHEROUS ST. GEORGE REEF. YOU STAND TODAY, AS YOU HAVE DOWN THROUGH THE YEARS, A TRIBUTE TO HUMANITY AND WORTHY OF OUR HIGHEST RESPECT. CUT FROM THE SOUL OF OUR COUNTRY, YOU HAVE VALIANTLY EARNED YOUR PLACE IN AMERICA'S HISTORY. IN YOUR PASSING, THE ERA OF THE LONELY SEA SENTINEL HAS TRULY ENDED. MAY MOTHER NATURE SHOW YOU MERCY. YOU HAVE BEEN ABANDONED, BUT NEVER WILL YOU BE FORGOTTEN. FAREWELL, ST. GEORGE REEF LIGHT.

Pictured here is the last entry in the station log, CPO James Sebastian's tribute to Ballantyne's masterpiece and its service to mariners. Sebastian held great respect for the builders and the near century of service performed by the lighthouse: "They will never be able to cut these things again . . . I hope we save the main light; it is extraordinarily beautiful." (From a copy of the official document donated to SGRLPS by Pat Griffin.)

Sebastian and crew are finished testing the large navigation buoy that is designed to replace St. George. Priced at $350,000, it is still less than the costs of maintaining the last manned station on the Pacific coast. On May 13, 1975, after Sebastian and Seaman James Denham exit via the Billy Pugh, the two men operating the boom don wet suits and join the *Carter*. (*Triplicate*, Steve Yarbrough.)

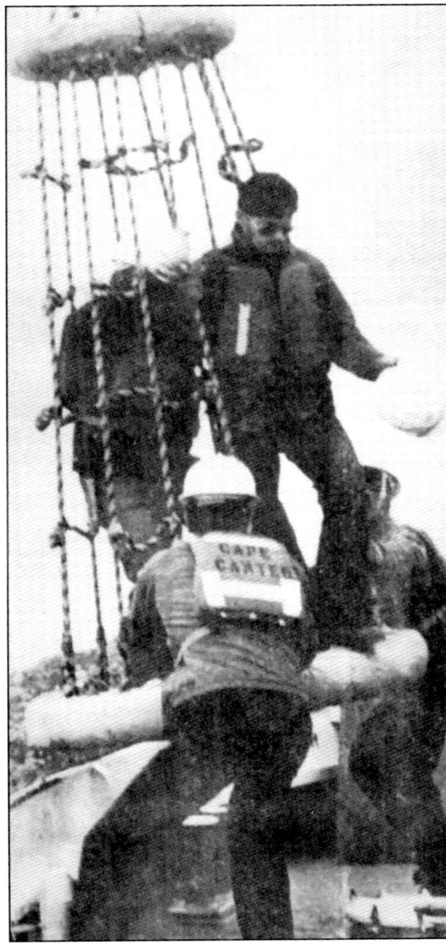

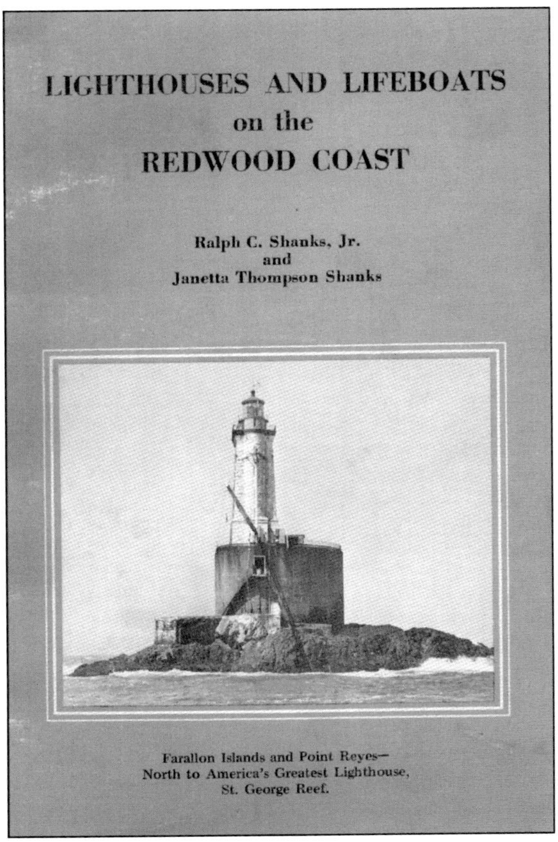

Among the first steps taken to preserve the station's history came in January 1976, when Humboldt Bay Coast Guard commander Tom Allen presented the St. George visitors' log to the Del Norte County Historical Society. Prior to this, a national and international lighthouse preservation ethic had been developing, spurred on by the works of lighthouse historians such as Jim Gibbs and Ralph Shanks. (*Lighthouses and Lifeboats on the Redwood Coast.*)

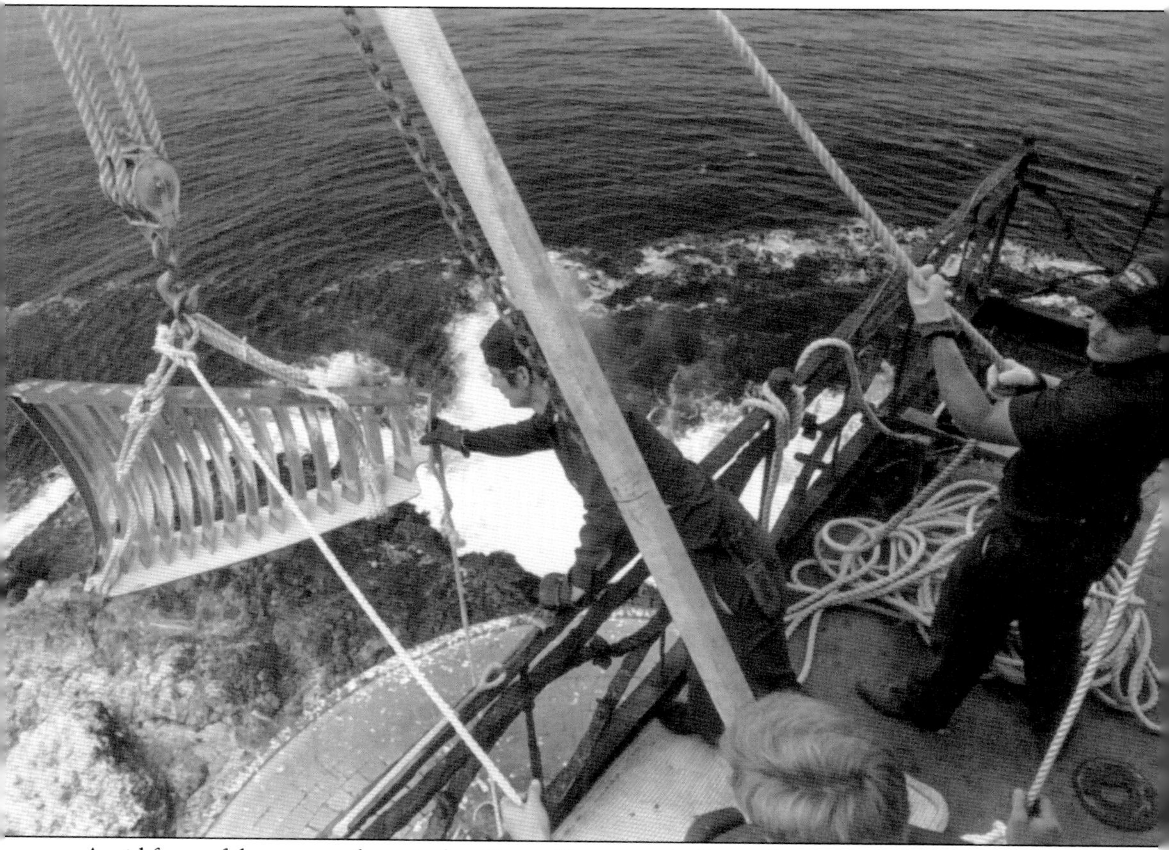

Amid fears of damage to the priceless Fresnel by a stray bullet and indecision by the government as to the final disposition of the optic, pressure was mounting by Crescent City officials such as city manager Mike Young, Bob Bolen of the historical society, and Wayne Wheeler of the US Lighthouse Society to house it in a new addition to the Del Norte County Historical Society Museum. After much planning (and incredible luck with the weather) the transfer was made in a remarkable four-day operation involving the Coast Guard buoy tender *Blackhaw*, commanded by Rick Brandis, and locally assigned cutter *Cape Cross*, commanded by Lt. (jg) Christian Quendens. On September 23, 1983, the *Blackhaw* moored off the lighthouse and assigned 12 crewmen, supervised by Bolen, Wheeler, and Dick Long, to dismantle the glass panels and send them by high-lead cable from the lantern room to the buoy tender. One bull's-eye was damaged, but all of the remaining panels were safely in the museum by September 26. Pictured here is the ticklish process of conveying the fragile lens pieces to the *Blackhaw*. (Coast Guard Historian's Office.)

Five

Abandoned but Not Forgotten

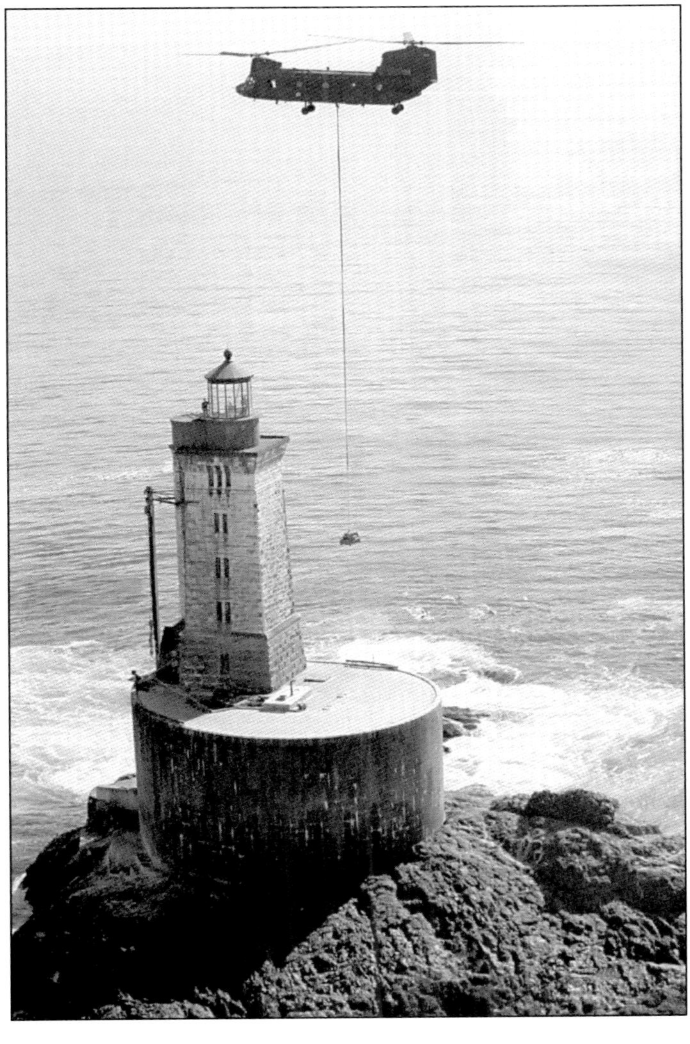

An Army National Guard helicopter hovering over the caisson deck is symbolic of the logistical challenges faced by volunteers of the St. George Reef Lighthouse Preservation Society. On this particular mission, the Chinook was needed to carry out a high-capacity air compressor, tons of sand for a sandblasting operation, and a large water container to wash fly-attracting bird droppings off the deck. (Steve Corley.)

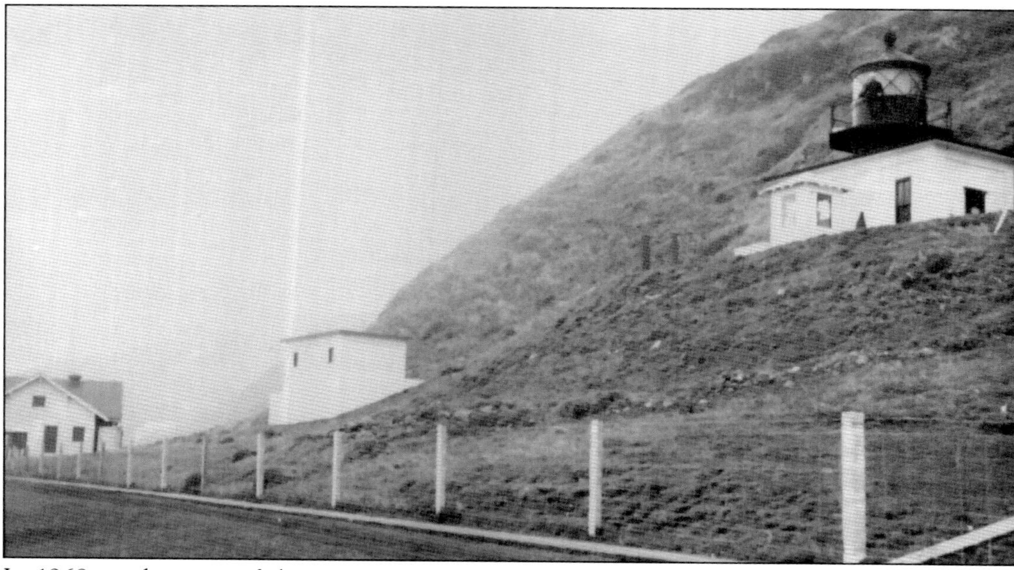

In 1968, exploration of the Punta Gorda Lighthouse led the author into the rich history of lighthouses. When he came to Crescent City in 1986, he learned that St. George was being offered for disposal by the government. He contacted Bob Bolen of the Del Norte Historical Society and formed the St. George Reef Lighthouse Preservation Society. (Coast Guard.)

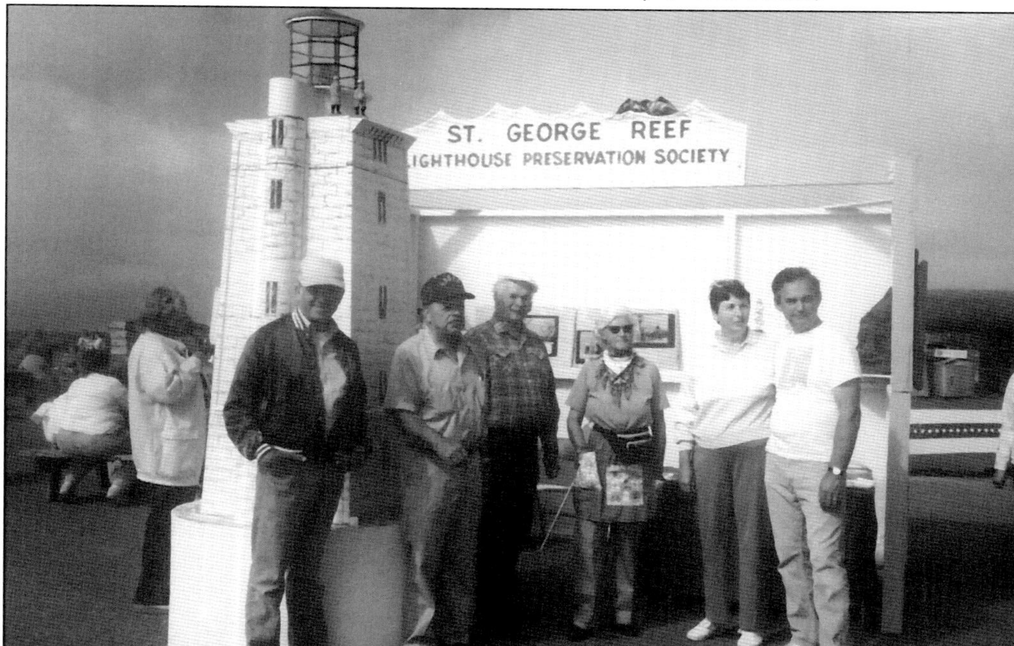

When the future of St. George was passed into the hands of SGRLPS by the Coast Guard, every effort was used to increase public awareness. Pictured at a display booth built at Crescent City Harbor by volunteers are some of the founding members of the group. They are, from left to right, Gene Olson, Bob Bolen, Jim McLaughlin, Dorothy Round, Alice Towers, and the author. (Author's collection.)

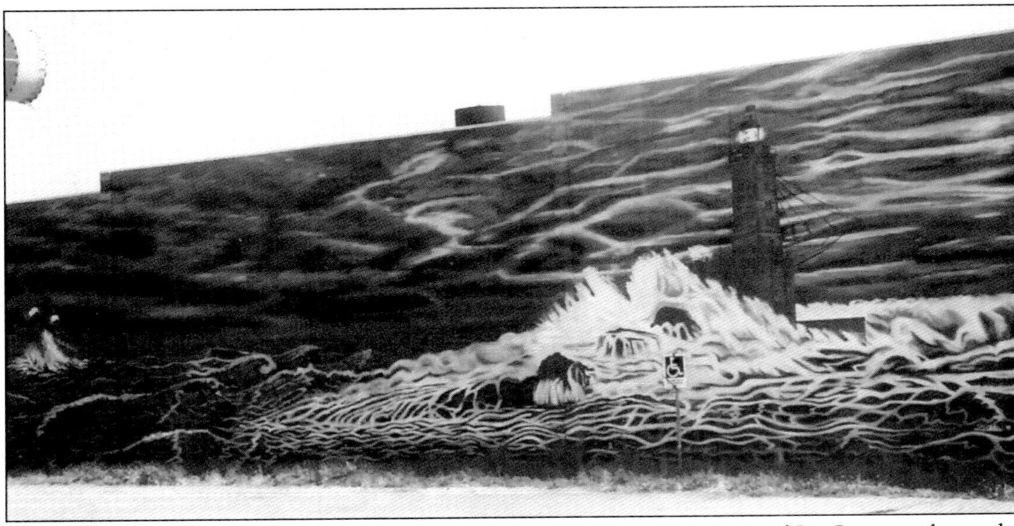

Among the first murals to be produced in Crescent City, this panorama of St. George adorns the side of Red's Theatre on G Street. The site, offered by theater managers Bert and Marcie Thomas as part of the public awareness program, was painted by artists Jim and Shannon Childs of Arcata in October 1991 and paid for by local donations. (Author's collection.)

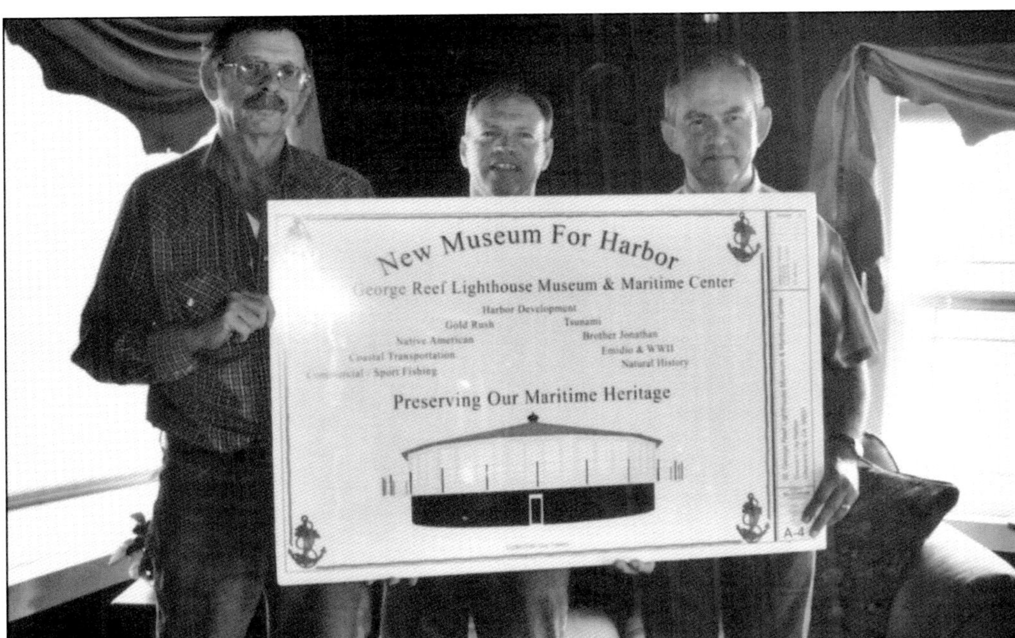

From its inception, the society began to collect a wide variety of material related to the history of the lighthouse with the goal of eventually building a museum in Crescent City to house and display the artifacts. Shown here holding a conceptual drawing of the planned two-story, 10,000-square-foot facility are, from left to right, John Vaughn (construction consultant), Bill O'Connor (draftsman), and the author. Construction is still pending. (Author's collection.)

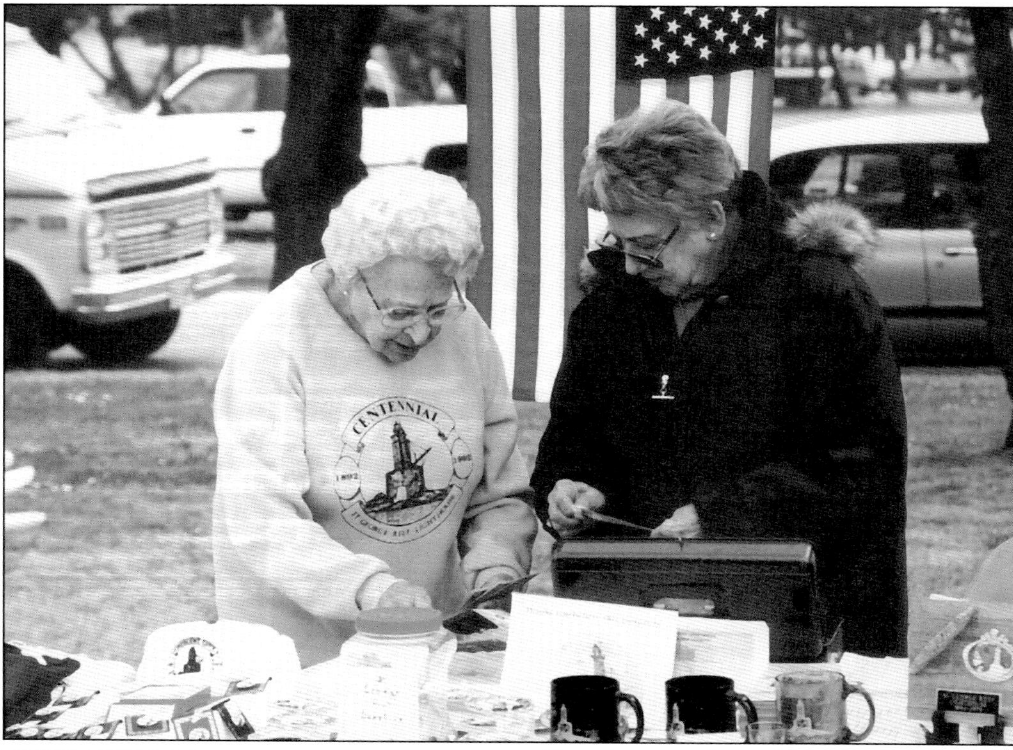

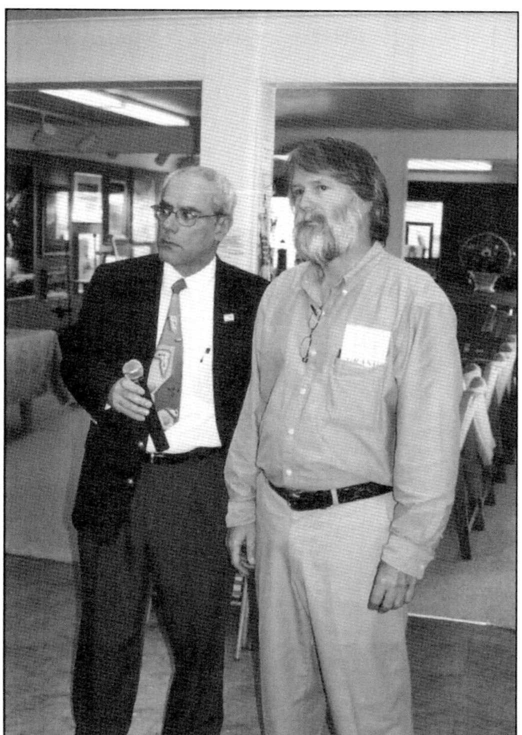

Founding members of St. George Reef Preservation Society Kay Thomas (left) and Eloise Ware are seen here at a fundraising event. The two sisters are known for their avid support of St. George. (Author's collection.)

Rick Bennett (left) and Rick Heiser are shown at a fundraiser for the lighthouse at the Harbor Art Gallery in Crescent City. Bennett is a local artist, and Heiser has performed many services for the restoration effort, from producing graphics to acting as a docent for tours at St. George. (Author's collection.)

After a decade of negotiations with the federal government, jurisdiction of the lighthouse was given to the St. George Reef Lighthouse Preservation Society. The structure and premises were deeded to Del Norte County, which in turn granted a 25-year lease to the society. On October 12, 1996, restoration workers and guests were flown out by Timberland Helicopter Services. Bob Bolen (left), the author (center), and Don Vestal hold signs marking the historic occasion. (SGRLPS Archives.)

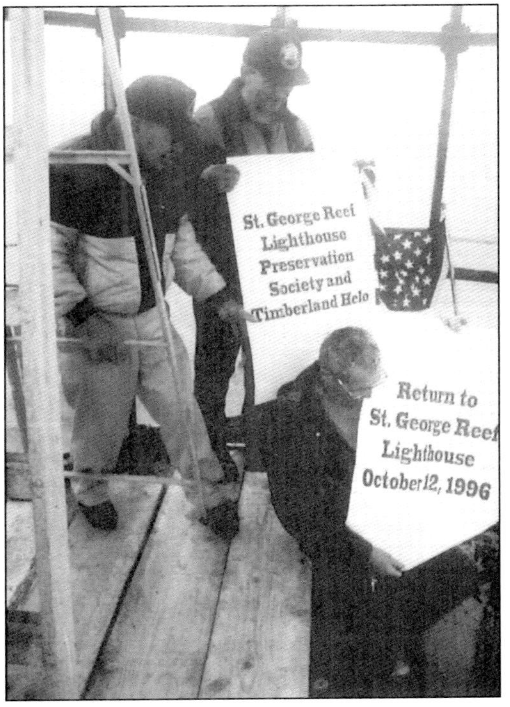

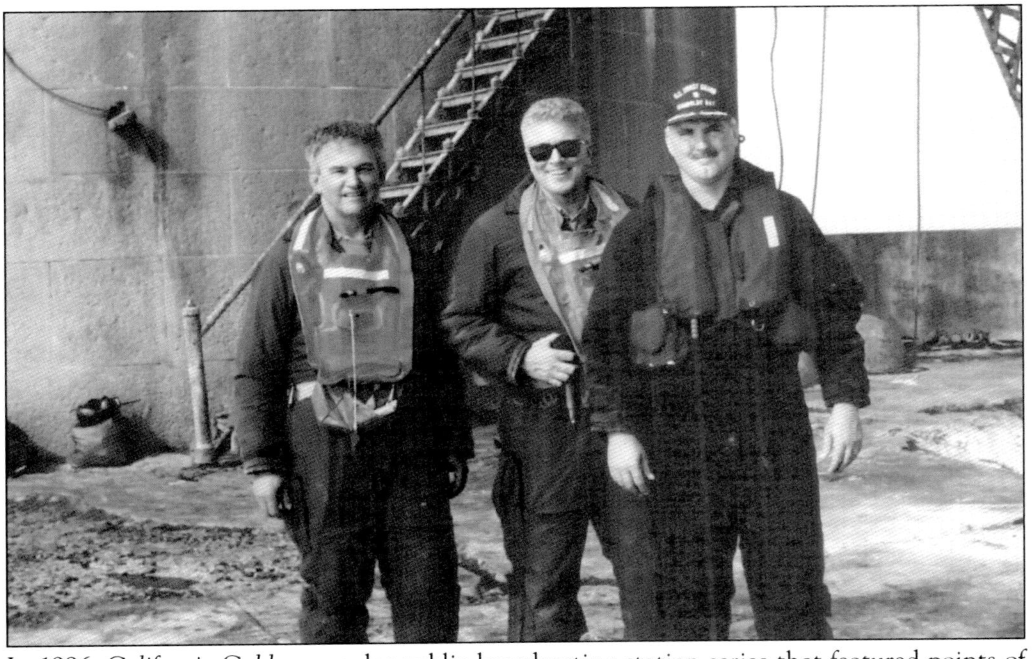

In 1996, *California Gold*, a popular public broadcasting station series that featured points of interest throughout the state televised the story of the lighthouse. Host Huell Howser and his cameraman joined the author and Coast Guard group commander Scott Allen, Humboldt Bay, for interviews and a tour of the structure. The author (left) poses with Howser (center) and Allen on the lower landing. (Author's collection.)

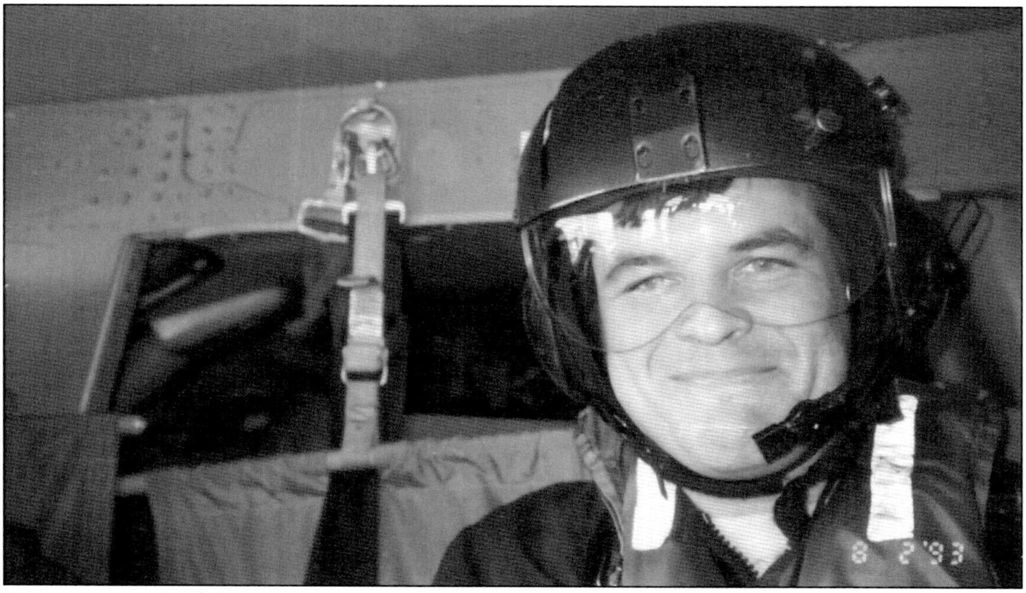

Representing the federal government in the transfer process was David Lingner, who conducted environmental screenings, which were part of General Services Administration procedures. Among his findings were that battery waste and a number of fuel containers needed to be disposed of before the transfer could be concluded. This was subsequently accomplished by helicopter teams from Humboldt Bay. (David Lingner.)

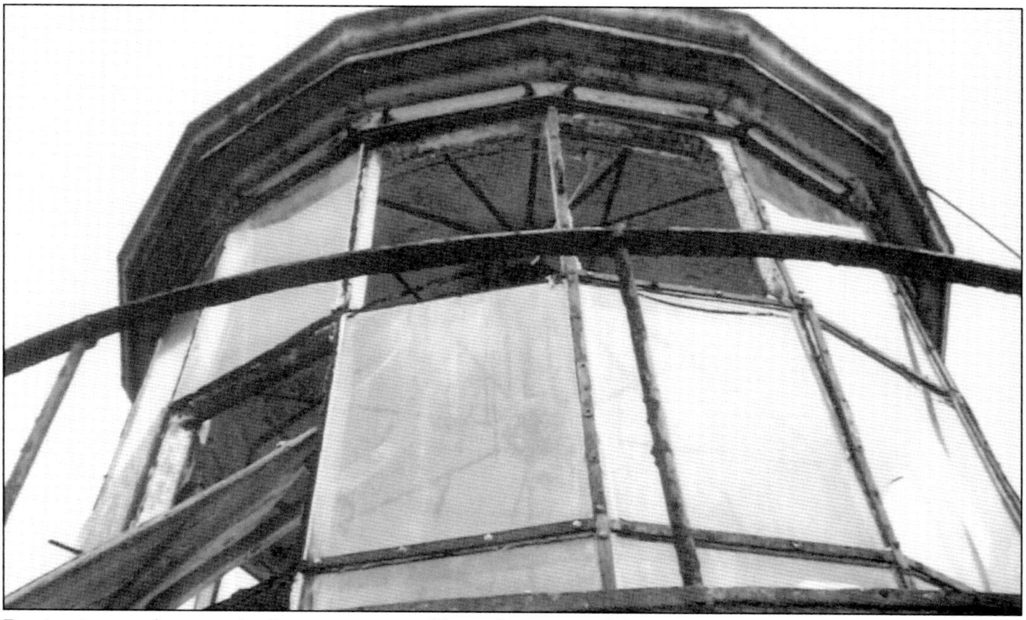

Beginning at the top, the lantern room offers a foretaste of the overall deterioration that has taken place. The windows had been broken out by the *Blackhaw* crew for lens removal. Initial plans called for in-place restoration, but nearly $45,000 and the service of two heavy-lift helicopters would ultimately be needed to approximate the craftsmanship of the original builders at Phoenix Iron Works. (David Lingner.)

Taken from a boat in March 1988, the photograph offers an overall assessment of the exterior: weathered paint, the dislocated boom hangs in the water, and rust streaks from crumbling handrails and lower-landing staircase stain the caisson. Restoration challenges are staggering, but aside from immediate safety concerns, priority must be given to the leaking lantern room. (Author's collection.)

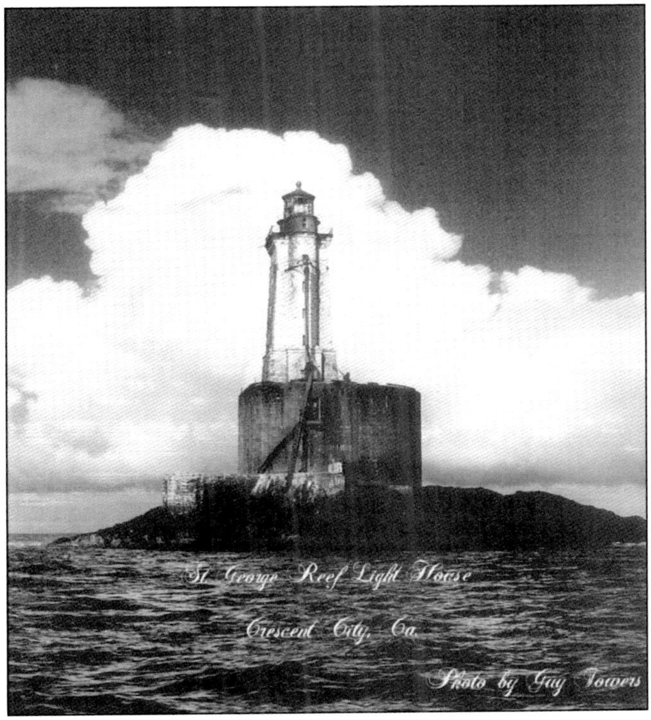

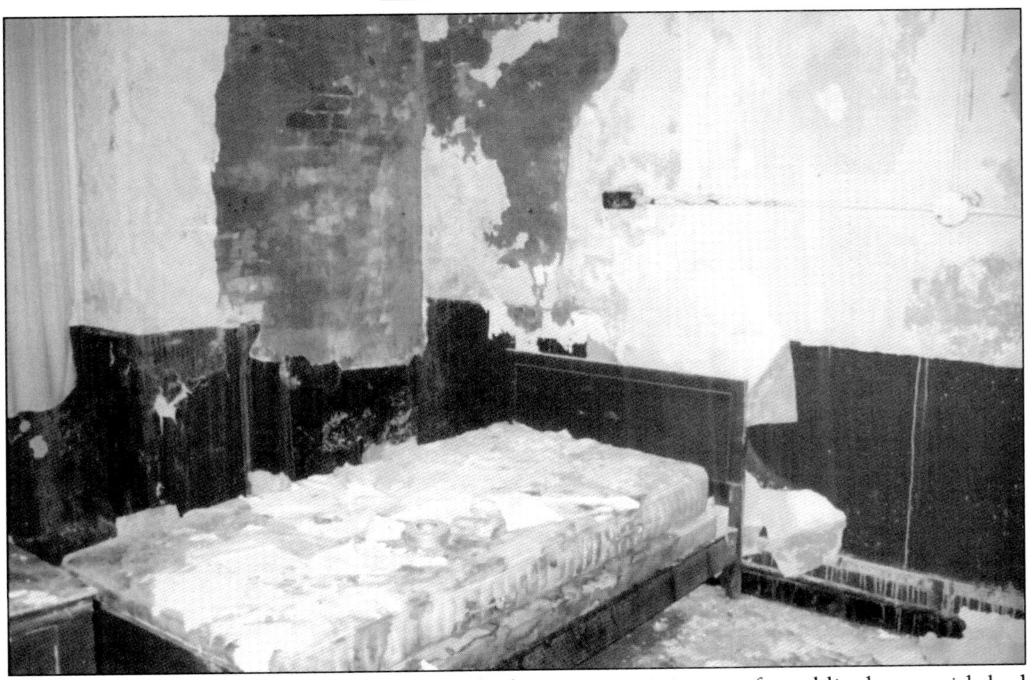

Descending to the keepers' rooms, Lingner finds scenes reminiscent of a public dump, with bed frames and dressers intact, but mattresses shredded and covered with peeling paint. Mounds of plaster litter the floors. It is dank and wet. The floor in the top room is totally rotted as the result of leakage from the watch room. (David Lingner.)

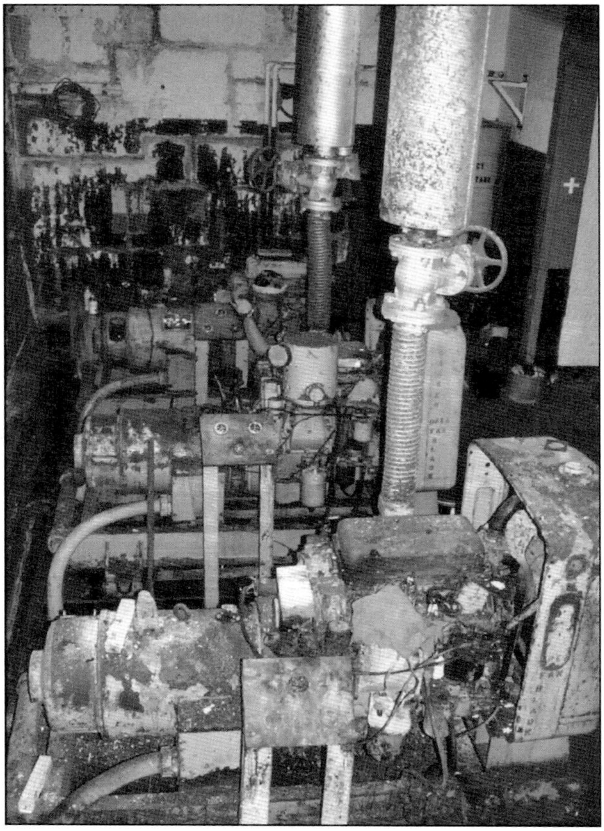

What confronted the surveyors in the engine room was a surprisingly intact time capsule of late 20th-century technology. Far from shipshape, the generators, air compressor tank, and banks of electronic equipment were corroded. The ceiling of the massive room showed the effects of drainage from the stonework on the catch deck and old skylight. Inch-thick scale covered the heavy metal beams supporting the ceiling. (Author's collection.)

The first major project was removal of the lantern room to shore for restoration in April 2000. The lift, by an Army Air Guard heavy-lift helicopter, went well; the lantern room sailed all the way to the harbor but then crashed in the surf. The pilots had come in too low. However, pieces were picked up by Dale Long of Fashion Blacksmith, who subsequently contracted with the society to repair it. In this photograph, the Chinook readies for the move. (Author's collection.)

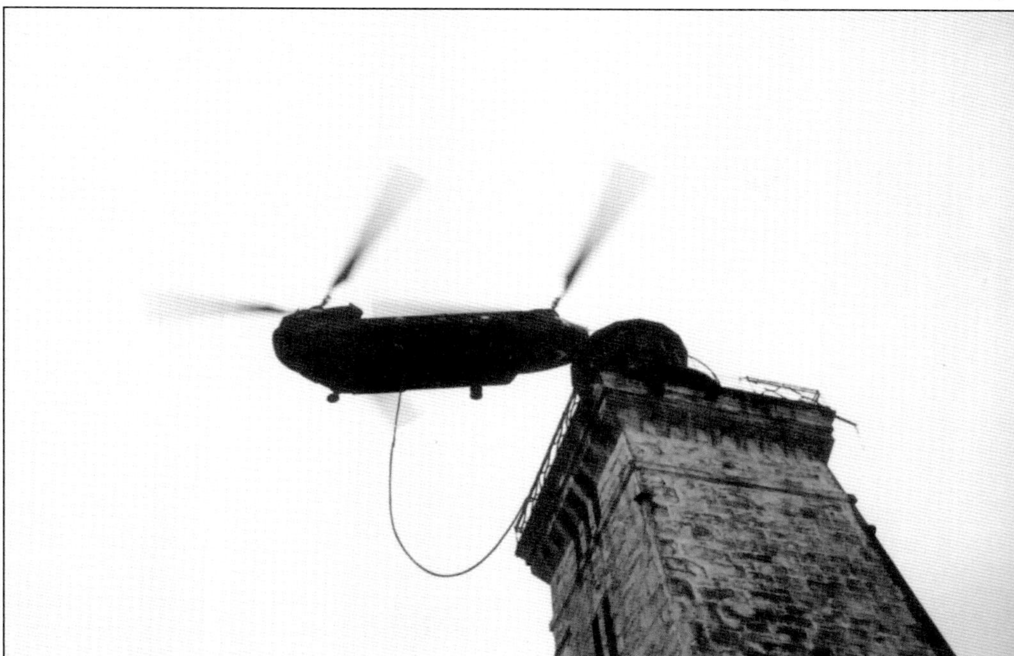

Dale Long and the employees of Fashion Blacksmith reconstructed the lantern room using stainless steel for the windows instead of cast iron, as it was originally. Additionally, a plastic material, similar to that used in boats would replace the glass panes. After two years, the project was complete. Pictured here, from left to right, are an unidentified Fashion Blacksmith employee, Dale Long, and his son Ted Long. (Author's collection.)

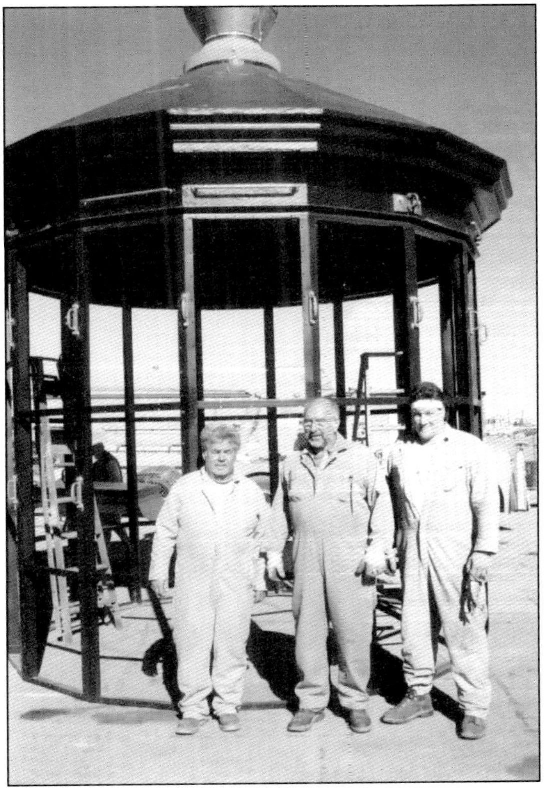

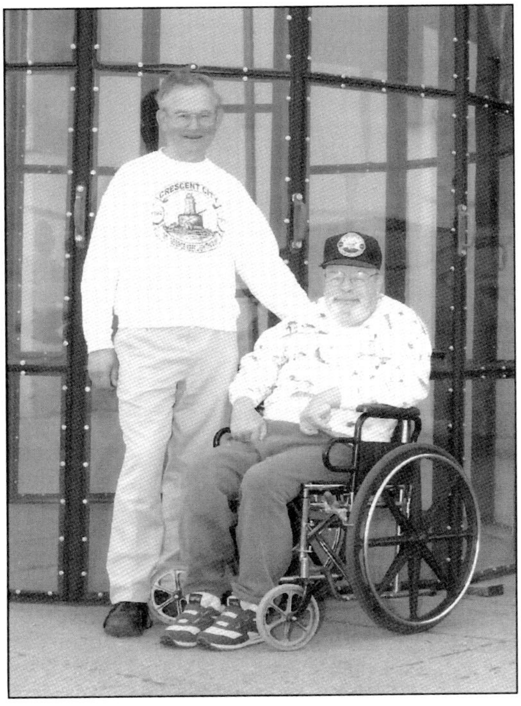

Bob Bolen (right) and the author pose beside the lantern room. Bolen fronted the $26,000 to pay Erickson Air Crane of Oregon to take the light housing home. He was a board member, former vice president of the St. George Reef Lighthouse Preservation Society, and a member of the Del Norte Historical Society. (Author's collection.)

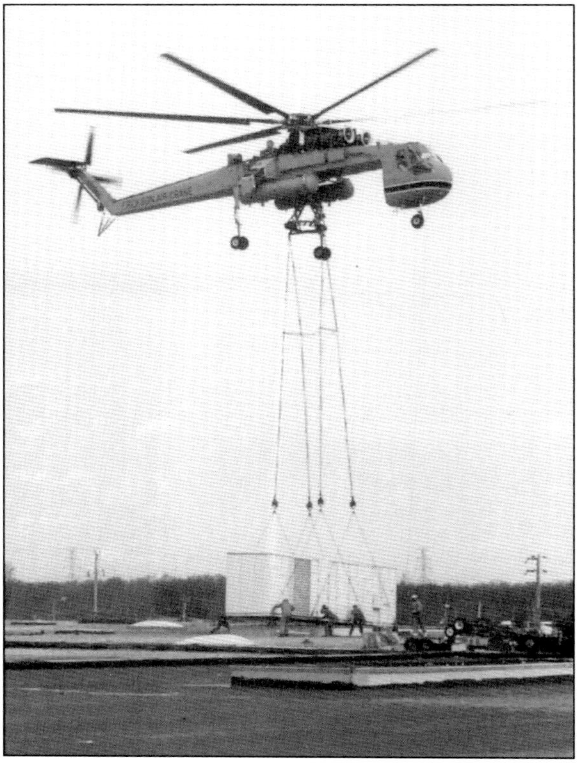

During the downtime for repair of the lantern room, work continued at the lighthouse: electrical rewiring, window repair, and painting and plastering of walls in the keepers' rooms. A pier light was donated by Coast Guard Group Humboldt Bay, but it was determined to be inadequate. The day of return finally materialized, and among much fanfare, the helicopter shown here put the crown on the "Queen of the Coast." (Erickson Air Crane.)

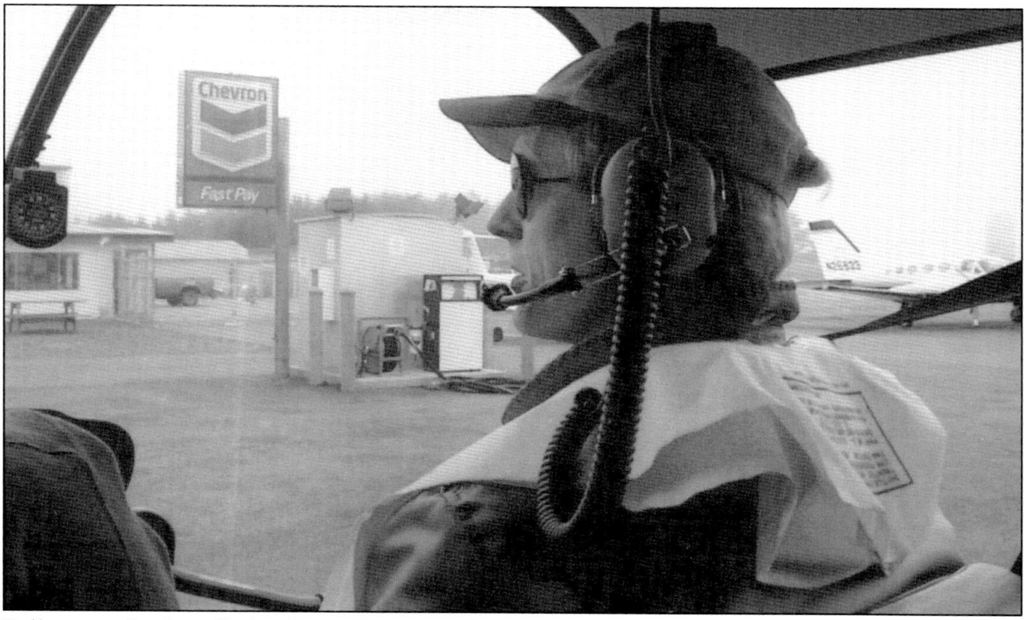

Following the first flight, Dave Everson, Shasta Wing and Rotor of Redding, California, has provided most helicopter services. Risking life and limb, he must fly over two mountain ranges, sometimes in bad weather, only to find fog so thick at Crescent City that he cannot find the lighthouse. (Nadine Perry.)

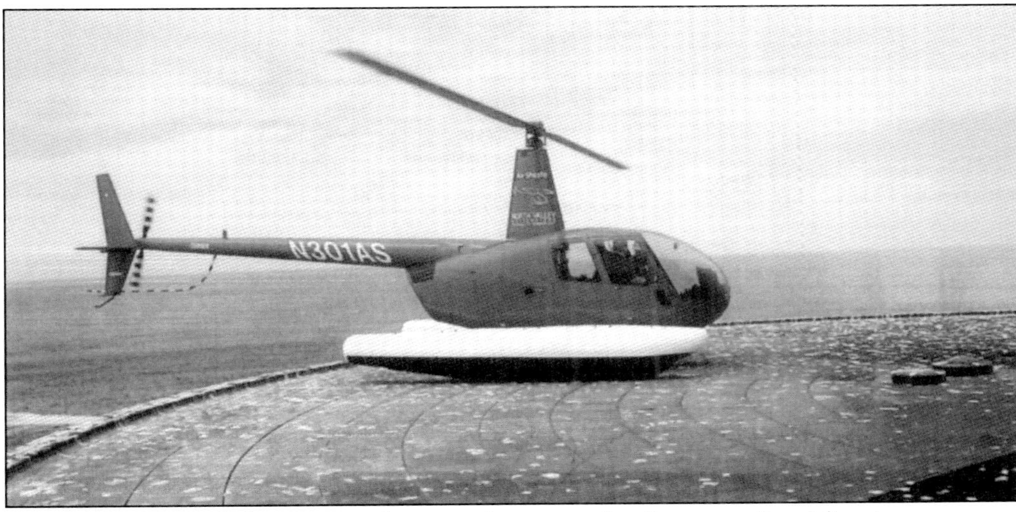

Dave Everson's R44 helicopter sets down on the caisson landing area after delivering passengers for tours and supplies for restoration work. The coverings on the craft's landing skids are flotation devices as required by Federal Aviation Administration rules when transporting paying passengers over water. The R44 can carry three passengers plus the pilot or a sling load of about 600 pounds. (Author's collection.)

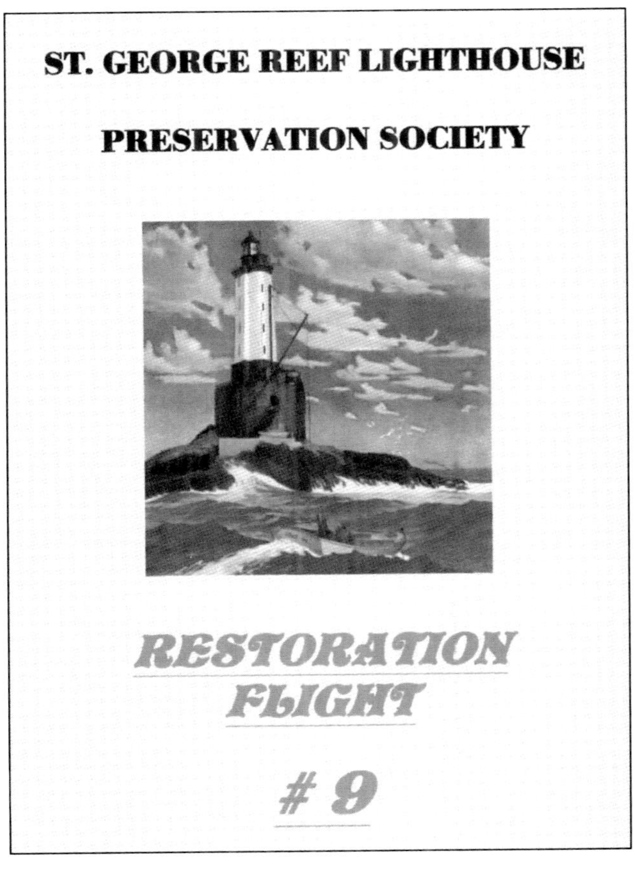

ST. GEORGE REEF LIGHTHOUSE

PRESERVATION SOCIETY

RESTORATION FLIGHT

9

In advance of each flight, the author and Terry McNamara discuss timing, goals, crew content, and work assignments as well as the tools and supplies needed. Pictured here is the cover sheet of flight No. 9, October 18,19, and 20, 2002, as compiled by McNamara. The main goal of No. 9 was the installation of a wind/solar power source for the new optic, in celebration of the 110th anniversary of the first lighting in 1892. (SGRLPS Archives.)

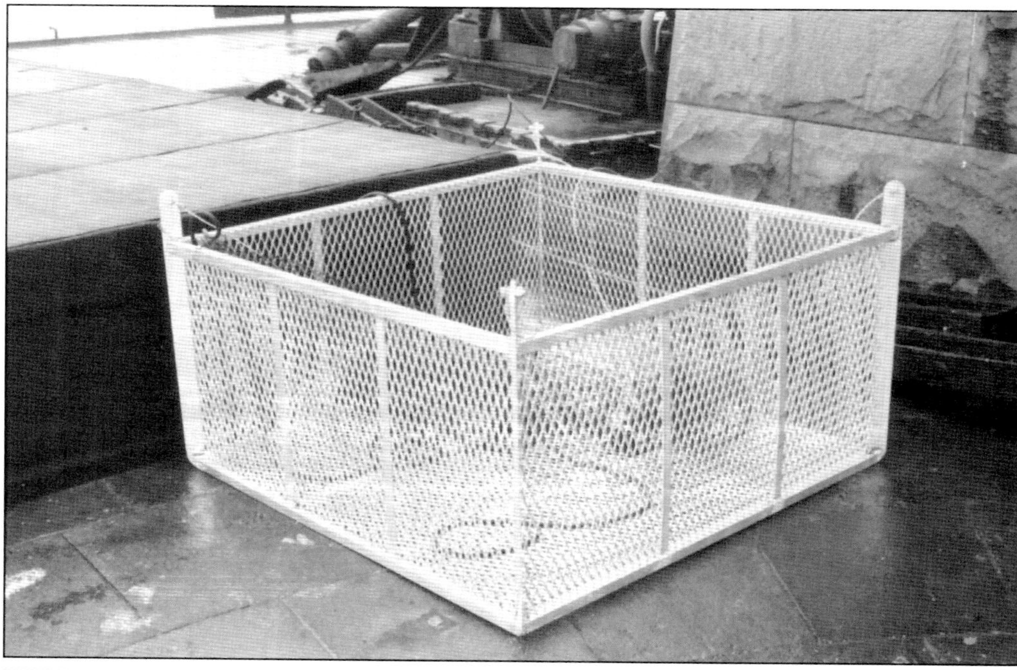

Early on, a cargo net was used, but after seeing valuable tools poking through the webbing, local volunteer and owner of Redwood Welding Don Nuss carefully crafted a metal cargo cage. Normal contents are sleeping bags, chests of food, carpentry, plumbing, and electrical tools and supplies, fuel, and water. On return trips, the cage might contain garbage or artifacts to be salvaged. (Author's collection.)

About this time, Glenn Williamson and his wife, Colleen, moved to Brookings, Oregon, with a view of St. George. She died unexpectedly but left money for Glenn to put a light in her favorite beacon. Preparations were made to install a solar/wind-powered optic with a range like the original. In honor of the first lighting, the new beacon flashed on October 12, 2002. (Steve Corley.)

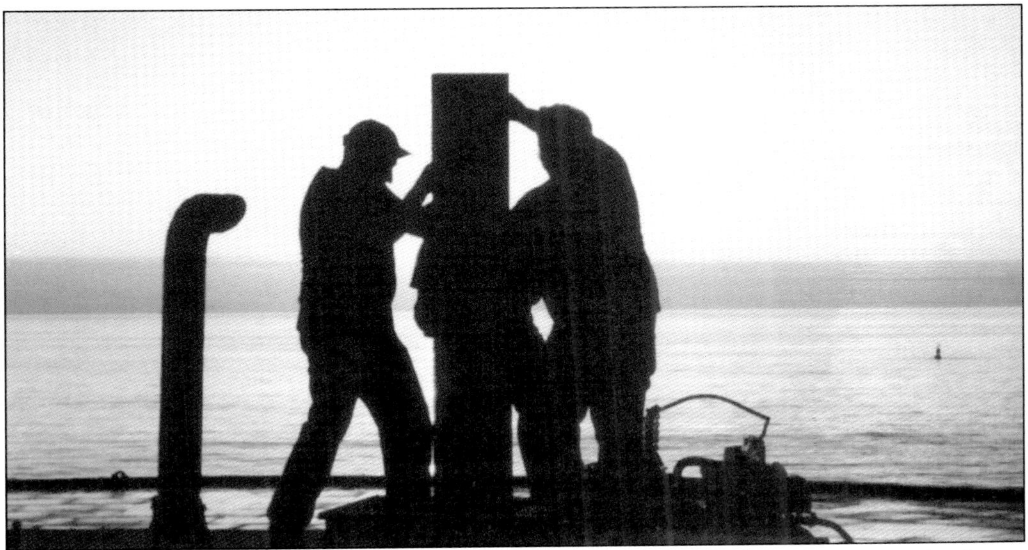

This silhouette of volunteers at St. George, framed against the setting sun, represents the dawn-to-dusk work ethic that is taken for granted as the hands-on, dirty, grimy, dangerous restoration tasks are accomplished. As soon as their feet hit the deck, the carpenter, plumber, electrician, painters, and jack-of-all-trades assistants unpack their gear and begin. These dedicated folk are doing what they love. (Author's collection.)

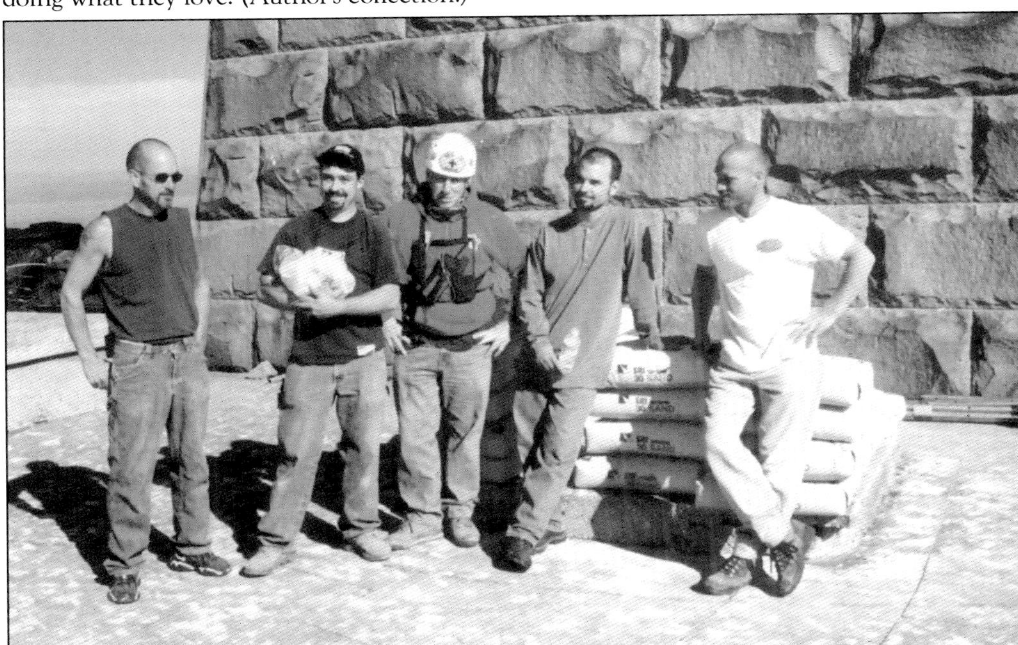

Pictured here on the catch deck as they take a quick break are, from left to right, Mitch Gianola (carpenter), Chris Bertolini, Terry McNamara, Randy Rogers (plumber), and Nick McNamara. Their next task is hauling the stack of 75-pound bags of blasting sand to the top of the tower, six stories above, where it will be used to remove rust from the metal roof of the watch room extension over the staircase. (Author's collection.)

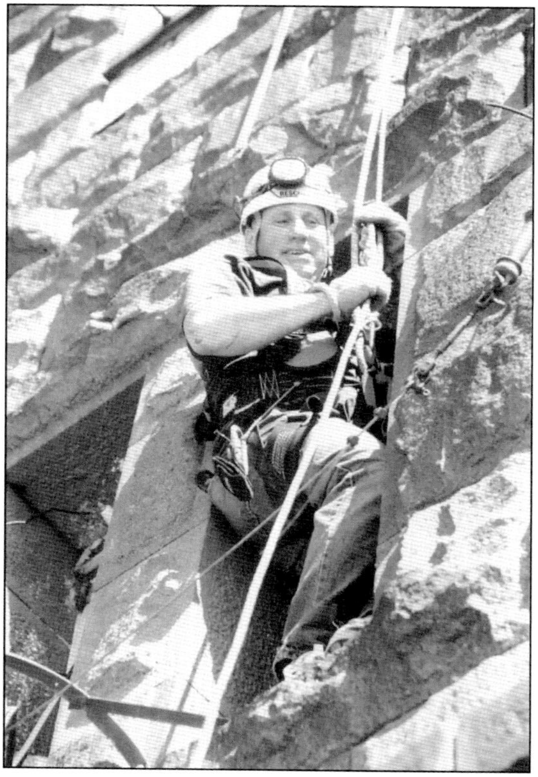

Terry McNamara rappels down the south side of the tower to repair storm shutters in the keepers' rooms. He is active in search and rescue where rope climbing is routine. Del Norte Search and Rescue volunteers have the important job of assisting passengers on and off helicopters for tours and restoration flights. (Author's collection.)

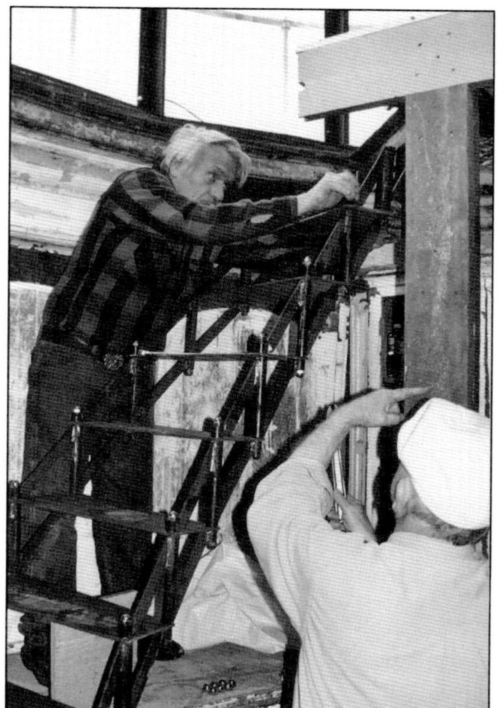

Don Nuss (left) is in the watch room installing the staircase, which he designed and fabricated. The original staircase was removed by unknown parties at some time after decommissioning. Dutch Dremmon offers help to align the bolt holes. (Author's collection.)

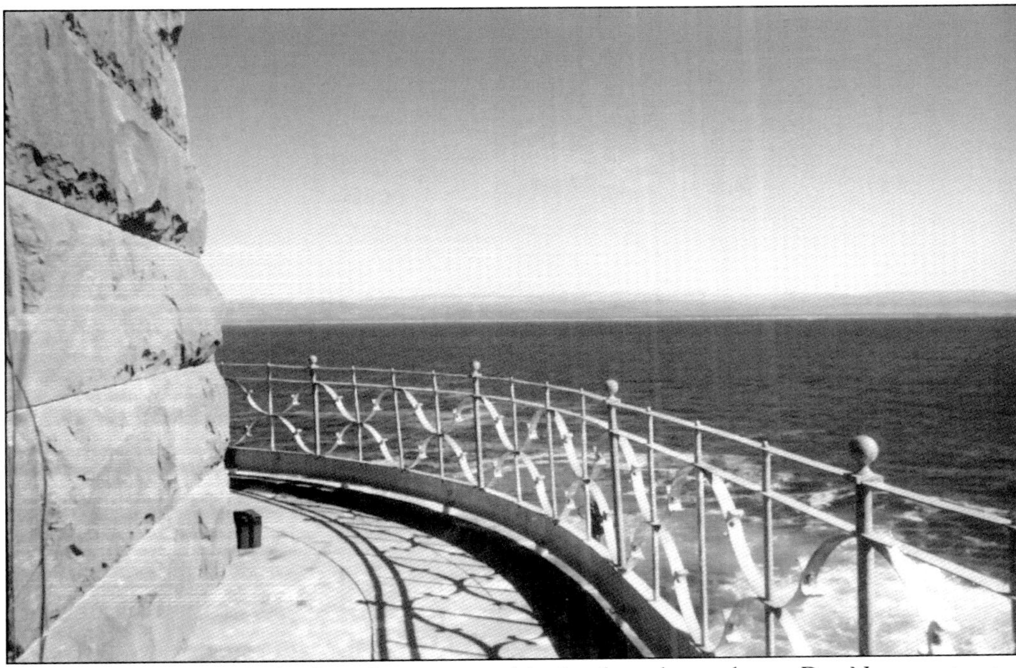

New stainless steel handrails adorn the caisson in this view from the southwest. Don Nuss constructed the handrails using a generous donation by the T.K. Foundation. (Author's collection.)

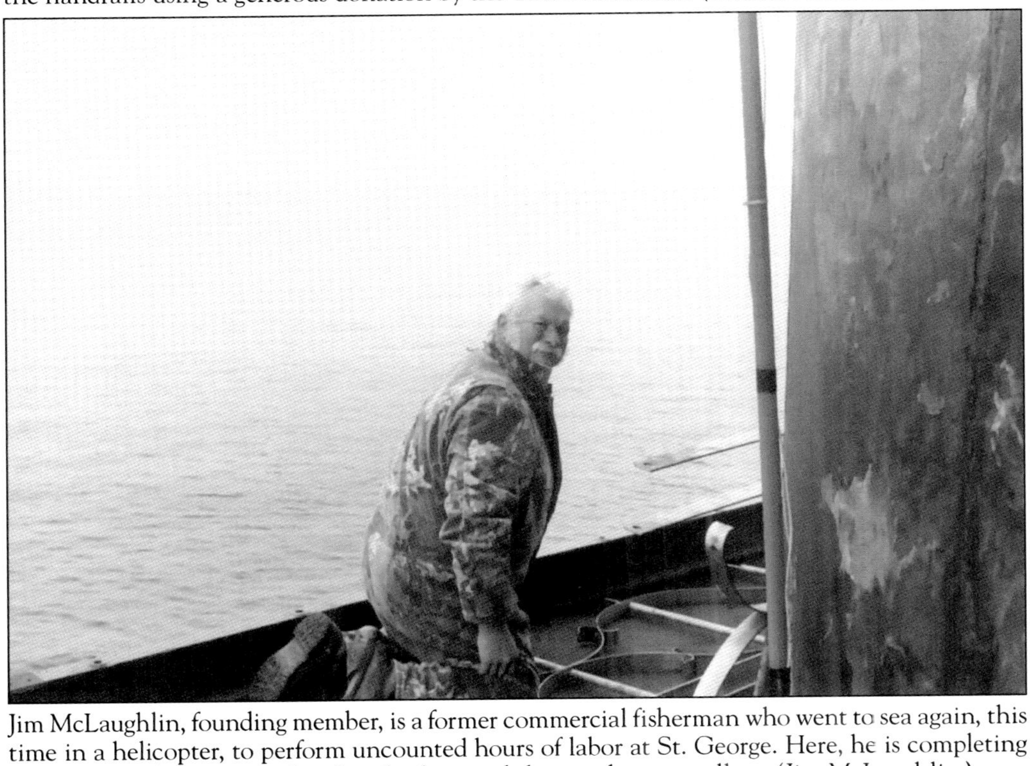

Jim McLaughlin, founding member, is a former commercial fisherman who went to sea again, this time in a helicopter, to perform uncounted hours of labor at St. George. Here, he is completing installation of the new replica handrail around the watch room gallery. (Jim McLaughlin.)

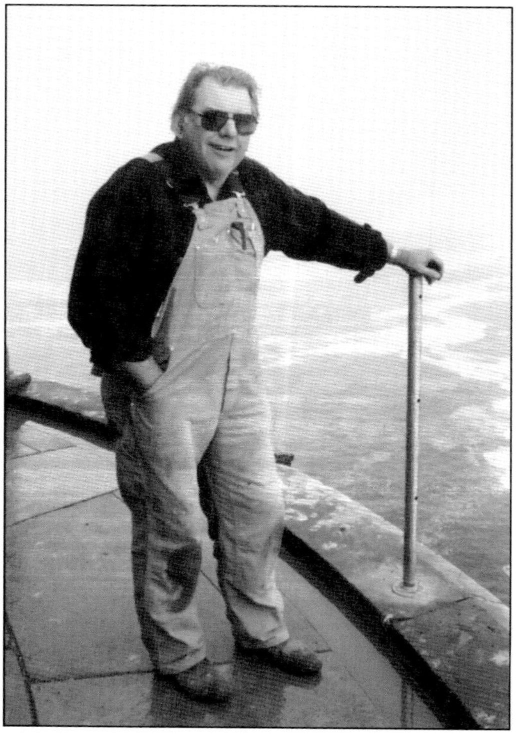

Long-term member, society officer, and former Coast Guard member Bill Barton is shown installing a temporary handrail around the edge of the caisson to replace the originals, which were completely destroyed by corrosion. (Author's collection.)

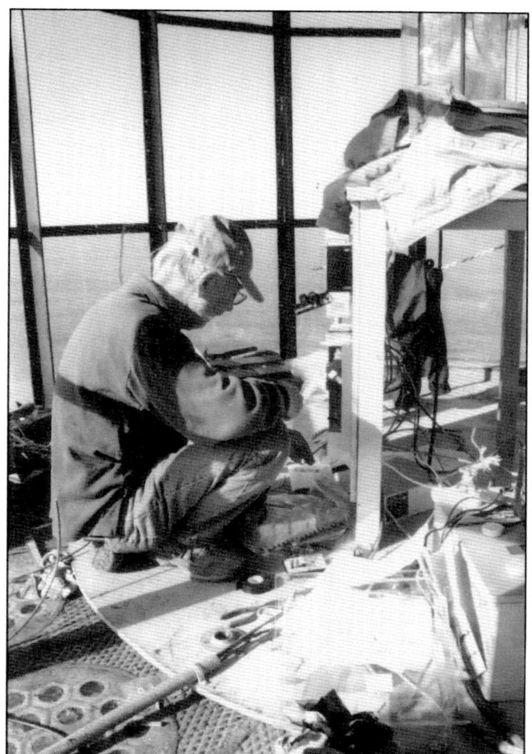

Glenn Williamson, retired electrical contractor, sorts out the complex wiring for the new St. George optic. (Author's collection.)

In a miracle of coincidence, Gary Foster, the last Coast Guard electrician to work at St. George before it was decommissioned, heard of the restoration going on at the lighthouse and volunteered to come from Sacramento, California, to refurbish the badly deteriorated lighting system. Foster (right) is shown here in the engine room with Roy Smith, of the Nutter Group electrical suppliers, which donated labor and materials. (Author's collection.)

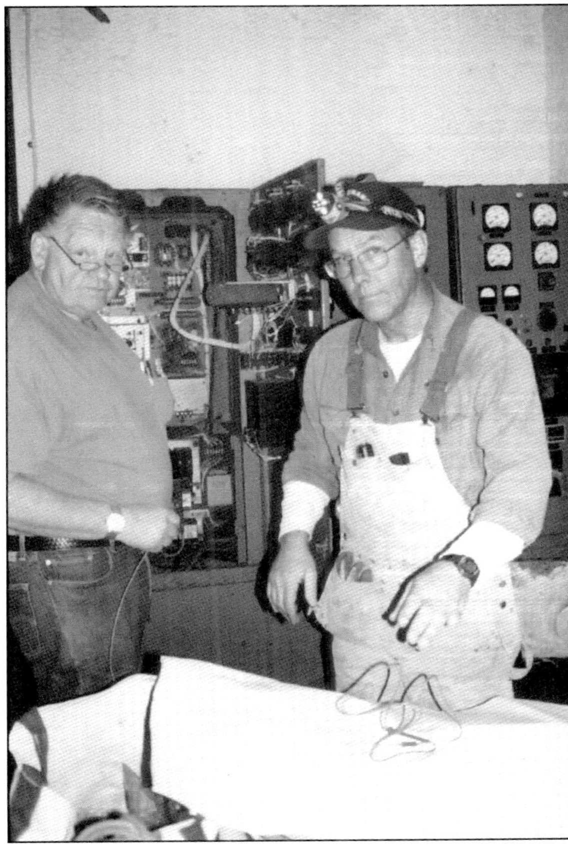

John Lambert, of Abstract Masonry, dangles in a harness high above the ocean while doing an inspection of the masonry below the lantern-watch room and face of the staircase. (Author's collection.)

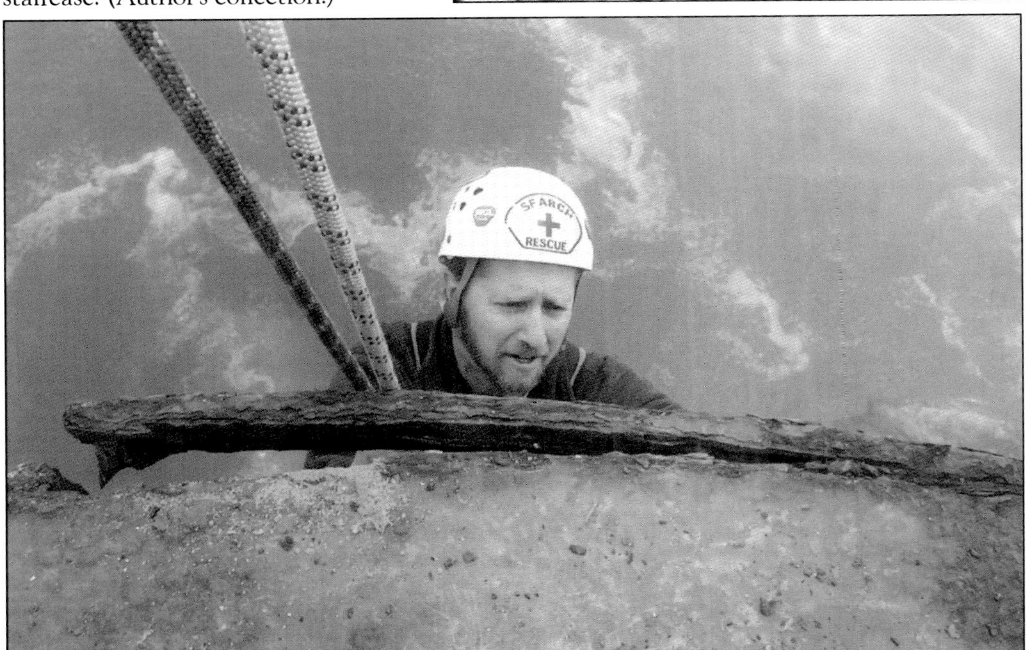

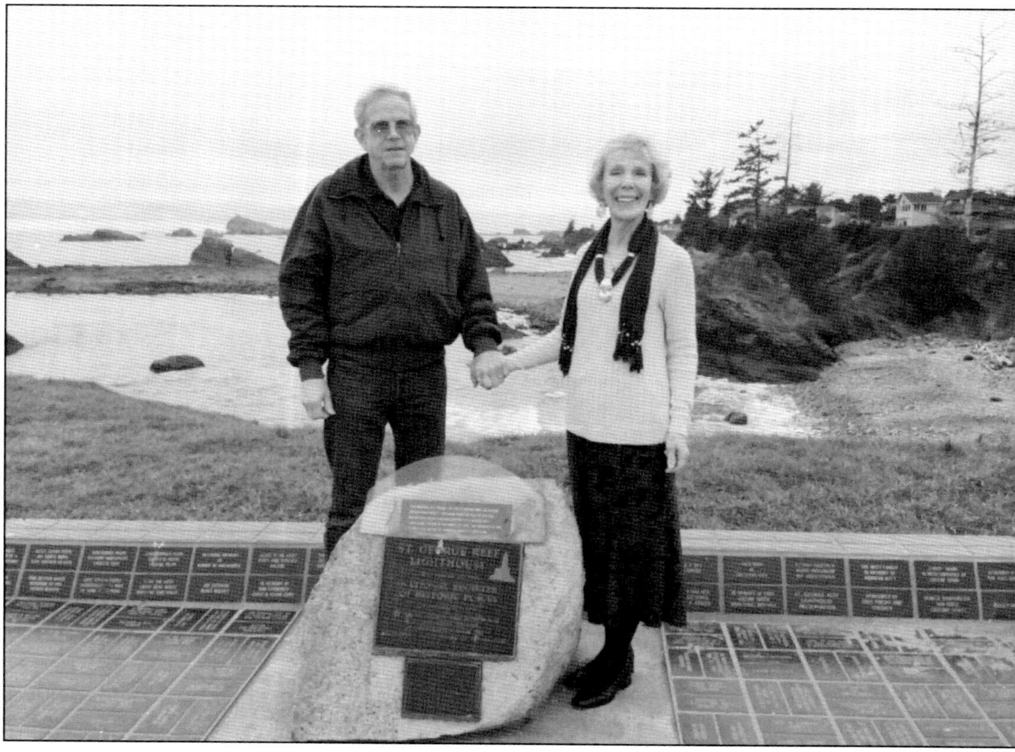

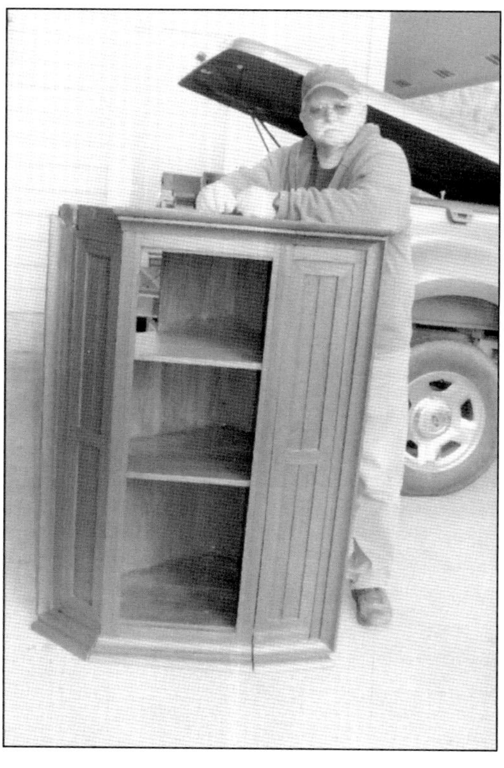

Exemplifying the teamwork needed in the restoration of St. George are Russ and Marshann Burnette of Crescent City, shown holding hands at the society's National Register of Historic Places marker and memorial plaza at Brother Jonathan Point. The Burnettes take on tasks ranging from sweeping floors to restoring masonry. (Russ and Marshann Burnette.)

Bill Monson, at his home in Crescent City, shows off a cabinet from the watch room, which he restored. Bill, retired, is a jack-of-all-trades and performs volunteer work all over the community with the support of his wife, Terry. (Author's collection.)

Framed in the doorway leading from the watch room to the watch room gallery is Mike Young, a local engineer who has donated much time and effort toward restoration. He was aboard a flight to determine the feasibility of using the lantern room roof and gallery to catch rainwater. Water in the existing cistern is polluted, and fresh water has to be hauled to the site. (Author's collection.)

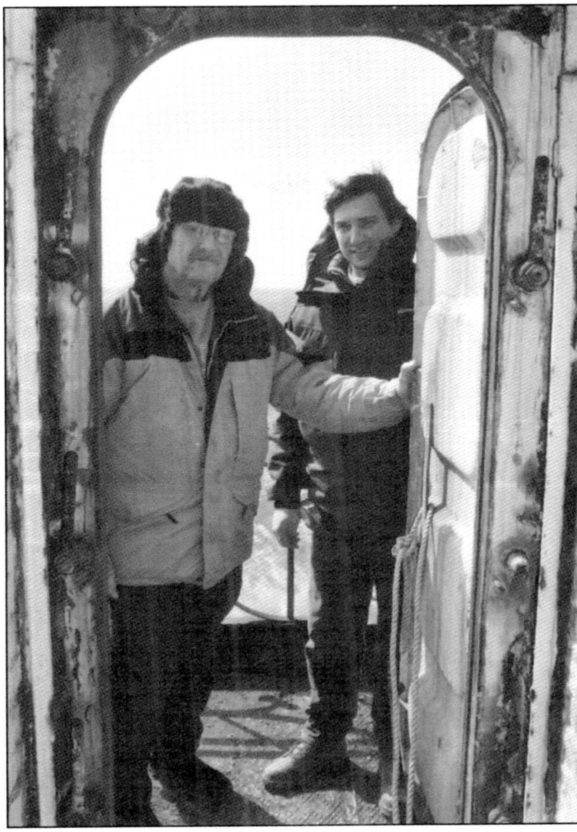

Larry Folsom and the author stand near the tower entrance. Behind Folsom are the remains of the boom-mast assembly. When not volunteering at St. George, where one of Folsom's main tasks was coordinating helicopter operations, he was a guard at Pelican Bay State Prison. The huge grounds of the prison can be seen from the lighthouse. (Author's collection.)

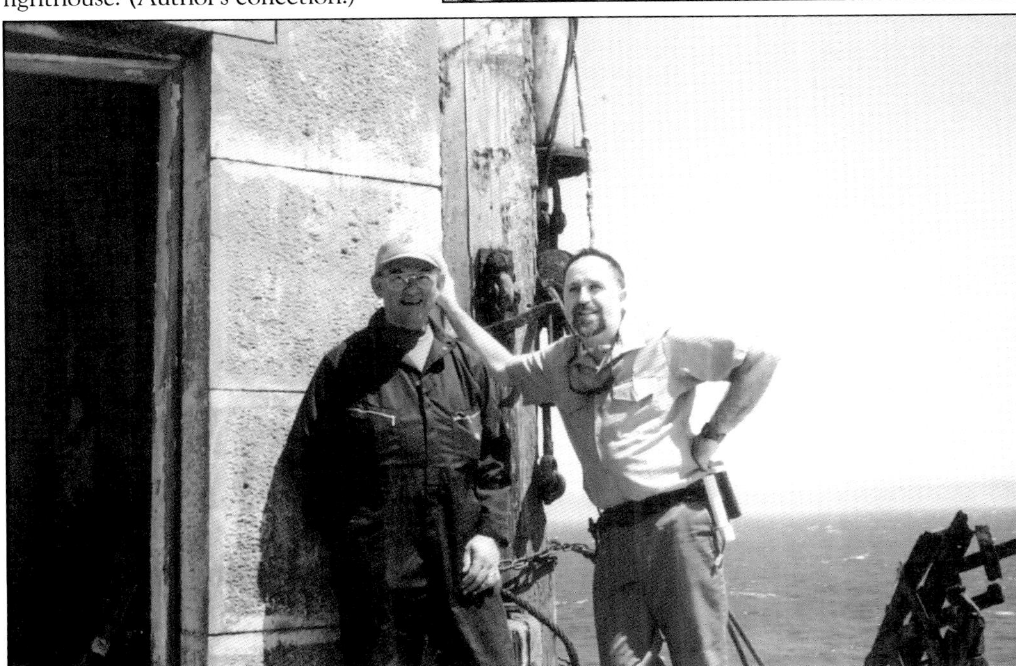

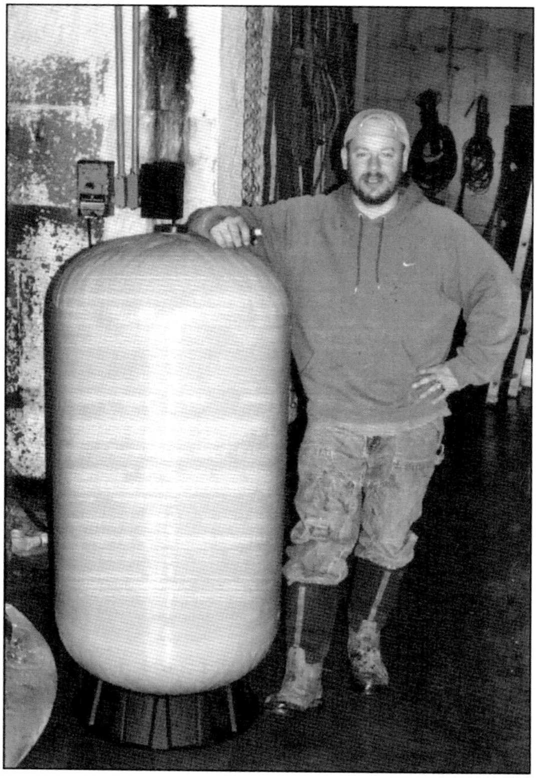

Randy Rogers, of Rogers Plumbing, stands by the new water tank that was just delivered in the cargo cage and will be installed in the engine room. With good humor and patience, Rogers has refurbished nearly all of the plumbing in the building, including the galley, which now has running water. (Author's collection.)

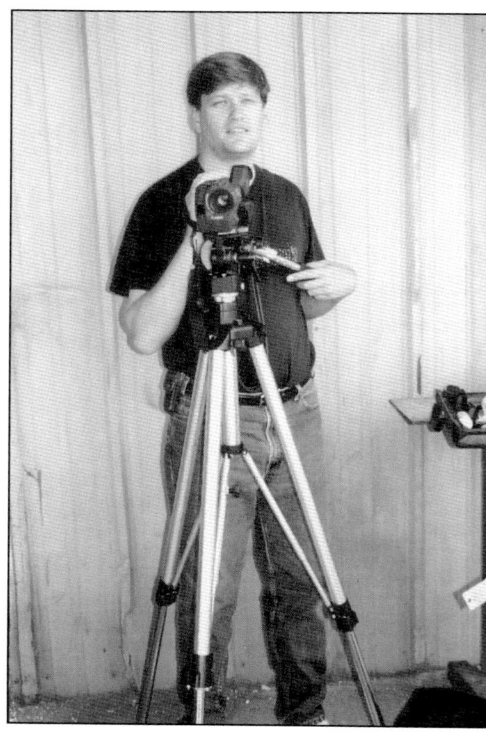

In addition to restoring and remastering *Last One Out, Turn Out the Lights!*, Bill Odonnell Jr. of Odonnell Entertainment Adventures of Shadow, LLC (aka Odonnell Entertainment) manages the society's website, www.stgeorgereeflighthouse.us, and has documented much of the restoration work on film. His plan is to use his copyrighted footage, which has no connection to SGRLPS, and have a unique documentary on St. George Reef Lighthouse produced in the near future. Bill and his father, Bill Odonnell Sr., helped in the formation of the St. George Reef Lighthouse Preservation Society, promoting it among several veterans' groups Bill Sr. founded. (Author's collection.)

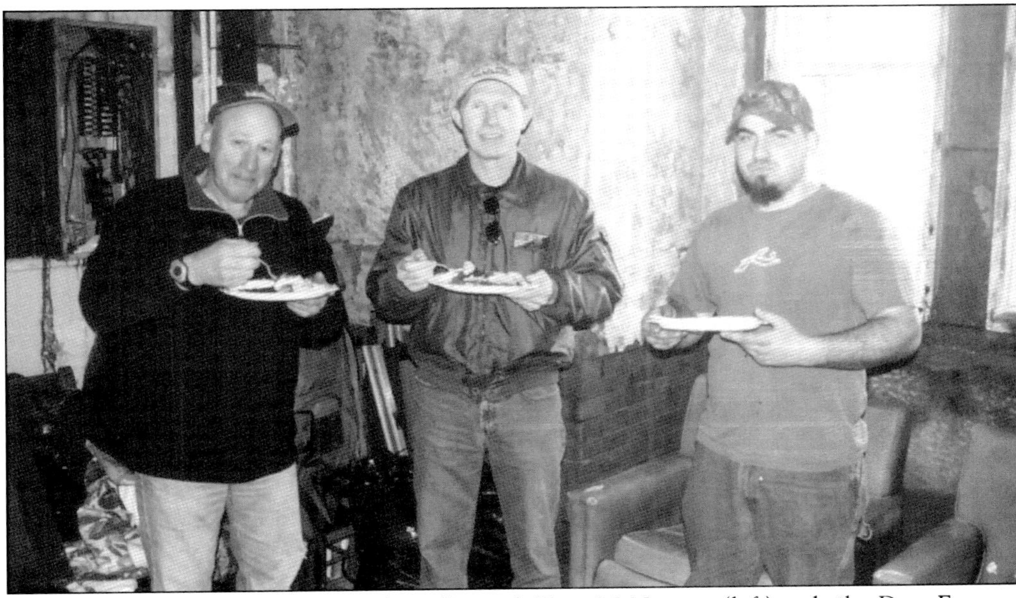

Aaron Duncan is at the far right in the galley with Terry McNamara (left) and pilot Dave Everson. Aaron is an all-around, get-it-done guy who likes best to work on the generators. In fact, with the assistance of Don Nuss, who made a new exhaust pipe, and Jim McLaughlin, one of the GMC engines ran for a short time. (Author's collection.)

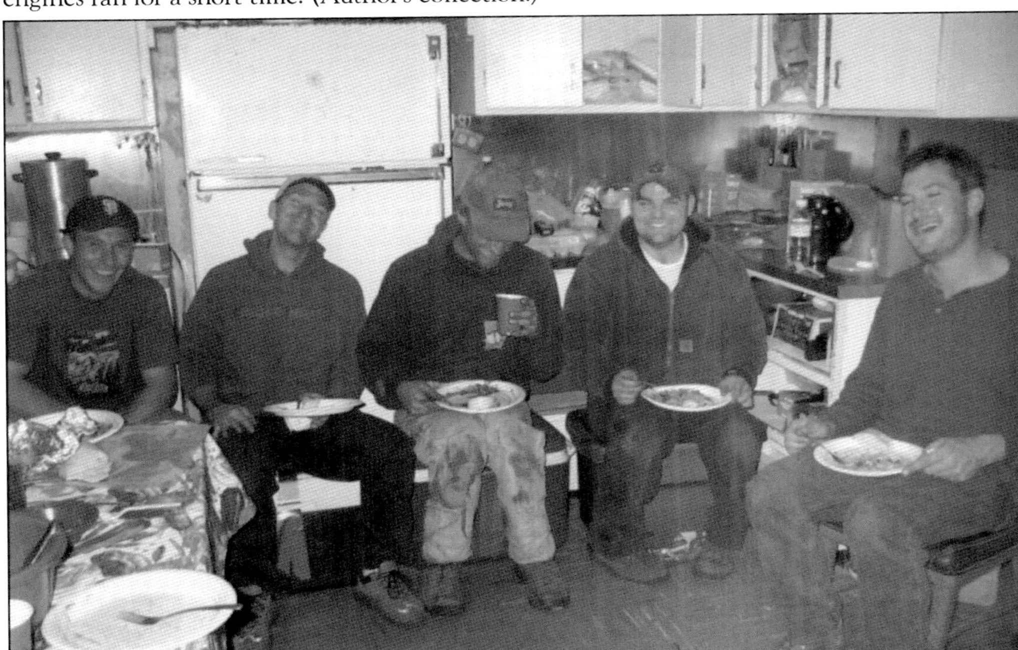

Although not in the spick-and-span condition of the Coast Guard era, the galley still serves up meals. These smiling volunteers make do sitting on ice chests as they chow down on food prepared by fellow worker Marilyn McLaughlin. From left to right are Bill Tedson, Israel Reagen, Nick McNamara, Aaron Duncan, and Roy Rook. (Terry McNamara.)

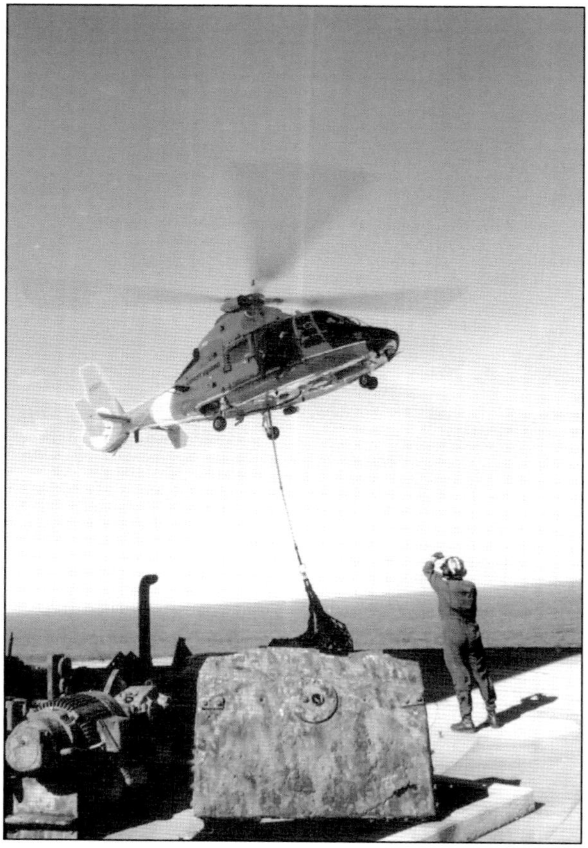

Coast Guard Group Humboldt Bay has been a key player in many projects at St. George. Helicopter pilots from the air station at McKinleyville have ferried out production crews to film three PBS documentaries. The Aids to Navigation Team of the group, stationed at Samoa, and cutters from the Crescent City station have participated in many memorial services and displays. Pictured here, a ground crewman directs the lifting of a load from the caisson deck. (Author's collection.)

Concurrent with the lighting, plans were in place to bring paid visitors to the lighthouse as a means to cover restoration expenses. The visitors would fly out on the last day of the monthly restoration flight and be led through the facility by docents stationed at several levels. Here, Terry McNamara (right) chats with famous test pilot Chuck Yeager and his wife, Victoria, on a tour. (Author's collection.)

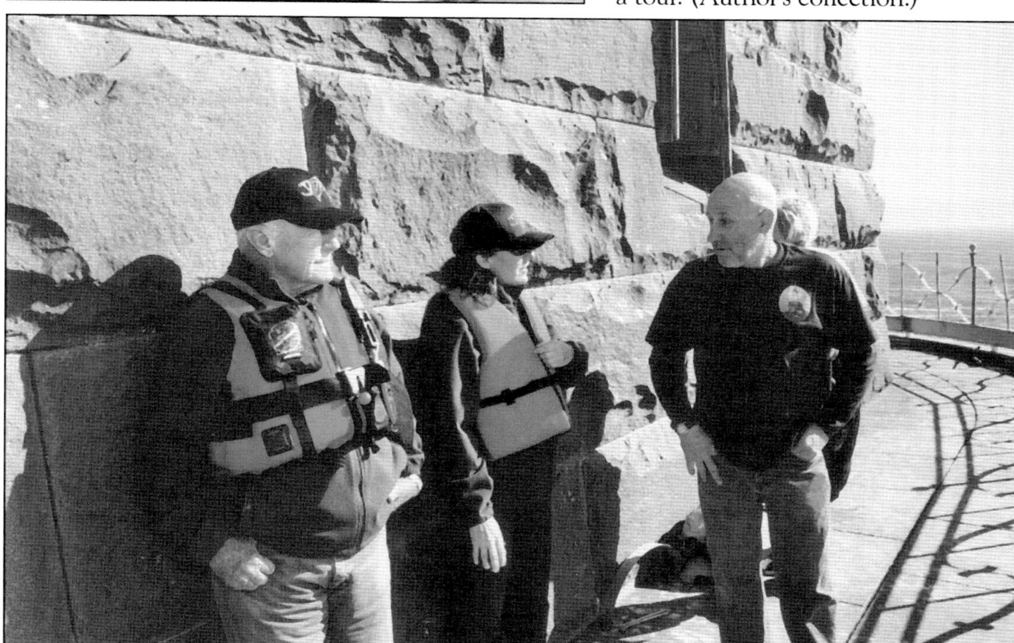

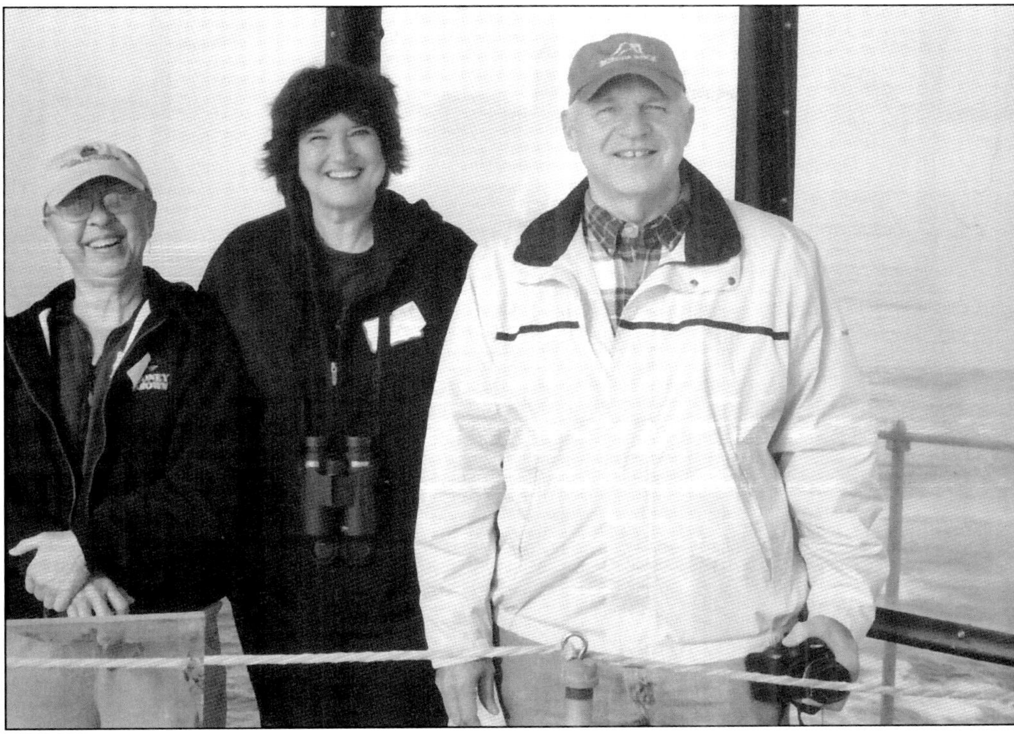

Derith Bennet (left) and unidentified guests have their photograph taken in the lantern room. St. George is a must-see destination for lighthouse lovers, and Bennet organized a large group to take the tour. (Author's collection.)

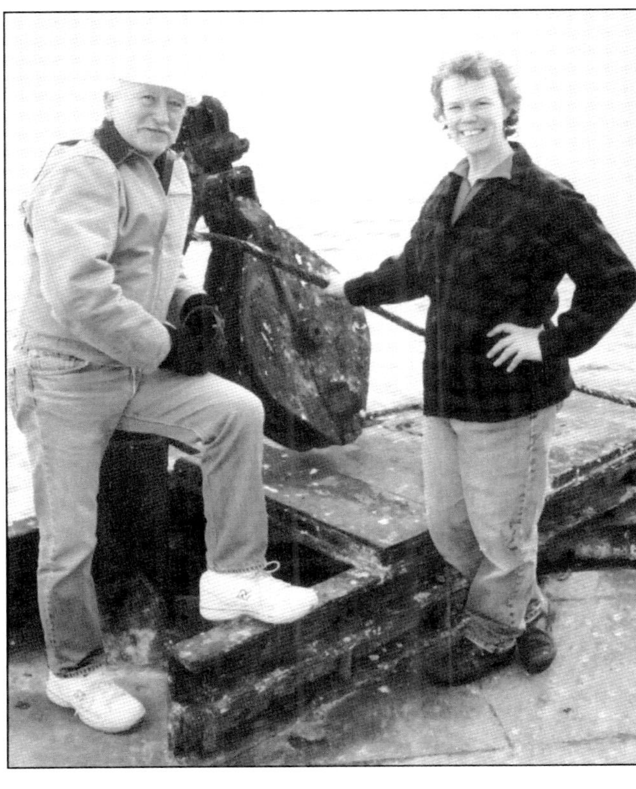

Susan Davis (right), restoration worker and tour docent, stands on the western edge of the caisson with Dutch Dremmon, photographer and graphic artist for the group, who has made his first visit to the lighthouse. Hanging between them is a pulley that was part of the boom-mast assembly. The pulley has since been taken to shore and restored. (Author's collection.)

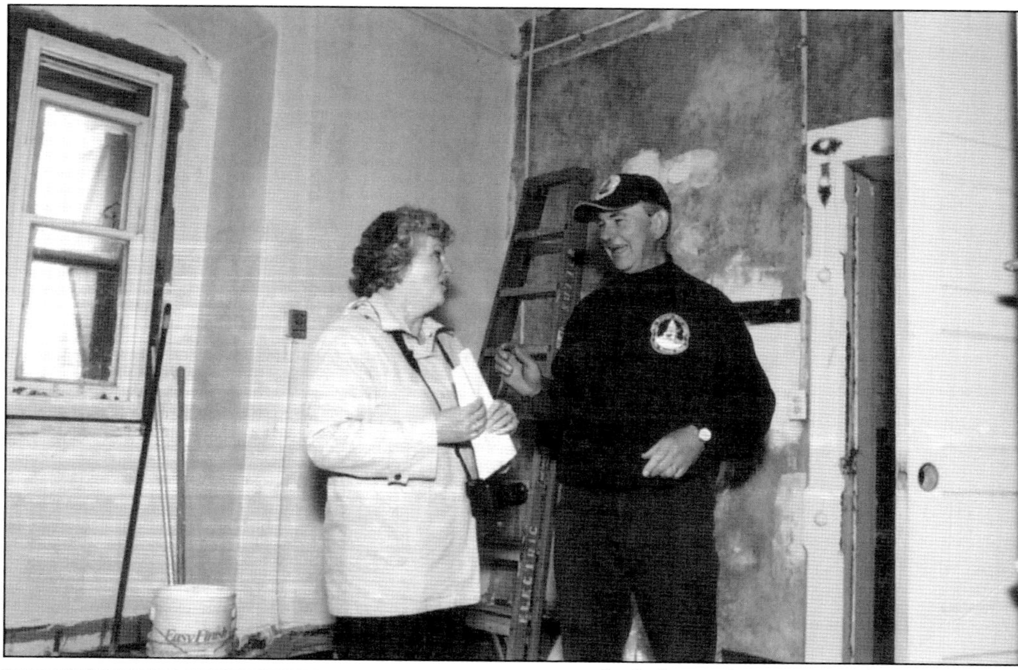

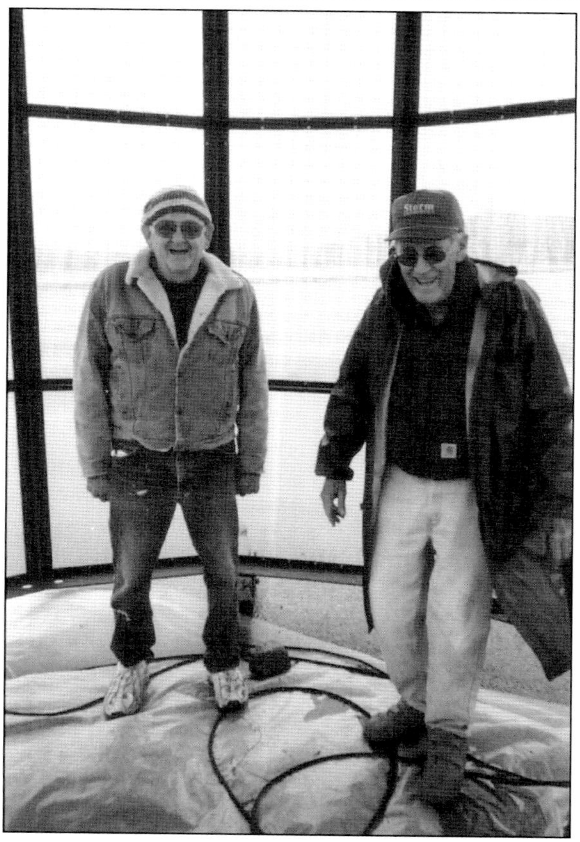

Lighthouse historian and writer Elinore Dewire comes in with other visitors to observe restoration progress at St. George. Here, she joins the author to see upgrades in a keeper's room. (Author's collection.)

Society members John Rogers (left) and Bob Faires put the finishing touches on the rebuilt lantern room just before it was carried to the lighthouse by Erickson Air Crane. (Author's collection.)

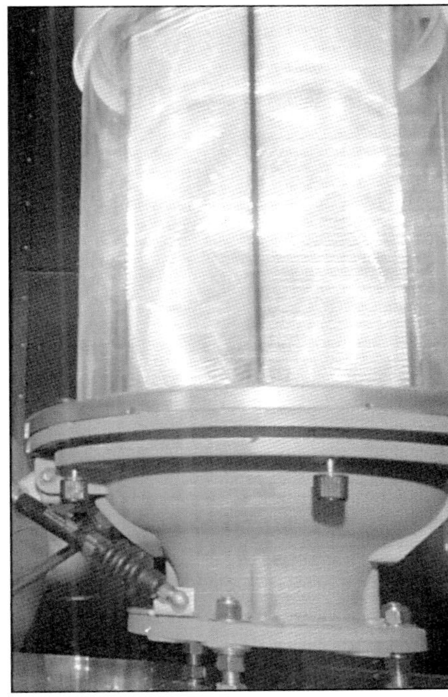

In order to operate the new light, the society needed permits from the Coast Guard and the National Marine Fisheries Service (NMFS). Guided through the process by Brian Aldrich, of the Coast Guard, and Monica DeAngeles and Jeanine Cody, of the NMFS, the complicated procedure required several years, but a reengineered system was activated on March 12, 2012. Shown here is Clark Moore, who designed and helped to install the equipment. (Right, author's collection; below, Clark Moore.)

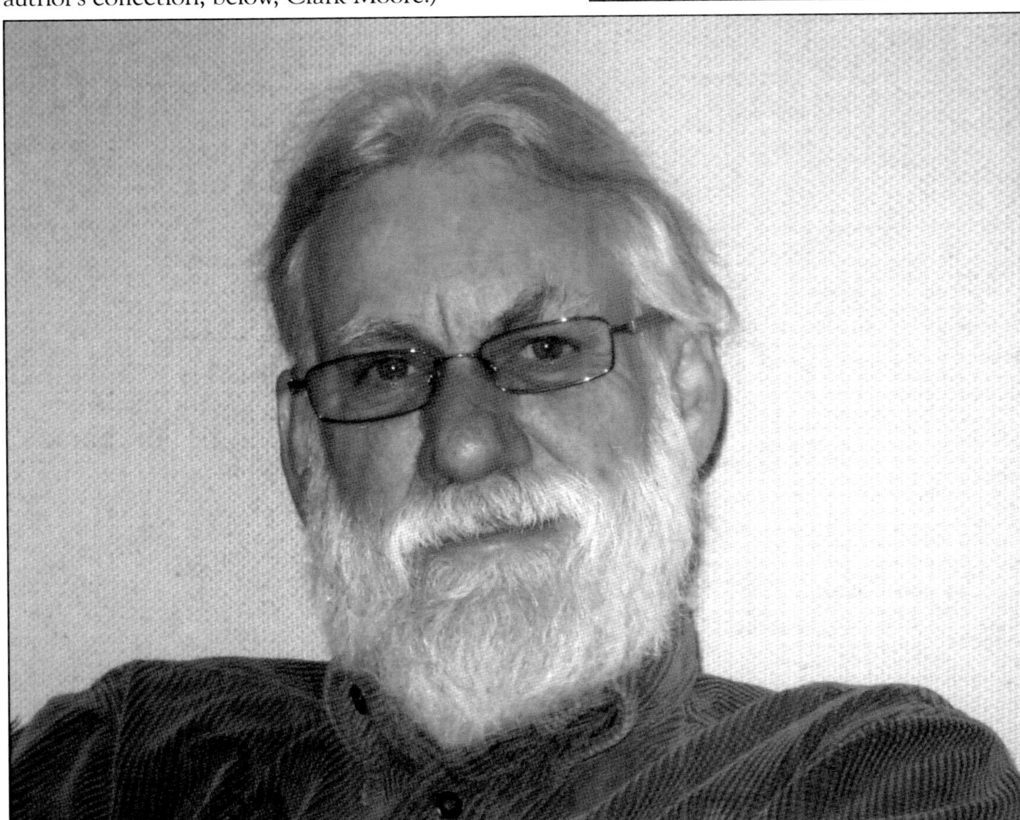

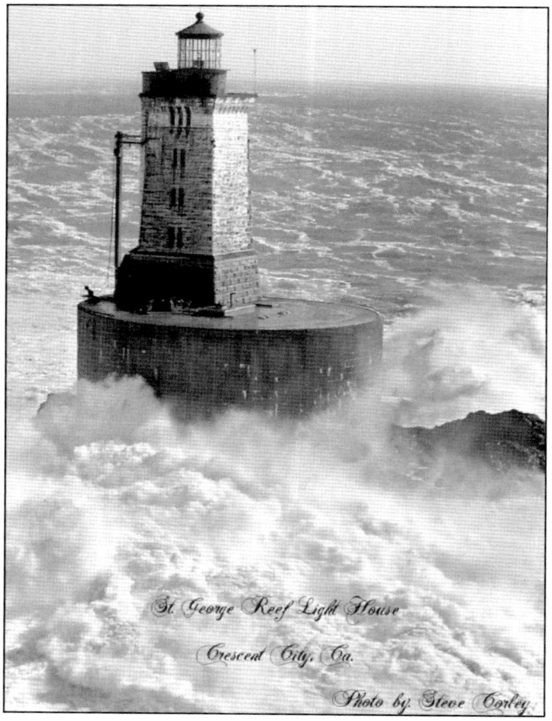

A *Rough Day at the Lighthouse* is what photographer Steve Corley named this shot of St. George being battered by a ferocious northwest swell. It is low tide; otherwise, the cresting surf would be washing over the caisson. This photograph, which served as a model for the watercolor print by Howard Koslow, was selected by the Postal Service to represent the lighthouse in its 2007 commemorative stamp series called Pacific Lighthouses." (Steve Corley.)

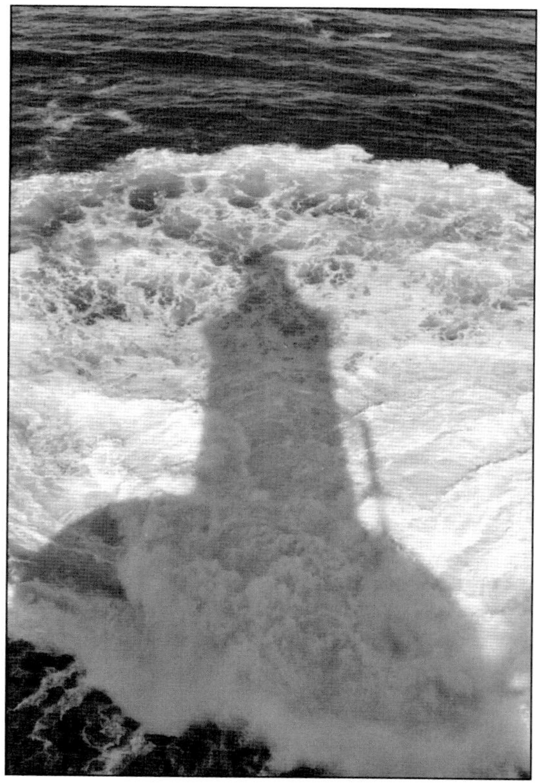

The future of St. George Reef Lighthouse is uncertain. It is as shadowy as this image of the tower cast upon the water. After a quarter of a century of work and an estimated outlay of $250,000, there is still work to be done. Huge gains have been made: a new light shines from a rebuilt lantern room, utilities are working, keepers rooms are redone, and masonry reinforcement has been started. Readers can help protect this effort and the legacy of its builders and keepers. (Author's collection.)

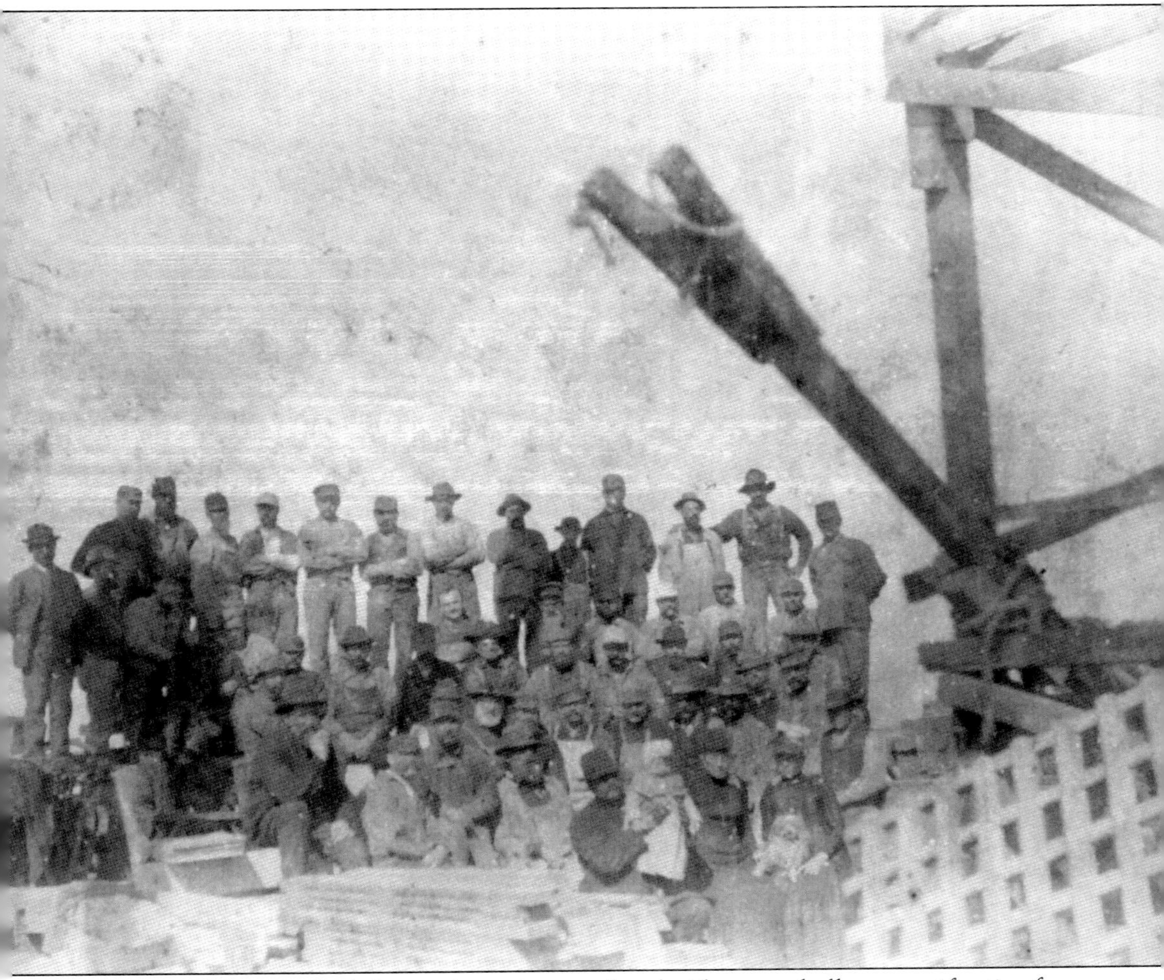

Immediately following the lighting, the society was faced with a new challenge: notification from the California Department of Transportation (CalTrans) that the landing space on the caisson did not meet Federal Aviation Administration (FAA) regulations for commercial helicopter operations and would have to be lengthened by about 30 feet before paid passengers could again visit the site. Happily, the commercial restrictions do not apply for volunteers flying out to do restoration work, but before activities can resume, the society must first apply for an access permit. The access permit is in process, and CalTrans is working to minimize modifications to the landing area. An appropriate addendum to the epilogue is this group photograph showing 47 men, their wives, and children (in lower right corner), posing at the base of the engineering marvel they have spent a decade constructing. They bid readers to consider the words of John Ruskin, that their labors will not be in vain, and the generations succeeding them do hold the stones of St. George to be sacred and their labors worthy of our homage. For information on tours and other inquires, readers can contact the St. George Reef Lighthouse Preservation Society at PO Box 577, Crescent City, CA 95531 or visit the group's website at www.stgeorgereeflighthouse.us. (National Archives.)

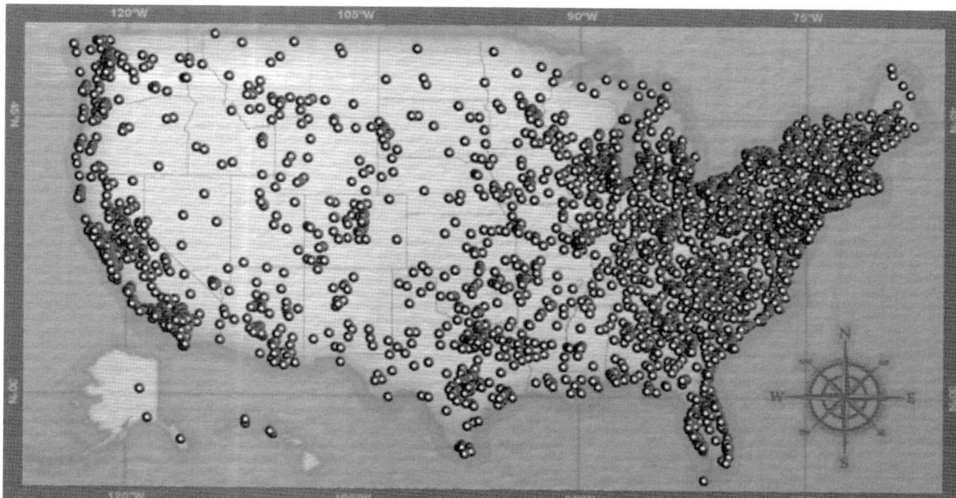